INVISIBLE CATHEDRALS

INVISIBLE CATHEDRALS

THE EXPRESSIONIST ART HISTORY OF WILHELM WORRINGER

EDITED BY NEIL H. DONAHUE

THE PENNSYLVANIA STATE UNIVERSITY PRESS

University Park, Pennsylvania

Library of Congress Cataloging-in-Publication Data

Invisible cathedrals : the expressionist art history of Wilhelm
    Worringer / edited by Neil H. Donahue.
        p.   cm.
    Includes bibliographical references and index.
    ISBN 0-271-01306-0 (alk. paper)
    1. Worringer, Wilhelm, 1881–1965—Criticism and interpretation.
2. Expressionism (Art)—Germany.   I. Donahue, Neil H.
N7483.W67I5   1995
709′.2—dc20   93-33979
                                                                  CIP

Published by The Pennsylvania State University Press,
University Park, PA 16802-1003

*To my wife, Christine
and our daughter, Alice Leslie*

Contents

List of Illustrations

Fig. 1.   Albrecht Dürer, drawing of a cube in his so-called Dresden Sketchbook, ink, 1520s. Dresden, Sächsische Landesbibliothek, Ms. R-147, fol. 168v. After the album *Albrecht Dürer in der königlichen öffentlichen Bibliothek zu Dresden*, ed. Robert Bruck, Studien zur deutschen Kunstgeschichte (Strasbourg, 1905), reprinted as Dürer's *The Human Figure: The Complete "Dresden Sketchbook,"* ed. Walter L. Strauss (New York: Dover, 1972)

Fig. 2.   Tony Smith, *Die*, steel, 72 × 72 × 72 inches (edition of three), 1962. (Photo by Geoffrey Clements, courtesy of the Paula Cooper Gallery, New York)

Fig. 3.   Adolf Loos, Moller House, Vienna, 1928. Interior staircase. (Photo by Roberto Schezen, courtesy of the photographer)

Fig. 4.   Tony Smith, *Free Ride*, steel, 104 × 104 × 104 inches, 1962 (edition of three with one artist's proof). (Photo lacking archival data)

Fig. 5.   David Smith, *Cubi XXIII*, steel, 76¼ inches high, 172⅞ inches long, 1964. (Photo lacking archival data)

Fig. 6.   Robert Morris, *Untitled (L-Beams)*, fiberglass; two units, each 96 × 96 × 24 inches (edition of three), 1965–67. (Photo courtesy of the Leo Castelli Gallery, New York)

Fig. 7.   Bruno Taut, *Crystal House in the Mountains*, ink drawing reproduced in Taut, *Die Auflösung der Städte; oder auch, Die Erde, eine gute Wohnung; oder auch, Der Weg zur alpinen Architektur* (Hagen, 1920)

Fig. 8.   Tony Smith, *Atlanta*, wooden mockup for bronze (edition of six), 48 × 31 × 24 inches, 1980. (Photo by Geoffrey Clements, courtesy of the Paula Cooper Gallery, New York)

Preface

A book on Wilhelm Worringer is long overdue. This volume aims to meet that long-standing need for a broad-based consideration of Worringer's work, its often lively reception, and its uncommonly extensive influence. *Invisible Cathedrals* seeks to focus discussion, for the first time, directly on a controversial figure in German Modernism, whose works in art history appealed to readers across disciplinary bounds and exerted considerable influence in very different areas. This volume thus deliberates, implicitly throughout and explicitly in the Introduction, on that peculiar situation: Worringer's wide reception outside his own scholarly discipline of art history along with his neglect within that field, due perhaps to the same attributes that account for his broader appeal. Yet a book on Worringer also, by the same token, faces a particular difficulty: on the one hand, Worringer remains largely unknown to many people, even in the areas where he has had an influence; on the other hand, he is too familiar to others, who maintain a fixed and limited conception of his work. Thus, a book on Worringer needs to provide both an engaging basic introduction to the figure and his works, along with a more profound and detailed reconsideration of his significance.

This volume does both and will serve equally the curious student and the scholar of the period by (1) introducing Worringer once and for all as a central (not just a peripheral) figure of German and European modernism; (2) supplying a bibliography of the scattered research in different fields as an aid to further research; and (3) bringing together essays by well-known scholars in those fields in order to establish lines of inquiry *within* and *between* the disciplines of art history and aesthetics, literary history and theory, cultural and social theory, and intellectual history.

The organization of the volume reflects that intention of creating interdisciplinary dialogue. The essays are arranged in chronological order of the principal works by Worringer that they discuss. The volume thus provides a linear perspective on his career for those unfamiliar with his work, yet that simple linear chronology is also continually qualified by the far-reaching approaches to his works in these essays. As a result, the reader of the volume as a whole is asked to step back constantly from his or her disciplinary habits (or even prejudices) in order to reconsider closely related material from new and unfamiliar perspectives. An alternate sequence that I considered would have divided the essays into two sections according to their methodologies: essays that represented more traditional historical scholarship would have formed one section of the book, and essays that represented more synthetic and theoretical approaches would have formed another section. Yet I felt that such a division would have split both the contributors and the readership into two camps, and would have thereby perpetuated a division that an interdisciplinary volume such as this one would prefer to supersede. The present sequence, I believe, highlights the fruitful dialogic quality of the volume by presenting different points of view on the same figure or even the same work. The volume carries the reader forward, but also at each juncture opens perspectives into different areas for further inquiry.

The work at bringing together scholars from different fields with an interest in Worringer began as preparation for a symposium that took place in April 1991 at Hofstra University. This volume is the culmination of the interdisciplinary dialogue about Worringer that began there. Five of the essays are revised and expanded versions of papers presented at the symposium. That event was made possible through financial and administrative support provided by the Hofstra Cultural Center, and I would like to thank the director Alexej Ugrinsky for his enthusiastic support of the initiative. Also, special thanks to Laura J. Labenberg of the Hofstra Cultural Center, for her practical help in planning that symposium: its success owes a great deal to her extraordinary efficiency. The German Academic Exchange Service (DAAD) generously provided additional financial support for the symposium. In particular, I would like to thank Heidrun Suhr of DAAD for her interest in the event. My colleagues in the Department of Comparative Literature at Hofstra were, as usual, wonderful in providing the good measures of wit and wisdom that make special events lively and daily life special. Barbara Lekatsas deserves extra appreciation for her skillful installation of an exhibition "The Other Side: German Expressionist Illustrated Books and Periodicals" from the remarkable Weingrow Collection of Avant-Garde Art and Literature at Hofstra. Along with the contributors to this volume, other scholars who participated in the symposium as speakers or respondents deserve thanks for their contributions: Rosemarie Bletter, Dorothea Dietrich, Mary Gluck, Elliot Jurist, Ralph Ley, Frederick Lubich, Robert Norton, Robert von Hallberg, and Rose Carol Washton-Long. I hope that this volume preserves some of the enthusiasm and spirit of intellectual adventure that all of the above individuals helped to create that day.

Several of the essays in this volume are reprinted with generous permission from the original editors and publishers. Chapter 1 appeared in *The Turn of the Century: German Literature and Art, 1890–1915*, ed. Gerald Chapple and Hans Schulte (Bonn: Bouvier, 1981), 197–223. © 1981 Bouvier Verlag. Reprinted by permission of the publisher. Chapter 2 appeared as "Crystalline Form, Worringer, and the Minimalism of Tony Smith" in Joseph Masheck, *Building-Art: Modern Architecture Under Cultural Construction* (New York: Cambridge University Press, 1993), 143–61. © 1993 Cambridge University Press. Reprinted with permission of Cambridge University Press. Chapter 7 appeared in *Deutsche Vierteljahrsschrift für Literaturwissenschaft und Geistesgeschichte* 66, 4 (1992): 765–82. © 1992 J. B. Metzler Verlag. Reprinted by permission of the publisher. Further, my editor at Penn State Press, Philip Winsor, and the respective members of the Press's very competent staff all deserve thanks for and appreciation for their friendly and reliable assistance, and their attention to the manuscript in all stages of its preparation.

In addition, I would like to express my gratitude to Peter J. Burgard and John Czaplicka for inviting me to Harvard University in the fall of 1991, after the symposium, to present my own essay on Worringer at the Center for European Studies, where they organized a stimulating forum for discussion. My colleague at Hofstra, Russell Harrison, has contributed thoughtful commentaries as well as practical assistance to this volume. Finally, also at Hofstra, ever since we first met to discuss Worringer, I have benefited often from the knowledge and moral support of Joe Masheck, who has been an ideal interlocutor about all matters relating to art history, both practical and speculative. My wife, Christine Rota-Donahue, has helped in many ways with this book in all its stages; I am pleased to dedicate it with much love to her and to our daughter, Alice Leslie.

Introduction:
Art History or "Sublime Hysteria"?

Wilhelm Worringer was an art historian, though an unconventional one. He enjoyed a very successful academic career, yet his ideas were never quite accepted by his academic colleagues; instead, those ideas seem to have insinuated themselves into areas outside, and even far removed, from his academic discipline. Unlike most art historians of the day, Worringer's works were read by painters and art critics, poets and novelists, in Germany and abroad, as well as by literary and social theorists,[1] and even early critics of film,[2] as well as psychologists.[3] Perhaps representative of his reception is the comment by the poet Rainer Maria Rilke in a letter to Lou Andreas-Salomé: "On my trip I read Worringer, in absolute agreement." In this country, after the Second World War, Worringer's ideas became the basis for Joseph Frank's influential theory of spatial form in literature.[4]

Now Worringer's name appears routinely in accounts of German Expressionism and European Modernism, but usually only as a brief reference in passing. From whatever perspective, Worringer's name almost invariably appears fixed in the background, on the distant horizon of the period's intellectual history. In fact, rarely has there been any attempt to bring his work out of the background and into the foreground for more critical examination, and rarely has Worringer received any direct attention in his own right. Until now, no single book has been available about Worringer or his influence, which cuts so widely across European Modernism and beyond.[5] The most significant work on Worringer, however, has been done by literary scholars, outside of the discipline of art history. In his own discipline, Worringer has received very little serious attention in terms of his own individual works or even his reception by other artists.[6] This neglect raises the question of why Worringer has not been taken more seriously in his own discipline. And why, in contrast, have scholars in other fields, with other sensibilities and different training, both studied and appreciated his work and influence?

The answer lies, I believe, in that Worringer's work is largely rhetorical. He was never primarily a systematic, "scientific" scholar, but rather a rhetorician and cultural theorist of art and aesthetics. He wrote about general ideas in aesthetics in broadly historical terms, with a simple, powerful rhetoric that assured both an audience outside the academy and deep suspicion or even resentment within it.[7] In fact, he seems to have considered himself a scholar-artist engaged *directly* in the production of culture, rather than a historical-positivist scholar engaged in the exploration of past cultures and their artifacts. Herein lies perhaps the principal paradox of his work as a whole: Worringer wrote mainly on historical topics, on the art of "primitive" cultures and of the Middle Ages, but his work almost unfailingly addresses artistic and cultural issues of his own day. Indeed, his study of Lukas Cranach demonstrates his awareness of the social context and market reception of art.[8] Worringer's career suggests a type of "activist" art historian, whose work on the art of past epochs provides historical justification for the art of his contemporaries.

Unlike his predecessor, Alois Riegl, who was the source of many of his ideas, Worringer himself used very few examples and illustrations in his works, and seemed unconcerned with the empirical validity of his theses. He promoted a certain vision of how art and society should be, even though that vision underwent certain modulations and even reversals over time. Therefore, it is not surprising that literary scholars and cultural historians have been drawn more readily to examine his work, and that often the most fruitful approach to his work has been through rhetorical analysis. That approach sets, in this volume, the foundation for the multiplicity of perspectives on Worringer presented here. This volume brings together scholars of art and literature, of visual and verbal style, both trained equally as intellectual historians, in order to examine closely the terms of Worringer's arguments, to situate them in the appropriate historical contexts, and thereby to broaden the basis for future study of his work. Most of these scholars have written on Worringer previously in another context. Taken together, their work defines, for the first time, Worringer's place in German Expressionism and European Modernism as well as his particular relations to his contemporaries, and our own. These exciting essays open new perspectives for further reconsideration of a figure both eccentric and fascinating.

Worringer established himself with the publication of his doctoral dissertation as *Abstraction and Empathy* in 1908; the book struck a nerve in the volatile art world of the day, was read widely and had a new edition almost every year for the next twelve years. Briefly stated, Worringer had developed, in outline but for the first time, an aesthetics for nonrepresentational art, whether it be Egyptian or African, Gothic or Baroque, or the works of modern abstraction that were just beginning to appear on the European art scene. As the subtitle indicates, Worringer proposes in *Abstraction and Empathy* a "psychology of style," whereby the formal and stylistic particularities of the work reflect the psychological disposition of the artist and, in turn, the historical period. For Worringer, art that realistically and recognizably depicts the natural world, from the ancient Greeks to the Italian Renaissance to French Impressionism, reflects a feeling of security, a metaphysical ease "at home in the cosmos," and thus the desire to identify, through empathy, with one's surroundings. In sharp contrast, however, nonnaturalistic art or abstraction reflects the psychic anguish of the individual in a hostile, threatening, and incomprehensible world, a primordial fear of open space that Worringer describes as "spiritual agoraphobia." Both urges are thus representational, but only of a *Weltgefühl* or "world-feeling," a certain psychic disposition toward reality. In the case of empathy, that disposition coincides with realistic representation in art. Abstract art, in contrast, subdues that existential anxiety or "spiritual agoraphobia" by eliminating the third dimension, the depth of naturalistic, perspectival space; abstract art allows an escape from the perilous contingency of existence into the geometric fixity of iconic, abstract, and transcendental form.

After a book on Lukas Cranach, also in 1908, Worringer offered the third book in his trilogy, *Form Problems in the Gothic* (1911), where he addressed the question of the psychological origins of Gothic art. Again, Worringer's bold thesis provoked outcries from his academic colleagues but was read by artists, like his first book, as a disguised manifesto for the new art of German Expressionism. Here, that condition of "spiritual agoraphobia" has been transmogrified into the "sublime hysteria" of the inspired German artist, the Gothic prototype for the modern Expressionist. Worringer's books and articles before the First World War made him a leading spokesman of the Expressionist avant-garde; however, Worringer's Expressionist phase was short-lived, and in 1920 his lecture "Questions about Contemporary Art" declared an end to that movement.

The essays in this volume cover Worringer's career from its beginning with his dissertation (1906) to his works of the late 1920s. During that time he taught as *Privatdozent* in Bern (1909–14) and then in Bonn (1918–28), where he became a professor in 1920. This volume makes only occasional reference to his work in later decades until his death in 1965. Worringer's subsequent career was distinguished enough but not otherwise distinguishable, as before, from his academic colleagues.[9] His archival estate or *Nachlaß* in the Germanisches Museum in Nuremberg contains and reveals little, since Worringer twice left his belongings behind: in Königsberg, where he taught from 1928 to 1944, and in Halle, where he was professor of modern art history after the war, from 1946 to 1950. He left the eastern sector in protest at the use of his name for propaganda purposes and moved to Munich, where he lived until his death in 1965.

Abstraction and Empathy (1908) is Worringer's most important and influential work, and the necessary starting point for all discussion of his thought. Accordingly, the first two essays in this volume, by Geoffrey Waite and Joseph Masheck, illuminate that classic text, though from very different angles; their two approaches, first intrinsic and then extrinsic in nature, complement one another and serve to frame this most important text. Geoffrey Waite's essay of 1981, here reprinted, provides a trenchant examination of Worringer's rhetoric of binary opposition in *Abstraction and Empathy*. Joseph Masheck's essay adopts a panoramic, "stereoptic" view of Worringer's aesthetic of "crystalline form" in order to show its earlier affinities in the history of art, its direct derivation, and what it anticipates in the postwar-to-contemporary arts scene.[10] As a survey in intellectual history, Masheck's essay complements, in turn, Geoffrey Waite's provocative new article, the last in the volume, where Waite situates Worringer in the field of postmodern cultural theory. Waite's two articles in this volume, separated by a decade, frame the rest of the contributions between his two approaches of close, rhetorical analysis and contemporary intellectual history, between Worringer's use of his own sources at the beginning of his career, and how others chose to use him later as their own source for their own purposes.

Whereas the first two essays concentrate primarily on the rhetorical and formal properties of Worringer's argumentation and examples in *Abstraction and Empathy*, the next two situate Worringer, critically, among the artists and intellectuals of his day, in the arts and beyond. Despite his alliance with the Expressionist avant-garde, and the centrality of his texts for that movement, Worringer's actual understanding of the art of the period has not received much attention. Magdalena Bushart examines the broad but contrary reception of

Abstraction and Empathy and *Form Problems in the Gothic* among artists and academic colleagues, both of whom linked Worringer's works, for better or for worse, with the new tendencies of Expressionism. Yet Bushart argues that the shared view of Worringer's two audiences conflicts with Worringer's own original intention in writing his soon-to-be-sensational dissertation and with his own "surprisingly conservative" taste in art! Bushart draws upon some of Worringer's earliest and seldom-cited writings in order to describe the genesis of his thinking and the ambiguity of his relation to the avant-garde. Her essay, in fact, demonstrates how Worringer's own understanding of what was avant-garde was deeply rooted in notions of *Stilkunst* (or art nouveau) from the generation preceding Expressionism. Thus, Bushart's essay defines the actual historical contours of Worringer's early thinking and its immediate derivation and development. By so doing, she calls into question Worringer's alignment with the avant-garde and presents his position as divided and, at best, ambiguous, but, at worst, duplicitous.

Michael W. Jennings also challenges the conventional perception of Worringer as an Expressionist of sorts in the academy. Whereas Bushart adopts a synchronic perspective, Jennings views Worringer from a diachronic perspective framed between Alois Riegl and Walter Benjamin. In that context of "materialist aesthetics," Jennings is able to reconsider the "subjectivist" bias in Worringer's reception (in how critics have conceived the relation of *Kunstwollen* to *Kunstwerk*, and of Worringer to Expressionism). Jennings focuses instead on the neglected matter of the *mediation* between the two in order to shift critical attention to a cultural interpretation of Worringer's work in social (not just formal and aesthetic) terms. Thus, Jennings's discussion revolves around the question of the "full materiality" of artist and artwork.[11] What Jennings undertakes here is his own sort of "epochal" shift in Worringer criticism: to read *Abstraction and Empathy* and its famous term *Platzangst* (spiritual agoraphobia or dread of space; literally, place [space]-fear [anxiety]) with a critical emphasis, for the first time, on the *Platz* and not on the *Angst*; that is, on the physical and social conditions behind the *Angst* and the art. He is able, thereby, to link Worringer, not to transcendent forms, but to the problems occupying social theorists such as Walter Benjamin, and then to define several aspects of Worringer's specific contribution to German Modernism.

Joanna E. Ziegler's essay "Worringer's Theory of Transcendental Space in Gothic Architecture" focuses on his second major work, *Form Problems in the Gothic* (1911), and argues convincingly for a full revision of Worringer's status in medievalist art scholarship. Worringer's reception by Expressionism, and the vivid contemporary impact of his text, as what I call a "disguised manifesto" for the avant-garde, ended up disguising also, in fact, his own real contribution to medieval scholarship. Ziegler reads that unacknowledged influence in terms of "imminence" and "truism," whereby the first term refers to the basic principles and rhetorical strategies of his work, its "spiritual" presuppositions; and the latter to "five analytical moments" in that text that have figured ever since as commonplaces in medieval scholarship, without acknowledgment of their source in Worringer's book on Gothic art. In other words, the same traits of Worringer's work that account for his enormous reception by the Expressionist generation also account for his systematic neglect, almost a direct refusal of acknowledgment, by later art-historical scholarship of pre-modern or medieval periods.

After that period of greatest "affiliation" with the artists and intellectuals of his generation, Worringer retreats from the collective euphoria of Expressionism. In an essay of 1919 entitled "Critical Thoughts on the New Art" (Kritische Gedanken zur neuen Kunst), Worringer began to reflect upon Expressionism and what it had aspired to achieve with its use of "rational means to suprarational ends" (*Fragen und Gegenfragen*, 93). He gives the movement credit for its attempt to attain a complete "spiritualization of expression" (96) and to determine whether or not the most intensely personal, individual expression can arrive at a collective validity equal to the great art of the past. Worringer begins, however, to hedge in his response when he maintains that only in the Expressionist's scream *(Schrei)* is the individual uplifted, sublated as it were, into the "illusion of suprapersonal context" (100). Expressionism is the "screaming cramp of the Self, whipped into a frenzy" (100) and "a heroic gesture of the decline of art" (104). Worringer's commentaries have begun to take on now a more sociological perspective, and to outline the impossibility of the Expressionist project in the historical conditions in Germany at the time. Yet in this essay, he is still deeply sympathetic with that project, as he explains in the passage that gives this volume its title:

> [T]his art has in the end become homeless. These images are not painted for rooms, they are not painted for exhibitions, they are painted as decoration for those invisible cathedrals of the spirit that tower above us. In other words: these homeless images are painted by a homeless Self onto the air. . . . The

modern spiritualism, born of nothing else than of the desperate intensity of the isolated, lost Self, had nothing else than only invisible cathedrals. (102)

That elegiac mood gives way, two years later, to a harsher tone in his famous essay "Questions about Contemporary Art" of 1921 (Künstlerische Zeitfragen), also known as the "funeral oration" *(Grabrede)*, where he declares the "End of Expressionism."

Years later, in 1934, Georg Lukács used Worringer's essay to suggest that Expressionism is really an "ideology of flight" from the material realities of class struggle, and a reactionary, Idealist mystification of class privilege. Worringer's notion of the artist's existential anguish at the core of abstraction, or of the Expressionist's "sublime hysteria," is for Lukács only the "spontaneous expression of the situation of their class." Despite Lukács's theoretical recognition of material realities, he does not enter at all in his essay into the historical context of the avant-garde (and the strident opposition to it) in Germany.[12] In light of what Geoffrey Perkins has called "the hysterical nature of much opposition to modernism" (29), as in Carl Vinnen's nationalistic *Protest of German Artists* (1911),[13] Worringer's category of "sublime hysteria" might appear—a surprise to Lukács!—a critical response to the reactionary "conservative front"; indeed, it could be considered as progressive, even *"subversive* hysteria."

Charles W. Haxthausen begins his examination of the *Grabrede* by taking exception to Lukács's misrepresentation of Worringer's essay, of which the latter third is ignored. There Worringer suggests that Expressionism has not died away but has simply found a new medium commensurate with an age when art itself no longer has expressive validity and, instead, only manages to subsist on the margins of society. For Worringer, Expressionism has migrated into works of historical inquiry, into scholarship:

> No, art has not been replaced by scholarship, rather scholarship has begun itself to become art. . . . And here there is a spiritual impulse at work that embodies the phenomenon of Expressionism more authentically, in a manner more appropriate to our times than in Expressionist painting. . . . The true Expressionism of the times lives not in the new optics of the eye, but in that of our minds. (*Fragen und Gegenfragen,* 124–25)

Thus, Worringer still advocates Expressionism, as Haxthausen shows, but a scholarly Expressionism that picks up where artistic Expressionism has left off. To my mind, Haxthausen's exploration of this aspect of Worringer's famous essay rightly raises a question that pertains to all of Worringer's work, and all the essays in this volume: Does Worringer's work have merit as scholarship, or is it itself an expression of the German avant-garde that Worringer sought to defend and promote? Is Worringer an art historian in any conventional sense, or is he, by his own definition, a "sublime hysteric," an Expressionist in academic garb?

In a review of Worringer's essays in the 1920s, with instructive comparisons to other art historians of the day, Haxthausen suggests an answer to that question: he completes his trenchant examination of Worringer's development in this period by focusing on his reading in 1925 of Carlo Carrà's painting *Pine by the Sea* (1921). Likewise, my own essay on Worringer's study of *Egyptian Art* (1927) adopts his understanding of Expressionist scholarship, stated above, in order to read his own scholarship not in terms of its putative object, but rather as a symptomatic document that reveals widespread anxieties at the time about Weimar Germany and its place in the modern world. Those anxieties concentrate in the surprising comparison Worringer draws, around which his study is organized, between ancient Egypt and modern, twentieth-century America. His denunciation of both cultures, in order to preserve an ideal image of German culture, relies however on a reversal of his famous and influential position on "primitive" cultures in *Abstraction and Empathy*. The hysteria of his argumentation is now no longer subversive or "sublime," yet its expressionistic (lower-case) qualities prefigure the "rhetorical sublime" of contemporary, "postmodern" theoretical discourse, as I demonstrate in a comparison of Worringer's America in *Egyptian Art* (1927) to Jean Baudrillard's text *America* (1986).

That shift to Worringer's profile in contemporary theory continues and is expanded in Geoffrey Waite's second essay in this volume, where he tracks down, like a *film noir* detective, the filiations of Worringer's thought in two "arenas" or "videodromes" of technoculture: that of "MassCult" (futuristic science-fiction literature and film, along with related subgenres and theories) and that of postmodern *political* theory, which includes contemporary theory of (cyber) warfare. After the other essays have explored, but by no means exhausted, Worringer's affinities to his artist and theorist contemporaries, and his influence(s) upon them, Waite locates Worringer's thought among *our* contemporaries and among the forms of *our* contemporary culture. Like my own essay, which reads Worringer's text on Egyptian art for its expressionistic, performative, and symptomatic aspects, Waite also moves beyond the distinction between scholarly-critical and artistic discourses in order to see Worringer as he saw himself, engaged directly in the production of culture.

Yet whereas I present Worringer, in his "rhetorical excesses," as a historical precursor of postmodernism's "rhetorical sublime" as it appears in Baudrillard's *America*, Waite engineers a bold, complex, and exciting anachronism, presenting Worringer as a "protocyberpunk warrior" in order to demonstrate his relevance to contemporary culture in its outermost reaches, in the avant-garde of its futurity. If Worringer's work was a "transitional object" for the emergence of Modernism in Germany, then it has also served, in a more ramified and attenuated way, as a "transitional object" to postmodern theory and postmodern culture itself. As such, Worringer's texts have helped crystallize historical developments (and the thinking about such developments); now, therefore, they also prove useful for articulating and understanding those changes. In effect, Waite reads the Expressionist idealism of Worringer's "invisible cathedrals" of the spirit as the "virtual reality" of our time and (techno)culture, both of which are always (borrowing another metaphor from Worringer) pregnant with the future.

NOTES

1. For points of Worringer's influence on and affinity to Theodor Adorno, Walter Benjamin, Georg Lukács and Georg Simmel, see my *Forms of Disruption: Abstraction in Modern German Prose* (Ann Arbor: University of Michigan Press, 1993).

2. See Rudolf Kurtz, *Expressionismus und Film* (Berlin: Verlag der Lichtbildbühne, 1926). Jean-Michel Palmier makes the connection of Worringer to Kurtz (and to Lotte Eisner) in his substantial introduction, "Rudolf Kurtz et l'esthétique du cinéma expressioniste" (7–36), to the French edition of Kurtz's *Expressionisme und cinéma* (Grenoble: Presses universitaires de Grenoble, 1986). Palmier compares Kurtz's work to *Abstraction and Empathy* and explores his debt to Worringer for the first aesthetics of German cinema. To my knowledge, Palmier, a well-known scholar of Expressionism, is the only critic to have made this important connection to Kurtz. Lotte Eisner, in *The Haunted Screen: Expressionism in German Cinema and the Influence of Max Reinhardt* (Paris: Le Terrain Vague, 1952; Berkeley and Los Angeles: The University of California Press, 1973), herself begins her study with a brief discussion of Worringer.

3. Such as C. G. Jung, Otto Rank, Franz Alexander, and Zevedei Barbu. See Masheck's "Raw Art: 'Primitive' Authenticity and German Expressionism" in his *Modernities: Art-Matters in the Present* (University Park: Pennsylvania State University Press, 1993), 185 n. 99. Otto Rank's *Art and Artist* is heavily indebted to Worringer, whom he cites frequently and discusses at length.

4. In *Forms of Disruption*, I examine Frank's theory and return to his source in Wor-

ringer's *Abstraction and Empathy* in order to propose a new reading of the relationship between German Modernist (and so-called Expressionist) prose and the ideal of visual abstraction. Although Worringer's ideas and Frank's use of them mainly provide a framework, along with a vocabulary of terms and concepts, for my study of imaginative prose in the period between 1902 and 1947, I am also able to establish there Worringer's direct influence on writers such as Rainer Maria Rilke, Carl Einstein, and Gottfried Benn.

5. Because of Worringer's extensive influence across very different fields of scholarly inquiry and of artistic expression, a collection of essays by experts in different fields is particularly appropriate and useful. Though a monograph on Worringer would be welcome (and is long overdue in the discipline of art history), it would be difficult for a single author to do justice to his influence in those different areas.

6. Magdalena Bushart's *Der Geist der Gotik und die expressionistische Kunst* (Munich: Silke Schreiber, 1990) is a notable exception and deserves translation. Ann Stieglitz's fascinating article, "The Reproduction of Agony," *Oxford Art Journal* 12, no. 2 (1989): 87–103, which examines the thesis of Worringer's *Formprobleme der Gotik* and the ideologically revealing changes in its many editions during the war period, also exemplifies the type of historical research that is necessary in this area. In order to understand the failure of art history to deal with figures such as Worringer, Donald Preziosi's reflections in *Rethinking Art History* are germane. Although in his terminology he belabors his allegiance to Foucault, Preziosi's discussion of "crisis" in the discipline directs attention to the historical developments and the "rhetorical framings" (xvi) of art history.

7. In his interesting study *Artwriting* (Amherst: University of Massachusetts Press, 1987), David Carrier examines the "use of rhetoric in interpretation" (1) and several art historians and art critics in terms of the narratives they construct, the historical plot they delineate that attributes significance to some artists or styles, and not to others. He notes aptly that "[a]rtwriting aims to be suasive. . . . The value of contemporary art, however, remains to be established, so art criticism, unlike art history, is never disinterested" (9). This distinction is useful in the present context: Worringer is, on the one hand, an art historian who creates a narrative of the past that favors nonnaturalistic art (and which is thereby antithetical to Gombrich's history of naturalistic art in *Art and Illusion*), and, on the other hand, an art critic who employs in his early books an engaged and, by all evidence, highly persuasive rhetoric that addresses that historical narrative to the art of his contemporaries. He thus brings his historical narrative and his immediate rhetoric to bear on the unsettled questions at the time of the value and significance of abstract and Expressionist art.

8. See Donahue, *Forms of Disruption*, 33 n. 11. Also of interest in this context is Reinhard Piper's account in *Mein Leben als Verleger* (Munich: Piper, 1964) of his own appreciation of Cranach, his commissioning Worringer to write the book on Cranach, and his disappointment and even outrage at Worringer's unexpected approach to the topic, which emphasized the workshop and collective nature of graphic production, instead of the individual artist. Piper's correspondence with Worringer (see *Briefwechsel mit Autoren und Künstlern, 1903–1953*, ed. Ulrike Buergel-Goodwin and Wolfram Göbel [Munich: Piper, 1979]) also reflects on this momentary dissonance in their otherwise cordial relationship.

9. In excerpts from his otherwise unpublished memoirs (in *Kunsthistoriker in eigener Sache*, ed. Marina Sitt [Berlin: Dietrich Reimer, 1990], 225–26), Heinrich Lützeler gives his impressions of Worringer at the university in Bonn, which had the oldest program of art history in Germany at the time (see Dilly, *Deutsche Kunsthistoriker, 1933–1945* [Munich: Deutscher Kunstverlag, 1988], 28) and where Worringer was *Privatdozent* and Lützeler a student, both in art history. In a short but dense characterization, Lützeler recalls Wor-

ringer's "Souveränität" and his reputation as "ein glänzender Redner," but also his "problematische Natur" due to his sense of unfulfilled early promise. Lützeler recounts: "Er sagte 1925 einmal zu mir, er sei ein Wunderkind gewesen, was ein fragwürdiges Los sei. Ob er einmal ein Wundergreis sein würde? / Er wurde es nicht."

10. In *Artwriting*, David Carrier characterizes Masheck's method, on display here, according to another example: "Masheck's strategy is to draw parallels between contemporary painting and icons and crucifixes from the Byzantine tradition. If we thus relate recent art to works from a very different culture, we may escape the limitation of theories that derive abstract painting from earlier naturalistic works. Masheck's goal is neither to assert that the abstract artists of our time are influenced by the Byzantines nor to imply that abstract art is inevitably spiritual; rather, he seeks a model for abstraction that does not define its identity by appeal to a historical narrative. This also was the goal of the semiotic theoreticians, but where they proceeded in large part by abstract argumentation, Masheck offers a series of examples . . . [and] makes visual comparisons without constructing a genealogy . . . . Masheck seeks 'to draw on the memory bank of culture to claim for contemporary artists the traditions to which they . . . contribute' [Masheck, *Historical Present*, 206]. His narrative, in which there is no *subject* whose development we can trace, is inherently harder to follow than a historical analysis or even an account of presentness. Compared with Greenberg and Fried, Masheck offers many examples, giving no explicit thesis that can be stated in so many words. He aims to tell a story without *subject*, dramatic beginning, or definite conclusion; such a text, perplexing for the reader who is accustomed to a strong narrative line, makes sense if we give up the belief that artwriting needs such a structure" (*Artwriting*, 98 and 102).

11. In *Forms of Disruption*, I also focus attention, for the first time, on Worringer's emphasis on the materiality of the artwork, the concrete "particularities of style" *(Stileigentümlichkeiten)*, though my understanding of that "materiality" is more phenomenological than historical-dialectical, as is Jennings's. Thus, Jennings's discussion gives an additional, more fully historical dimension to that word and to Worringer's theory of art.

12. This contradiction between a theoretical position and actual critical practice in this case seems to have determined in large part Worringer's later critical reception, which exaggerated the mystifying anguish in his thesis and underplayed the historical and social dimensions. Worringer subsequently became, for many lesser critics than Lukács, a convenient target for reductive generalizations. Lukács's position on Worringer, though usefully provocative and certainly not entirely wrong, is nonetheless facile and self-serving. This volume aims to promote a more historically grounded and critically differentiated (yet not necessarily always positive and appreciative) understanding of Worringer's place in German and European modernity. See also *Forms of Disruption*, 30–31 n. 1. In Chapter 8 Geoffrey Waite aptly points out also that Worringer's critics, for the most part, commit the same fault that they seek to discredit him for: inadequate reflection upon and awareness of the ideological and economic determinations of their discourse.

13. Geoffrey Perkins, *Contemporary Theory of Expressionism* (Frankfurt: Herbert Lang, 1974), and Carl Vinnen, *Ein Protest deutscher Künstler* (Jena: Eugen Diederichs, 1911).

1

Worringer's *Abstraction and Empathy*: Remarks on Its Reception and on the Rhetoric of Its Criticism[1]

Geoffrey C. W. Waite

In appearance, discourse may be of little account but the interdictions imposed on it very quickly reveal its proximity to power and to desire. And this is hardly surprising: for discourse—psychoanalysis has shown this—is not simply what reveals (or conceals) desire, it is also itself the object of desire; history never ceases to teach that discourse is not simply what translates conflicts or systems of domination, but the objective and the means of the conflict—the power one is trying to appropriate.

—Michel Foucault, *L'Ordre du discours*

A few introductory remarks:[2] The aporia which I would first like to discuss is only obliquely (not to say nominally) involved with questions explicitly posed by Wilhelm Worringer's *Abstraction and Empathy: A Contribution to the Psychology of Style*, a text arguably of crucial significance for European modernism. My real, underlying, and frankly tendentious concern is rather with a problematic I think is shared by that text (indeed by any historical document), by the pretexts involved when we read and use it, and by our own critical discourse. I should try, therefore, to make explicit some presuppositions behind my argument as to texts (and I deliberately blur distinctions between literary and critical writing by attending to the literariness of both),[3] about what we do when we read them, and about why we read them at all.

Texts do not necessarily mean what they say; they are in fact symptoms of, or, put differently, constituted by other determining factors. This is hardly an original notion: it is an insight of the three most powerful explanatory discourses of our present historical moment. I agree fully with Louis Althusser:

> However paradoxical it may seem, I venture to suggest that our age threatens one day to appear in the history of human culture as marked by the most dramatic and difficult trial of all, the discovery and training in the meaning of the "simplest" acts of existence: seeing, listening, speaking, reading—the acts which relate men to their works, and to those works thrown in their faces, their "absence of works." And contrary to all today's reigning appearances, we do not owe these staggering knowledges to psychology, which is built on the absence of a concept of them, but to a few men: Marx, Nietzsche, and Freud.[4]

As a consequence of their work, there are no innocent documents, no innocent readings, no innocent eyes. And this is the case not merely, to paraphrase Nelson Goodman, because all come always ancient to their work, obsessed by their own past, but also because they are always obsessed by ulterior motives. One way of stating this problem is to say that any document exists not as an entity but as a function or relation that is thrice determined. It is determined genetically and structurally and in terms of its reception. Texts also must be referred to their *pretexts*. They exist in relation to inter- or pretexts, to their often unconscious and duplicitous relation (Harold Bloom's term "misprision" is precise) to other anterior and contiguous texts (in the widest sense) that produce them. Texts exist in relation to the critical and especially ideological assumptions, the pretexts, of their consumers.

The text/pretext nexus is mutually implicatory. Its understanding is, or should be, a consciousness of standing in a still operant history.[5] But—and perhaps hermeneutical understanding is most vulnerable at this point[6]—we must be prepared to read not only the truth that texts reveal to us in open-ended dialogue with them, not only what they say, but also the misprisions, the ruptures, the absences within their textual space, their differences with the ideologies that determine them and that they produce. We must read—and as Marx, Freud, and Nietzsche demonstrate so forcefully, we must read precisely— what the document does *not* say. Texts are undeniably repressive not merely because they exclude or mislead readers during secondary revision, nor even because they rigorously interdict any apodictically final or proper meaning, but because, as Foucault has suggested in quite another context, they impose unseen standards and bars on those who have most positively received them.[7]

If this powerfully negative feature of texts is to be taken into account, some form of symptomatic reading is exigent.[8] But then many assumptions made by "close" reading, however pluralistically they be deployed, will necessarily prove insufficient.

> One might say . . . that the text's *relation to itself* is problematical because it is simultaneously a relation to certain ideological problems. The text is thus never at one with itself, for if it were it would have absolutely nothing to say. It is, rather, a process of *becoming* at one with itself—an attempt to overcome the problem of itself, a problem produced by the fact that the text itself is the production, rather than reflection, of an ideological "solution."[9]

The "deconstruction" of the document—its dismantlement to uncover its implicit rhetorical (figural and persuasive) and ideological strategies—requires a concomitant commitment to its redistribution in a larger problematic by one's own critical discourse. Such redistribution will necessarily appear to many—not least to the formalist or historicist—as a willful and tendentious manipulation of the historical document. But the work of symptomatic reading is not to "do justice" to the document,[10] but to analyze its gaps, its problematic structures that are often spontaneous and unconscious, which is to say ideological, and then to locate it within larger contexts. The task is, one might say, to make the document "interesting," if that word can ever again be restored to its radical etymology.

My desire is to make, through the kind of symptomatic and rhetorical analysis adumbrated above, *Abstraction and Empathy* "interesting" in this sense and, as far as I can, at least begin to explore its problematic, that is, "the objective internal reference system of its particular themes, the system of questions commanding the answers given by its ideology,"[11] and the relation of the problematic to the text's (continuing) reception, without the deluded assurance that we can easily escape these questions, this ideology, or its discursive formulations.

This is the aporia I think responsible criticism should address; the presumptuous desire of my discourse is that the way into an aporia be (as it was for the Greeks) also the desire for a way out.

II

Let us begin by recalling and reworking an old, perhaps familiar insult. "My friend, the Professor of Greek, informs me that the classics have made him what he is today. This is, if well founded, a serious charge." Worringer's dissertation *Abstraction and Empathy*[12] has been read as a classic text by many of the most significant artists, writers, and critics of modernism; indeed, it has been read as a crucial text for the critical activity itself. Worringer himself remarks in an introduction to one of the many editions published between 1908 and the present that this text was the "open sesame" to the modern movement as a whole. Part of my purpose now will be to suggest strongly that his claim is, if well founded, a serious charge indeed.

Art historians and literary critics alike typically mention *Abstraction and Empathy* in the same breath with Kandinsky's *Concerning the Spiritual in Art*. Although one might do well to include Weininger's *Sex and Character* in this (unholy) family of texts, this is at least an indication of the importance of Worringer's text for the modern movement. Indeed, Albert Soergel, in his influential study of developments in Germany, placed Worringer in the elite company of Dilthey, Freud, Bergson, Husserl, Simmel, Scheler, Kierkegaard, and Buber—all, according to Soergel, the "spiritual base" of the period.[13] A more recent literary historian has implied that a typology of all modern literature can be extrapolated from Worringer's thesis.[14] First published in 1908, Worringer's text appears in hindsight to be poised strategically indeed. It emerged almost exactly with Picasso's *Demoiselles d'Avignon* and Schönberg's second quartet,[15] and less than four years before the Sonderbund Exhibition in Cologne, the first major "antinaturalistic" art exhibition on a European scale. For many artists and writers later (including Worringer himself), the Sonderbund was the practical reaction to the "salutory shock"—as Werner Haftmann called it[16]—of Worringer's theses.

Although a systematic, critical discussion of the influence of *Abstraction and Empathy* on artists and writers of Expressionism has not been written, there is ample material for such a study.[17] Perhaps typical is Marc's enthusiastic letter to Kandinsky in 1912 describing Worringer's "fine mind" and "incredibly scholarly thinking," that "we can well make use of."[18] Worringer's influence on Expressionism includes not only his first book, lectures, and conversations with the Expressionists themselves. Well documented is his role in "inventing" the term "Expressionism"—or rather in assuring its adoption and in making propaganda for it.[19] In some sense, he may indeed have "interpreted and guided the feeling of a new generation."[20] If so, his is an influence that penetrates many areas: for example, Spengler's notion of "Magian" culture in *The Decline of the West* and Gottfried Benn's "Kunst und Macht"—and quite beyond the autochthonic issues of the German Problem as well.

Worringer's impact is nowhere stronger than in England, where T. E. Hulme's appreciative albeit impressionistic montage of *Abstraction and Empathy* exerted considerable influence on both the theoretical underpinnings and the poetic practice of the Imagist movement:[21] particularly, to varying degrees, on Pound, T. S. Eliot, Wyndham Lewis, and Yeats, and the aesthetician Herbert Read. This Anglo-American reception of Worringer's text is characterized by uncritical enthusiasm. Hulme, in his rearguard action against the "circumambient gas" of the sensitivity he calls "Romantic" ("the pouring of treacle over the dinner table"), and in his effort to ground a new style of thinking, culture, and society on "objective," "Christian," "abstract" values, found in Worringer's thesis "an extraordinarily clear statement" of his own ideological position and for the practice of Imagism.[22]

This uncritical response to Worringer was subsequently exported to North America, where it found sanctuary in American academic criticism, notably in Joseph Frank's influential collection of essays on "Crisis and Mastery in Modern Literature."[23] In *Abstraction and Empathy* Frank found "the key" to the problem of spatial form (50), a problem that, in turn, provides its own key to what he calls the major change in aesthetic form and sensibility of the modern period: "modern literature has been engaged in transmitting the time world of history into the timeless world of myth. And it is this timeless world of myth, forming the common content of modern literature, that finds its appropriate expression in spatial form" (60). Indeed, for Frank, it is precisely Worringer who provides the theoretical model that can analyze "the complete congruity of form" (57) that is shared by fine art and literature.[24] Frank's seminal but uncritical adoption of Worringer's categories (not to say value judgments) has shaped the reception of Worringer's thesis by North American criticism and by some poets.[25]

Frank's essay—and explicitly his positive valorization of Worringer—has come under attack by William Spanos,[26] one of the very few sustained attacks on Worringer's position we have. Spanos's polemic is directed against New Criticism (which is linked by him to the theories of the Imagists), against analogies between plastic art and literature (which are inappropriate to [post]modernity), against contemporary "Neo-Formalist critic-disciples" (Susan Sontag is mentioned) and other neo-New Critics (Lévi-Strauss, Marshall McLuhan). It would seem that Spanos's most exigent concern is to propagate neo-Heideggerian awareness, that is, "critical openness," a "dialogic evaluative process" (102) that can confront the radical "thrownness" and temporality of "modern man's" situation and of "his" literature. Spanos locates Worringer at the root of the stance he attacks. *Abstraction and Empathy* is exposed for its "transcendental" ideological position, a "microcosm of an essentially Gnostic macrocosm; that is, of a universe in which the temporal world (alive and changing objects) is discontinuous with the world of eternity (dead and permanent form) and qualitatively inferior, infected as it is by the corrupting (i.e., evil) powers of time" (93). To replace such bad faith, Spanos proposes an "engagement" that "cuts radically across Worringer's distinction" between abstraction and empathy (95). Spanos provides not the tools for a critique of Worringer (his subtitle aside, however) but rather a polemic emerging from the "existential option" (95) that, quite apart from any imagined correctness or incorrectness, does not engage Worringer's text itself. In this respect, the very spontaneity of his broadside obscures more than it reveals. The privileged and authoritative position of any text can only be strengthened by an attack on it that does not scrutinize the structures and rhetorical strategies of that text and the mechanisms of the reception these strategies determine.

In any event, the authority of *Abstraction and Empathy* has been strengthened by an important discussion of it by William Holdheim.[27] He has carefully analyzed the text's reception but in order to suggest the necessity of "a liberating infanticide" to counter the anxious influence it has received. Holdheim would return us, in effect, to the text itself and to what was undoubtedly Worringer's stated original intention, namely to mediate between the polarities he found in his most crucial predecessors: Alois Riegl (abstraction) and Theodor Lipps (empathy). Holdheim's own intention is to moderate between Frank (spatial form) and Spanos (hermeneutic or existential open-endedness) in order to suggest a more "dialectical" model for reading both Worringer's text and, by extension, modern criticism itself.

Holdheim's would then be the most ambitious literary-critical attempt to rehabilitate *Abstraction and Empathy*.[28]

Clearly, a study of the reception of Worringer's thesis should not ignore critics of Worringer who speak from within the context of aesthetics and art history. Among them are major voices. Emil Utitz, a contemporary of Worringer's, anticipates already in 1914 and 1920 many later criticisms of Worringer's theoretical position.[29] More recent objection to it may be found in the work of such major scholars as Rudolf Arnheim,[30] Erwin Panofsky,[31] Edgar Wind,[32] and E. H. Gombrich.[33]

Yet the most consistent and sustained attack on Worringer's position comes neither from an "existential option" nor from professional art historians and aestheticians, but from a radically different source that they all ignore. Georg Lukács, from his "Heidelberger Philosophie der Kunst" (1912–14) on into the fifties, has extensively and repeatedly polemicized against Worringer and "bourgeois aesthetics of the imperialist period from Worringer to Malraux."[34] Lukács's analysis is crucial to us because it is an analysis of Worringer's ideology. From this perspective, Worringer is seen to be determined by an ideological stance that is subjective and nationalistic at its base and in its influence. Worringer appears as "the major theoretician" of the "nordic," antirealistic "essence of art," and is representative of that imperialistic ideology that intends to "dethrone" classical antiquity and the Renaissance for the sake of Germanic values. Worringer's thesis is characterized by a fascination with inorganic forms, by an antihuman, irrational formalism. The obsession with the "chaos of reality," "fear of space," etc., is the specific, historically determined and consistent reactionary ideology that Worringer shares with the Expressionists for whom he wrote "the most influential program."[35]

Thus the entire issue of the "abstracting away of reality" as presented by Worringer in fact hides a deeper problematic:

> It is a theory which has the modish pretention of establishing highest objectivity of art. This is very representative for theories of the imperialist period which never step forward openly but which always offer their propaganda in masked form. . . . [T]he theory of abstraction, which later became the theoretical basis of Expressionism, is a culmination of the subjectivistic emptying of aesthetics; it is the theory of subjectivistic ossification and decay of artistic forms in the period of putrefying capitalism.[36]

There is, for Lukács, a direct line implicating the spontaneous flight from reality (from *in*human conditions into *trans*human solutions) and the grounding of an artistic practice that is determined by such flight and that necessarily manifests itself in *anti*human forms.[37]

Of immediate interest to the problem of reception is that Lukács's discussion of Worringer's *Abstraction and Empathy* has been disregarded by all the art historians (and artists) and literary critics (and writers) we have just reviewed. This ignorance, suppression, or repression is hardly surprising, perhaps, since they themselves are implicated by Lukács's interpretation. Indicative of the virtual silence on the problematics exposed by Lukácsian analysis is the following remark in one of the most influential histories of modern art. During a discussion of Worringer's influence on modern art and theory, the author writes: "This is not the place to test the validity of Worringer's concept of history, to here and there make minor corrections or to place in doubt his conclusions made about the psychology of race and religion." What indelibly remains for this writer is Worringer's "literally inexhaustible" discovery of abstraction.[38] But if this is true, if, as the writer further suggests, Worringer's text demonstrates that "art historical reflections can have an immediate, topical influence and importance";[39] if Worringer indeed "interpreted and guided the feeling of a new generation" (currying particular favor among writers on the political right), then the question of the relationship between Worringer's ideology and his thesis cannot be passed over in silence or ignorance.

Our own question is to the rhetorical structure of Worringer's text. For what kinds of ideological distortions operated it so as to enable such an ideologically distorted reaction? What kinds of alternative reading are possible and necessary? We must initiate a rhetorically aware reading of *Abstraction and Empathy*—a reading that might link the text's structural idiosyncrasies with its determinate ideology and persuasive strategy.

III

Worringer's text is divided into two main parts, "Theoretical" and "Practical," and each of these is subdivided respectively into two or three subsections. The first theoretical subsection elaborates what Worringer calls the two fundamental artistic drives, urges, or wills: abstraction and empathy; the second subsection discusses the residual products of each: in turn, the "form" of style (abstraction) and naturalism (empathy). The second main part, the practical, applies the theoretical model to examples of genre and period: in turn, first, Ornament; second, Architecture and Sculpture; and third, the Northern Pre-Renaissance. This last subsection (and the book in its original form) concludes with an analysis of the "apotheosis" of "abstract tendencies of Northern artistic volition," namely, the treatment of drapery (119 [163]).[40]

The text was supplemented with new prefaces as it was reissued through its many editions. Of particular interest to us will be the first main, theoretical part of the text proper; the 1948 preface (which describes the "conception" of the text in the Trocadéro Museum in Paris); the long epilogue of 1959 that has not been translated into English; and the appendix that was first added to the third edition of 1910, "Transcendence and Immanence in Art," in which the drives of abstraction and empathy and their concomitant forms of style and naturalism are linked to their respective "metaphysical"—the term is Worringer's—equivalents of transcendence and immanence.

The argument presupposes and proceeds in tension with a number of pretextual sources and in a variety of theoretical contexts. Gombrich has provided a sovereign overview of the tradition from which many of the salient features of *Abstraction and Empathy* emerge. He discusses the work of Hildebrand, Wölfflin, Wickhoff, and Riegl (but not Lipps) in the context of the evolution of the psychology of vision from the Greeks on. The reader is directed to Gombrich for this context.[41]

The major positive influence on Worringer was Riegl's "Kantian revolution" in art history (the analysis of art in terms of how it is articulated according to two basic epistemological and perceptual categories, the haptic and the optic) and his postulation of changing modes of perception, artistic volition, and intention *(Kunstwollen)*.[42] Riegl's work was directed, for Worringer (and Riegl himself), against Gottfried Semper's brilliantly reductive thesis that art emerges from the three-part nexus of raw material/utilitarian purpose/technology *(Können)*.[43] But Worringer's major point of departure in *Abstraction and Empathy* was less Riegl or Semper than the work of Theodor Lipps, in particular his elaboration of the notion of empathy first used by Robert Vischer in *Über das optische Formgefühl* (1873). Lipps's famous formula for empathy, the foil to Worringer's entire thesis, was "aesthetic enjoyment is objectified self-enjoyment" ("ästhetischer Genuß ist objektivierter Selbstgenuß").[44] For Worringer, Lipps's thesis conceals an inevitably provincial, "Eurocentric"

(99 [141]),[45] and ahistorical bias (*pace* Lukács). There are instead only two primary binary aesthetic urges, abstraction and empathy, with their respective forms.

> Just as the urge to empathy as a pre-assumption of aesthetic experience finds gratification in the beauty of the organic, so the urge to abstraction finds its beauty in the life-denying inorganic, in the crystalline, or in general terms, in all abstract law and necessity. (4 [36])

In Worringer's schematic periodization, empathy signifies Greek antiquity, the Italian Renaissance, and the art of Western Europe to the end of the nineteenth century; in terms of theory, it exerts a dominant, even repressive, influence on contemporary aesthetics. Abstraction signifies Egyptian art and architecture, Byzantine mosaic, ornament, and Romanesque sculpture. In complicated ways, the Northern Gothic represents a synthesis of both tendencies.

As his subtitle suggests, Worringer is concerned with a "psychology of style." Thus he makes what was to become a portentous argument for an existential grounding of these urges and realizations. The primary source of empathy/naturalism is delectation of an organically structured, ordered, secure, meaningful universe. Its "psychic precondition" is "a happy pantheistic confidence between man and the phenomena of the external world" (15 [49]). The urge to abstraction/style, however, takes root in an awareness of temporality, contingency, and in a state of abject terror: "the immense dread of space," and "the flux of happening" (15 [49]). Born as it is of the desperate psychological need for faith, repose, and stability, it is this existential imperative which, as we have seen, struck such responsive chords in writers, artists, and critics:

> Tormented by the entangled inter-relationship and flux of the phenomena of the outer world, such peoples (scil. the civilized peoples of the East) were dominated by an immense need for tranquillity. The happiness they sought from art did not consist in the possibility of projecting themselves into the things of the outer world, of enjoying themselves in them, but in the possibility of taking the individual thing of the external world out of its arbitrariness and seeming fortuitousness, of eternalising it by approximation to abstract forms and, in this manner, of finding a point of tranquillity and a refuge from appearances. Their most powerful urge was, so to speak, to

wrest the object of the external world out of its natural context, out of the unending flux of being, to purify it of all its dependence upon life, i.e. of everything about it that was arbitrary, to render it necessary and irrefragable, to approximate it to its *absolute* value. Where they were successful in this, they experienced that happiness and satisfaction which the beauty of organic-vital form affords us; indeed, they knew no other beauty, and therefore we may term it their beauty. (16–17 [50–51])

Now there are (at least) two consciousnesses at work in passages like this one: one described and the other inscribed. The description of "such peoples" at the beginning and the rhetorical "we" at the end are only nominally different. The speaker (and by extension his sympathetic listener) who can understand (Lipps will say, as we shall see shortly, "empathize" with) them is in a privileged position and is already inscribed in the ostensible description. For it is but a small step to project or translate this "we" into "such peoples." Such inscription was, in any event, precisely made by so many in the modern movement.

The author of *Abstraction and Empathy* himself steps forward in many guises. He is a historian and psychologist of style, a critic of culture (especially of technology, positivism, and realism), a scientist (in the peculiar German idiom), a kind of technician of the sacred (a priest of abstract art as redemption [*Erlösung*]), and, not least, a psychoanalyst of that anxiety and dread that lie at the very root of all authentic artistic activity. And Worringer outlines a helixlike morphology of art in which "primitive" and "foreign" forms are potentially recurrent in history, since they are ontologically and psychologically primary. The enormous influence of his text was due to, and manipulated by, all these roles.

A critique of this polyphonous text and its influence can profitably continue with a closer look at Worringer's use of Theodor Lipps since Lipps's theory stands, as Worringer says, *pars pro toto* as "foil" for his entire thesis (4 [36]). Worringer's use of this pretext's notion of empathy can be designated precisely as "misprision" since he "creatively" misreads Lipps in order to gain space for his own thesis. That his discourse states its insight in the mode of blindness is doubly ironic since few writers have been at greater pains than has Lipps to make an argument transparent.

For Lipps, the use of the term "empathy" has corresponded too often with abuse, a situation he sets out to rectify. "Empathy" has a long history, extending in the German tradition deep into early Romanticism.[46] As Lipps construes it, empathy is neither a simple, spontaneous occurrence in you but rather the fact that you move yourself and are moved when you perceive anything whatsoever. It is not a feeling *(Gefühl)* that is valorized (it is not pleasure or displeasure). It is rather "self-objectification" in which both terms, self and object, receive diacritical stress. Empathy is a mode of self-objectification, Lipps argues, that is not limited in a necessary manner to the natural or organic order of things *(pace* Worringer). Lipps's first example, in his 1906 essay "Einfühlung und ästhetischer Genuß," is the case of our *apperception* (the neo-Kantian term conveys for him the temporal modes of recollection and anticipation)[47] of a discrete, abstract line in geometry. From this minimal example, Lipps extrapolates in ascending order of complexity visual examples from nature, intersubjectivity, and finally aesthetics. He then reflects on the aesthetic dimension of all perceptual encounters.[48] It should be noted that for Lipps the verb *sich einfühlen* is something more than a reflexive verb (again *pace* Worringer). It is not so much a projection *(sich einfühlen)*, although it is this, but rather an activity of objectification *(eine Tätigkeit)*. Empathy is closely related to translation (and thus, we swiftly note, to a figural and rhetorical process of metaphor-making), to translating something felt in you into an object. But this object is something, as Lipps repeatedly insists, that makes counter-demands *(Förderungen, Zumutungen)* on you. The relation between the object and the subject is thus precisely circular, part transcendental, part naive. It is, *in fine*, a dialogical relation,[49] for which Gadamer's term "fusion of horizons" is appropriate. This would be the case if, when Lipps writes "ich bin in etwas eingefühlt," he can be interpreted to mean "I *am* in so far as I am felt to empathize in something or someone else." Whether this strong ontological interpretation is legitimate or not, however, Vernon Lee is correct when, in her own discussion of empathy, she insists that it should not be construed to be a reflexive action alone, nor as a "metaphysical, quasi-mysterious *projection of the ego* into the object under observation."[50] Lee's intervention here is, to be sure, intended as a critique of Lipps; yet Lipps in facts avoids just this confusion ascribed to him by Lee and Worringer. Empathy for Lipps is never the deluded, naive, or permanent self-identification or fusion of the ego and the object of perception.[51]

Two important dimensions of Lipps's argument are suppressed in *Abstraction and Empathy.* First, the description of empathy as an active, intentional participation, not a static state of consciousness;

second, the thesis that "abstract figures" (including geometric lines) can be aesthetically significant *independent* from their appearance in nature.[52] In the light of this suppression, Worringer's value-charged notion of empathy as "a relationship of confidence between man and the external world," as an "unproblematic sense of being at home in the world," as "the naive anthropomorphic pantheism or polytheism," as "world-revering naturalism" (45 [83]), etc., can only be read as a severe ideologically motivated distortion of emphasis.

This is not to deny that, from a broader perspective than Worringer can assume, the notion of empathy (in Lipps's sense) can be viewed as "radically subjectivizing" and as a "specifically philistine aesthetic theory."[53] Lipps's theory is quite obviously born of an ideology of complacency and the rationalization of lived social conditions. Particularly revealing in this regard is the example of the leper cited in the 1906 essay and, especially, the last paragraphs of that essay. There a relationship of art to "true humanity" is indeed eulogized.[54] Nothing could be closer to what has been called "complicities of communion in the complacent breaking of the humanist bread, the complicity which confirms the spectator in his spontaneous ideology."[55] Horatian injunction *tua res agitur* demands not aestheticized empathy nor even ideological recognition, but rather a deeper empathy with the totality of lived relations and a knowledge of the abstract relations that determine them. But our question here involves not Lipps but Worringer, since in all this problematic he is not only not in advance of Lipps through his criticism of him but in retreat. And this is in large measure due to his suppression of the complexity of Lipps's argument, his turning of it into a mere foil to his own argument on behalf of abstraction. Pretexts triumph here over the text, a triumph repeated by the text's reception.[56]

Misprision operates in *Abstraction and Empathy* on many levels. It is reflected, for example, in what is in effect Worringer's betrayal of his *own* intention and self-understanding. For Worringer does not initially set out to argue on behalf of abstraction, but rather for the need for a synthesis of the terms of his binary opposition. The first paragraph of his text proper calls for the "clear delimitation" of the aesthetics of natural beauty from that of the work of (plastic) art (3 [35]). The mechanism that apparently operates the polarity of abstraction and empathy in history is, however, left vague. His spirit in the machine is similar, it would seem, to the agonistic model used by Nietzsche in the *The Birth of Tragedy* (45 [82]). The text is intended to understand this teleology, whatever its mechanism, and to achieve precisely "an approximately complete picture of the evolution of human artistic activity" (34 [70]). Worringer insisted on this intention repeatedly and made it explicit in his appendix of 1910 (126–27 [172–73]). This desire for synthesis is certainly reflected, too, in his vision of the Gothic (nationalistically, even racially, oposed to cisalpine art) (48 [86] and 114–15 [157]).[57] The Gothic is the "approximate" synthesis of Naturalism and Style. It is—and note the organic metaphor—"the puberty of modern man" (115 [158]). Worringer also describes a specifically *Germanic* need for the Gothic:

> The need for empathy of this inharmonious people does not take the nearest-at-hand path to the organic, because the harmonious motion of the organic is not sufficiently expressive for it, it needs rather that uncanny pathos [*jenes unheimliche Pathos*] which attaches to the animation of the inorganic. (77 [116])

But we are well advised by Freud not to let the uncanny slip by unnoticed. What is often strangest and distant in time (the Gothic) may well be what is closest to home (Worringer's text, which would lead us there).

His later introductions function to reiterate the sense of strangeness he felt in the presence of his own text. He cannot get over it: "The compass of my instinct had pointed in a direction inexorably pre-ordained by the dictate of the spirit of the age [*vom Diktat des Zeitgeistes*]" (vii–viii [7–8]). As early as 1910 he had written:

> [T]he most recent movement in art has shown my problem to have gained an immediate topicality, not only for art historians, whose concern is with the evaluation of the past, but also for practicing artists striving for new goals of expression. Those misconstrued and ridiculed values of the abstract volition, which I sought to rehabilitate through scientific analysis, were simultaneously—not arbitrarily, but from inner developmental necessity—re-established in artistic practice as well. Nothing has given me greater satisfaction and corroboration than the fact that this parallelism has also been spontaneously felt by artists devoting themselves to the new problems of representation. (xiv–xv)

In the last introduction (1959), this sense of "topical vitality" was undiminished and "astonishing" to him ([15–16], German only). This fascination with topicality is precisely the interference with the hope for a synthesis of abstraction and empathy. Such intent is waylaid by the Expressionists and later by other writers, artists, and critics. The persuaded reception of abstraction is an uncanny reception.

But such interference is amply present "in" the text proper itself. It is indicative, for example, that when Worringer describes "primitive man's" search for order in a chaotic world he shifts suddenly into the present tense: "Having slipped down from the pride of knowledge, man is just as lost and helpless *vis-à-vis* the world-picture as primitive man" (18 [52]). If this is true, however, only abstraction (not synthesis) can save "modern man" as it had once saved the "primitive"; and where else can such salvation be provided, at least initially, than by his own text itself? Yet it is a text overdetermined by unreflected value-judgments: pejorative depictions of empathy (and reason) and enthusiasm for abstraction (and the irrational).[58] *Abstraction and Empathy* is the absolute conflation of normative and descriptive modes of discourse.

Certainly Worringer could never entirely obviate the need if not for empathy then for sympathy, "the only sentiment to which no character of man is indifferent" (David Hume, *Enquiries*, 223). An ostensibly "scientific" text that can so badly conceal its desire to be topical and programmatic cries out for empathy. That writers need readers as much as readers need them is not an anonymous vagary: it has been confirmed by schools of criticism that otherwise violently disagree. But there is no need to import a foreign term to describe this fact: one name for it is empathy (Lipps) but not empathy (Worringer). And when "the psychic presuppositions for the urge to abstraction" are to be sought, it is still "we" who must seek them: "We must seek them in these peoples' feelings about the world, in their psychic attitude toward the cosmos" (15 [49]). But how could we possibly recognize these "feelings" there if we did not know them already, to some extent, in ourselves? Indeed Worringer is compelled, quite in defiance of his propaganda for abstraction, to make this point explicit: "we cannot suppose man to have picked up . . . the laws of abstract regularity, from inanimate matter, it is, rather, an intellectual necessity for us to assume that these laws are also implicitly contained in our own human organization" (20 [54]). A great deal is at stake for Worringer at this historical juncture.

> Our knowledge of phenomena is complete only when it has reached that point at which everything which seemed to be a boundary becomes a transition, and we suddenly become aware of the relativity of the whole. To have known things

means to have penetrated to the innermost nucleus of their being [*bis zu jenem innersten Kernpunkt ihres Wesens vorgedrungen zu sein*], where they disclose themselves to us in the whole of their problematic. (126 [172])

But this depiction of the desire of Worringer's entire discursive enterprise is formulated not in the language of alienated, crystalline, inorganic abstraction but in the discourse of hermeneutics. It is a discourse far closer to Lipps than Worringer could allow himself to imagine. He has no choice, however, but to *use* the empathy he has misread if he is to advance his thesis and convey it to his text's implied reader.

Once again we note the powerful irony at work. The use of empathy in Worringer's text is especially ironic if irony is considered as a trope. For tropes, in what Nietzsche called the extramoral sense, are used mechanically and unconsciously but never without ulterior motive. "Truth" (for Worringer, his desire for *aletheia* of "the innermost nucleus") is itself, in part, an army of rhetorical figures, drawn up by the unknown commander of language ("syntax" *means* to draw up an army) in order to do battle with a foe and, ironically, with itself. It is tropes that are precisely abstract in Worringer's sense of "primary," "originary," "fundamental." Vernon Lee's deceptively quiet suggestion is this: "Empathy is what explains why we employ figures of speech at all, and occasionally employ them . . . when we *know* perfectly well that the figure we have chosen expresses the exact reverse of the objective truth."[59] The issue of abstraction versus empathy leads us not out to an empirically existing style of Egyptian sculpture or cisalpine naturalism but into a much deeper problematic.

Just as "Theodor Lipps" became little more than a synecdoche for a distorted view of empathy, the "pure" Greek as Worringer presents him in "confident surrender to the outer world, the sensuously secure feeling of being at ease and at one with creation," etc. (101 [144]), surely never existed empirically. He is a metonomy for Worringer's nostalgic desire for order and meaning, his hope for efficacy. Did Worringer know nothing of the Nietzschean birth of tragedy? The referentiality of Worringer's description of, say, Byzantine ornament is equally open to the same analysis. And what now is the function of the Gothic in Worringer's text? To this last question we shall return, but we see already that the Gothic must be some figure for Worringer's own abstracting attempt to impose order on an alienated view of history and on a deep confusion within the order of discourse within which he writes. Harold Osborne had located one important feature of this confusion:

> [M]any leaders of abstract movements in twentieth-century art
> have been attracted towards a revelatory theory of art and
> have believed that abstract works of art body forth a vision of
> ultimate verities or reflect a metaphysical reality beyond the
> world of the senses. Although in common with the trend of
> the time their attitude to their art has been in the main non-
> naturalistic, this element of Idealistic naturalism has often re-
> mained and they have felt that their works were not only new
> creations complete in themselves but could convey an emo-
> tional revelation of a reality beyond themselves.[60]

In this light, it is particularly interesting that Barbara Harlow, in
regard to Alois Riegl's major text, poses the question of whether
Riegl describes confusions in his object of study (as he believes) or
rather his own distorted state and frame of reference, in which case
the confusions are in that text (and, in a sense, always already known
by it).[61]

Some of the confusions in *Abstraction and Empathy* involve rather
obvious shifts of emphasis. Worringer, as we saw, speaks of both
abstraction *and* empathy as "artistic urges" that have ontic manifestations and reflect ontological choices (transcendence or immanence).
But there is in Lipps's discussion of empathy—or in any discussion
of empathy until Worringer's—never a strong claim made that "empathy" depicts the artistic activity *sensu stricto*. Lipps is not talking
about artistic creation; he is talking about perception. Worringer
would seem to have shifted the axis of consumption (empathy) onto
the axis of production (abstraction).[62] Now, his *text's* awareness of
this displacement from a psychology of perception to a psychology
of creativity coincides in direct proportion to *Worringer's* failure to
make it explicit. When he discusses abstraction his language becomes,
as we have seen, most empathetic and performative; when he discusses empathy, it becomes most anxious and, in Worringer's terms,
most abstract. It is then that it is manipulated by forces not in his
control. And so it is often extremely difficult, if not impossible, to
read *Abstraction and Empathy* in such a way as to have figure and
meaning correspond in any stable manner. "Objective description"
spasmodically fluctuates and yields. Most readers in point of fact have
been persuaded for the case of abstraction (*pace* Lukács) and against
its synthesis with empathy (*pace* Holdheim).

But the most striking evidence that empathy has not been banished
far from the surface of Worringer's argument is that the text is heavily
dependent on organic metaphors at crucial moments in the argu-

ment. For example, there is Worringer's only sustained effort at self-understanding, namely, his attempt to foreground his own text qua text. The first post–World War II preface (1948) is overdetermined by metaphors of, in order, sterility, insemination, conception, gestation, labor pains, maturation, and even death. Worringer begins by describing a day in Paris ("a grey forenoon destitute of all emotional atmosphere" viii [9]) at the Trocadéro when he was a young student. He was compelled to study "the rendering of drapery" and then, suddenly, the sterility of the moment was shattered by an interruption, the unexpected entrance into the room by Georg Simmel, then known to Worringer only by sight. In the silent presence of Simmel the following event is said to have taken place:

> [I]t was in the ensuing hours spent in the halls of the Trocadéro with Simmel in a contact consisting solely in the atmosphere created by his presence, that produced in a sudden, explosive act of birth the world of ideas which then found its way into my thesis and first brought my name before the public. (ix [10])

He continues: "I shall not describe the state of spiritual intoxication in which the hours of conception left me. Nor shall I speak of the pangs [*Geburtswehen*] that accompanied the subsequent birth of the written word" (x [10]). The "miraculous sequel" to this story was that it was Simmel who, years later, was "of all men the first to react, with a spontaneous call, to the surprise afforded him by the chance reading of my trains of thought!" (ix [10]). Simmel, having been sent a copy of *Abstraction and Empathy* by their mutual friend Paul Ernst, was "the secret and unconscious midwife at the birth of my inspiration," and "the first to react to the paper in which the seed of this hour came to fruition" (xii [13]). And thus a "bridge, both mysterious and meaningful was established to my happiest hour of conception" (xii [13]).[63]

Now, this is empathetic discourse in the crudest sense. Its function in Worringer's text is neither gratuitous nor meaningless. It is precisely *rhetorical* in the double sense of the word: it is powerfully figural and it desires to persuade. Worringer himself writes of why he tells the story at all: "I am sacrificing to the god in which I believe most deeply, the *deo ignoto* of chance, if I recall these enigmatic concatenations today and if I feel the urge to enable others to experience them in retrospect" (xii [14]). And, equally important, this story gives Worringer's own text the most perfect, organic, and natural shape possible: circularity. For the text proper of *Abstraction and Empathy* ends, we remember, with a description of Gothic drapery, itself like Worringer's text a fusion of "uncanny pathos."

We are confronted here with what French deconstructionists term a *pli*: a fold in drapery and in the text, an undulating strategem and, perhaps, a message. But what is the message? And how should we read it? What is a text like *Abstraction and Empathy*? A conflation of history, theory, and practice? A self-consuming artifact? An allegory of bad faith? Do precisely such questions constitute the definition of what we mean by an "Expressionist" text? Yet, even these intractable aporias are, I would like to suggest in conclusion, only partial.

IV

I would have most liked my discourse—itself determined by a number of often heterogeneous discourses and ideologies—to have broached a more fundamental problematic: What is the relation in the rhetoric of criticism between abstract trope and empathetic persuasions? Paul de Man's formulation of the theoretical issue is exemplary:

> Considered as persuasion, rhetoric is performative but when considered as a system of tropes, it deconstructs its own performance. Rhetoric is a *text* in that it allows for two incompatible, mutually self-destructive points of view and therefore puts an insurmountable obstacle in the way of any reading or understanding. The aporia between performative and constative language is merely a version of the aporia between trope and persuasion that both generates and paralyzes rhetoric and thus gives it the appearance of a history.[64]

This statement is in control of all the crucial questions but one: namely, *the question of control itself*. For history continues to operate, if not in spite of this luminous point zero of understanding, then because of it. Statements, including de Man's, continue to persuade (or dissuade) and thus to generate history (if only histories of reception). Other aporias still remain: Whom do statements persuade and why? Who or what is in control? And finally, to return to the inscription from Foucault, what power are *we* trying to appropriate?

In the specific context of this collection of essays, what exactly is our relation to our own historical documents? Does our scholarly discourse—to allude to the Marxist thesis that is *skandalon* at the aporia of our moment—in its desire to interpret the world (to glide on the path of least resistance into its pretexts), obviate the desire and the ability to change it? If this were the case, it would be the truer insult and the much more serious charge—to our friend the Professor of Greek and to Worringer's presentation of the problem of abstraction and empathy, but also, "in the last instance," to "us."

NOTES

1. Editor's note: This essay, written in 1977–78, appeared originally in *The Turn of the Century: German Literature and Art, 1890–1915*, ed. Gerald Chapple and Hans Schulte (Bonn: Bouvier, 1981), 197–223. It is reprinted here with slight revisions for several reasons: its importance as an interpretation of *Abstraction and Empathy* and as a useful documentation of sources (which need to be made more readily available), its pertinence in the context of this volume, and the perspective it gives on the changes in Geoffrey Waite's consideration of Worringer over the last decade.

2. Had this paper been written today, its theoretical position (under the influence, for example, of Sebastiano Timpanaro, *On Materialism* [London: NLB, 1975]) would be different, its style and tone more direct. With regard to secondary texts relevant to discussion of Worringer, two new groups of material have appeared since this essay was written that merit study: (1) the lively literary and political debate between Joseph Frank and Frank Kermode (and others) on the notion of "spatial form," which has found an arena in *Critical Inquiry* (Winter 1977, Winter 1978, Spring 1978), although nothing explicit is added there to the problem of reading Worringer's major text; and (2) the important, revisionist position on the significance of that text's reception in Germany before 1911 that is to be found in a long, lucid footnote in Peg Weiss, *Kandinsky in Munich: The Formative Jugendstil Years* (Princeton: Princeton University Press, 1979), 158–59. Weiss also demonstrates persuasively that Theodor Lipps's theory of empathy had direct, formative influence—as I think his readers might well expect—precisely on the theory and practice of nonobjective, "abstract" art, at least in its *Jugendstil* variant. For an exemplary analysis of the relation between ideology and rhetorical, narrative disruption in texts that emerged from a historical conjuncture and theoretical problematic not dissimilar from Worringer's, I enthusiastically recommend Fredric Jameson, *Fables of Aggression: Wyndham Lewis, The Modernist as Fascist* (Berkeley and Los Angeles: University of California Press, 1979).

3. See Paul de Man, *Blindness and Insight: Essays in the Rhetoric of Contemporary Criticism* (New York: Oxford University Press, 1971), viii and esp. 136–37. Here de Man defines the "literary" text as "any text that implicitly or explicitly signifies its own rhetorical mode and prefigures its own misunderstanding as the correlative of its rhetorical nature; that is, of its 'rhetoricity.' It can do so by declarative statement or by poetic inference. (A discursive, critical, or philosophical text that does this by means of statements is therefore not more or less literary than a poetic text that would avoid direct statement. In practice, the distinctions are often blurred: the logic of many philosophical texts relies heavily on narrative coherence and figures of speech, while poetry abounds in general statements. The criterion of literary specificity does not depend on the greater or lesser discursiveness of the mode but on the degree of consistent 'rhetoricity' of the language.)" On the problem-

atic implications of de Man's privileging of literary language in (even) this sense, see Timothy Reiss's chapter "Discursive Criticism and Epistemology," in *Interpretations of Narrative*, ed. Mario J. Valdés and Owen J. Miller (Toronto: University of Toronto Press, 1978), 38–47, esp. 43–47.

4. Louis Althusser and Etienne Balibar, *Reading Capital* (London: NLB, 1977), 15–16.

5. Gadamer's term is *wirkungsgeschichtliches Bewußtsein*. See Hans-Georg Gadamer, *Wahrheit und Methode: Grundzüge einer philosophischen Hermeneutik*, 3d ed. (Tübingen: Mohr, 1975), 343. For this translation of the term and a discussion of it, see David Couzens Hoy, *The Critical Circle: Literature and History in Contemporary Hermeneutics* (Berkeley and Los Angeles: University of California Press, 1978), 63 and passim.

6. This is a complicated and difficult issue. For Gadamer's response to early critics of *Wahrheit und Methode* on this point, see his 1967 essay "Rhetorik, Hermeneutik und Ideologiekritik. Metakritische Erörterungen zu 'Wahrheit und Methode,'" in *Theorie-Diskussion: Hermeneutik und Ideologiekritik* (Frankfurt am Main: Suhrkamp, 1975), 57–82. More recently, Gadamer has dealt (in discussions at the University of Iowa and York University) with the problem of texts that resist hermeneutical understanding. One of the most important statements of the necessity for a general theory of interpretation to account for both recollection of meaning (hermeneutics) and reduction of the illusions of consciousness (deconstruction or demystification) is Paul Ricoeur's discussion of Marx, Nietzsche, and Freud as the "three masters of the school of suspicion" in his *De l'interprétation: Essai sur Freud* (Paris: Editions du Seuil, 1965), esp. 29–44.

7. See the interview with Foucault, "Revolutionary Action: 'Until Now,'" in Michel Foucault, *Language, Counter-Memory, Practice: Selected Essays and Interviews*, ed. Donald Bouchard (Ithaca: Cornell University Press, 1977), 219.

8. Althusser and Balibar, 28–29. See also the discussion of this term in the glossary by Ben Brewster to Louis Althusser, *For Marx* (New York: Random House, 1970), 253–54. The concept of structured textual gaps *(Leerstellen)* is crucial to the aesthetics of reception of literary texts, especially the aesthetics of Wolfgang Iser and, in my opinion, is most persuasively argued in his essay "The Patterns of Negativity in Beckett's Prose," *Georgia Review* 29 (Fall 1975), 706–19. Cyrus Hamlin, whose ongoing work develops a hermeneutic of reading from Hegel's concept of negativity, discusses Iser's work in the context of the European tradition of narrative (catastrophe in Attic tragedy, conversion in the New Testament); see his important theoretical position paper "Strategies of Reversal in Literary Narrative," in *Interpretation of Narrative*, ed. Valdés and Miller, 61–73.

9. Terry Eagleton, *Criticism and Ideology: A Study in Marxist Literary Theory* (London: NLB, 1976), 89. I am aware that Althusser's notion of problematic does not fully accord with Eagleton's. On the relation of these two writers, see Thomas E. Lewis's "Notes toward a Theory of the Referent," *PMLA* 94 (May 1979), 459–75.

10. See Michel Foucault, *The Archaeology of Knowledge* (New York: Harper and Row, 1976), 6–7. Compare, however, the following qualification: "And the reading must always aim at a certain relationship, unperceived by the writer, between what he commands and what he uses. This relationship is not a certain quantitative distribution of shadow and light, of weakness and force, but a signifying structure that critical reading should *produce* . . . . To produce this signifying structure obviously cannot consist of reproducing, by the effaced and respectful doubling of commentary, the conscious, voluntary, intentional relationship that the writer institutes in his exchanges with the history to which he belongs thanks to the element of language. This moment of doubling commentary should no doubt have its place in a critical reading. To recognize and respect all its classical exigencies is not easy and requires all the instruments of traditional criticism. Without this recognition and this respect, critical production would risk developing in any direction at all and authorize

itself to say almost anything. But this indispensable guardrail has always only *protected*, it has never *opened*, a reading." Jacques Derrida, *Of Grammatology* (Baltimore: Johns Hopkins University Press, 1976), 158.

11. Althusser, *For Marx*, 67. For a discussion of the concept of problematic from a Marxian perspective, see Alex Callinicos, *Althusser's Marxism* (London: Pluto, 1976), 34–38. For a structuralist point of view, see Miriam Glucksmann, *Structuralist Analysis in Contemporary Social Thought: A Comparison of the Theories of Claude Lévi-Strauss and Louis Althusser* (London: Routledge and Kegan Paul, 1974), 3–13.

12. Wilhelm Worringer, *Abstraktion und Einfühlung: Ein Beitrag zur Stilpsychologie*. The edition I use is Munich: Piper, 1959; Serie Piper no. 122, 1981. The English translation, used when quoting Worringer in the main body of my text, is New York: International Universities Press, 1953. The translation is cited first in parentheses; the page reference to the German edition follows in brackets within the parentheses.

13. Albert Soergel and Curt Hohoff, *Dichtung und Dichter der Zeit: Vom Naturalismus bis zur Gegenwart*, rev. ed. (Düsseldorf: Gabel, 1963), 2:23–35, esp. 27–28. The first edition of 1925 is even less restrained in its estimation of Worringer's importance.

14. See *Handbuch der deutschen Gegenwartsliteratur*, ed. Hermann Kunisch (Munich: Nymphenburger Verlagsbuchhandlung, 1965), 20–45, esp. 20–21. For Kunisch, "Form als Geist" corresponds to Expressionism, "Form als Welt" to Worringer's terms "Einfühlung/Naturalismus," and "Form als Figur" is the logical extension of Expressionism in terms of "Abstraktion/Stil" in Worringer's sense.

15. See Roy Pascal, *From Naturalism to Expressionism: German Literature and Society, 1880–1918* (London: Weidenfeld and Nicolson, 1973), 63.

16. See Werner Haftmann, *Painting in the Twentieth Century* (London: Humphries, 1960), 129.

17. Some leads concerning Worringer's influence on artists are given in Will Grohmann, *Wassily Kandinsky: Leben und Werk*, 2d ed. (Cologne: M. Du Mont Schauberg, 1968), 85–88, and Herbert Read, *Art and Alienation: The Role of the Artist in Society* (New York: Horizon, 1967), 127–28, 142, 157. Kunisch is helpful on Worringer's interest for German writers, as is Soergel-Hohoff. On the theoretical significance of his theories for modern art, see especially Werner Haftmann, *Grundlagen der modernen Kunst: Eine Einführung in ihre symbolischen Formen* (Stuttgart: Kröner, 1966), 81–85, 109–10 and passim.

18. See Klaus Lankheit, "Wissenschaftlicher Anhang" to Wassily Kandinsky and Franz Marc, *Der Blaue Reiter*, dokumentarische Neuausgabe, ed. Klaus Lankheit (Munich: Piper, 1965), 253–304; here 277. Further discussion of Worringer and his contemporaries is on 254, 271–72, 286, 298. For a revisionist view of the relationship of Worringer to Kandinsky, see the interview with Worringer in Klaus Brisch, *Wassily Kandinsky (1886–1944): Untersuchungen zur Entstehung der gegenstandslosen Malerei an seinem Werk von 1900–1921* (Dissertation, Bonn 1955), 22. This work contains a wealth of information and documentation concerning the entire period.

19. See in particular Paul Pörtner, "Zur Begriffsbestimmung der Ismen," in *Literatur-Revolution 1910–1925: Dokumente, Manifeste, Programme* (Neuwied am Rhein: Luchterhand, 1961), 1:13–25.

20. Pascal, *From Naturalism to Expressionism*, 62.

21. T. E. Hulme, *Speculations: Essays on Humanism and the Philosophy of Art*, ed. Herbert Read, foreword by Jacob Epstein (London: Kegan Paul, 1936), 82–91. For a discussion of the importance of Worringer for Hulme, see Alun R. Jones, *The Life and Opinions of T. E. Hulme* (London: Gollancz, 1960), 101–17.

22. T. E. Hulme, *Further Speculations*, ed. Sam Hynes (Lincoln: University of Nebraska Press, 1962), 120.

23. Joseph Frank, *The Widening Gyre: Crisis and Mastery in Modern Literature* (New Brunswick: Rutgers University Press, 1963). See in particular the chapter "Spatial Form in Literature," 3–62, which first appeared in the *Sewanee Review* in 1945. Further page references are in the main body of my text.

24. Thus Frank in 1945 would have answered Heinrich Küntzel's suggestion in 1969 that it might be possible to show that *Abstraction and Empathy* "kann einen tieferen Grund für die Gemeinsamkeit der bildenden Kunst und der Literatur in der Zeit um 1910 abgeben, als ihn Motivparallelen anzeigen." See Küntzel's article "Alfred Lichtenstein," in *Expressionismus als Literatur: Gesammelte Studien*, ed. Wolfgang Rothe (Munich: Francke, 1969), 398–409, here 408.

25. See Nathaniel Tarn's ambitious essay "The Heraldic Vision: A Cognitive Model for Comparative Aesthetics," *Alcheringa, Ethno-Poetics Issue* (1976), 623–41.

26. William Spanos, "Modern Literary Criticism and the Spatialization of Time: An Existential Critique," *Journal of Aesthetics and Art Criticism* 29 (1970–71), 87–104.

27. Unpublished lecture delivered 6 March 1978 at the conference on contemporary criticism at the State University of New York at Binghamton sponsored by *boundary 2*, "Worringer and the Polarity of Understanding." My recollection of this important paper is guided by notes, but I take full responsibility and apologize for any inaccuracies. See the bibliography to this volume for the published version of Holdheim's essay and the rejoinder by Joseph A. Buttigieg.

28. Actually, many of Holdheim's theoretical concerns find expression in the work of the *Strukturforschung* school of art criticism, especially that of Guido von Kaschnitz-Weinberg. See Sheldon Nodelman, "Structural Analysis in Art and Anthropology," in *Structuralism*, ed. Jacques Ehrmann (Garden City, N.Y.: Doubleday, 1970), 79–93.

29. Emil Utitz, *Grundlegung der allgemeinen Kunstwissenschaft*, 2 vols., reissue, ed. Wolfhart Henckmann (Munich: Fink, 1972). Utitz agrees with Worringer's intention to free aesthetics from a dependency on the theory of beauty, but he considers his theoretical position (in particular his extension of Riegl's concept of *Kunstwollen*) relevant only to a mistaken notion of what a general aesthetics should entail (1:37, 279–80). He criticizes Worringer's work on the Gothic (1:37–38) and Worringer's stress on religion and metaphysics (1:282–83). He further accuses Worringer of having insufficient knowledge of the work of contemporary art historians (1:284–86).

30. Rudolf Arnheim, "Abstraction and Empathy in Retrospect," *Confinia Psychiatrica* 10 (1967), 1–15. Arnheim sees some value in Worringer's criticism of modern and "Europacentric" bias in art history, but he is critical of Worringer's linking of abstract artistic form with a psychological attitude of "withdrawal" and "refuge." He sees a potentially dangerous theoretical split in Worringer's theory between two kinds of art, both of which, according to Arnheim, require abstraction whatever their respective relations to "nature" may be. See his *Visual Thinking* (Berkeley and Los Angeles: University of California Press, 1969), 188–91, for further remarks on this matter.

31. Edwin Panofsky, *Meaning in the Visual Arts: Papers in and on Art History* (Garden City, N.Y.: Doubleday, 1955). On the misunderstanding in Worringer of the distinction made in classical aesthetics between "reality" and "nature" and the transformation of one into the other, see "The Fundamental Question," 265–85, esp. 266–67.

32. Edgar Wind, *Art and Anarchy: The Reith Lectures 1960*, rev. and enlarged ed. (London: Faber and Faber, 1963). Wind describes Worringer's diction as being dependent on an "antiquated psychology" that classified all impulses as volitions (128–29, 170–72).

33. E. H. Gombrich, *Art and Illusion: A Study of the Psychology of Pictorial Representation*, 3d ed. (London: Phaidon, 1968). Gombrich continues, in effect, Utitz's critique of Worringer. "By throwing out the question of skill" a valid psychology of stylistic change

is obviated. Further, and more disturbingly, he finds the "ghost in the machine" mechanism in Worringer's notion of history, which sanctions an anti-intellectual, metaphysical, and even racial explanation of change (16–18). In *Art and Alienation*, Herbert Read has attempted to "defend" Worringer's position by suggesting to Gombrich that "the conventions that are said to determine what and how the artist paints are of an equally supra-historical and intangible kind" (74, 107–8). A discussion of Worringer's fate in studies of, say, Egyptian or Gothic art would carry our present problem too far afield.

34. Georg Lukács, "Einführung in die Ästhetik Tschernyschewskijs," *Werke* (Neuwied am Rhein and Berlin: Luchterhand, 1969), 10:164.

35. See Lukács, *Ästhetik II, Werke,* 12:701, and *Ästhetik I, Werke,* 11:343–51. Compare also "Karl Marx und Friedrich Theodor Fischer," *Werke,* 10:284, and "Reportage oder Gestaltung," *Werke,* 4:63. Of most importance is Lukács's extensive discussion of Worringer's thesis in the historical context of the inability of the period from Romantic idealism to Expressionism to address the problematic of capitalism. See his seminal essay "'Größe und Verfall' des Expressionismus," *Werke,* 4:109–49. For an elaboration of "Fluchtideologie" and "Entleerung des Begriffs Revolution," see also Jost Hermand's analysis "Expressionismus als Revolution," *Von Mainz nach Weimar (1793–1919): Studien zur deutschen Literatur* (Stuttgart: Metzler, 1969), 109–49.

36. Lukács, "Kunst und objektive Wahrheit," *Werke,* 4:615–16.

37. Lukács, *Die Zerstörung der Vernunft, Werke,* 9:708.

38. Hofmann, 82.

39. Ibid.

40. The text of *Abstraction and Empathy* will be cited first in the pagination of the English translation, then the German original.

41. Gombrich, 3–18. Further background material and discussion of the context of Worringer's thesis are found in Melvin Rader's introduction to chapter 10 of *A Modern Book of Esthetics: An Anthology,* ed. Melvin Rader (New York: Holt, Rinehart and Winston, 1973), 353–57.

42. On Riegl, see Nodelmann and in particular Barbara Harlow, "Realignment: Alois Riegl's Image of Late Roman Art Industry," *Glyph* 3 (1973), 118–36.

43. For Riegl's critique of Semper, see Alois Riegl, *Historische Grammatik der bildenden Künste,* ed. Karl M. Swoboda and Otto Pächt (Graz and Cologne: Böhlau, 1966), 212–14, 254–55.

44. Quoted by Worringer (7/40); see Theodor Lipps, *Ästhetik: Psychologie des Schönen und der Kunst,* 3d ed. (Leipzig: Leopold Voss, 1923), 2:102–3. In *Abstraction and Empathy,* however, Worringer makes far more use of Lipps's popularized version of his thesis on empathy. This important essay in "Einfühlung und ästhetischer Genuß," *Die Zukunft* 54 (20 January 1906), 100–114. The quotation is on 100.

45. "Europa-zentrisch" seems to be Worringer's neologism. I prefer the translation above to "Europacentric."

46. A central early text in the German tradition is the following passage from *Die Lehrlinge zu Sais:* "Ein Blindgeborener lernt nicht sehen, und wenn man ihm noch so viel von Farben und Lichtern und fernen Gestalten erzählen wollte. So wird auch keiner die Natur begreifen, der kein Naturorgan, kein inneres naturerzeugendes und absonderndes Werkzeug hat, der nicht, wie von selbst, überall die Natur an allem erkennt und unterscheidet und mit angeborner Zeugungslust, in inniger mannigfaltiger Verwandschaft mit allen Körpern durch das Medium der Empfindung, sich mit allen Naturwesen vermischt, sich gleichsam in sie hineinfühlt." Novalis, *Schriften,* ed. Paul Kluckhohn and Richard Samuel (Stuttgart: Kolhammer, 1960), 1:105. On the face of it, this usage by Novalis would seem to justify Worringer's equation of empathy with a "naive" and "pantheistic

worldview." But such a reading avoids the issue of the context of the passage in Novalis's text and the underlying current of precision, negativity, and even "abstraction" demanded by Novalis himself. Worringer's own sense of the history of the term "empathy" is heavily indebted to Paul Stern, *Einfühlung und Association in der neueren Ästhetik: Ein Beitrag zur psychologischen Analyse der ästhetischen Anschauung* (Hamburg: Leopold Voss, 1898). The passage from *Die Lehrlinge zu Sais* was known to Worringer, since it appears here (in slightly different from) on 3.

47. See Carl Müller, *Die Apperzeptionstheorie von W. Wundt und Th. Lipps und ihre Weiterführung in der Gegenwart* (Langensalza: Hermann Beyer, 1910), 30–41.

48. Why, he asks, is the viewing of a picture of a leper qualitatively different from seeing a leper in reality? (Lipps, "Einfühlung," 113–14). We shall return briefly to this important and problematic example.

49. Holdheim stressed this aspect of Lipps's theory.

50. Vernon Lee [pseud. for Violet Paget], *The Beautiful: An Introduction to Psychological Aesthetics* (Cambridge: Cambridge University Press, 1913), 66–67. On the interchange between Lipps and Lee, see her discussion in *Beauty and Ugliness and Other Studies in Psychological Esthetics* (with C. Anstruther-Thomson), (London: John Lane, 1912), 45–76, 351–53. Also Rader, 353–55.

51. See Lipps, *Ästhetik*, 1:121–26.

52. See Lipps, *Ästhetik*, 1:225–56, for this important point. There are surprising parallels between Lipps's work and Husserlian phenomenology (especially the *Cartesian Meditations*). One would stress the active, apperceptive role Lipps accords perception and cognition, and the dialogical relationship between subject and object that is implicit in his *Ästhetik*. In Husserl, however, one finds a far more rigorous language into which Lipps could be translated. I am thinking of the role granted in the *Cartesian Meditations* to empathy, "analogical appresentation or apperception," "objectivity," and especially "intentional overreaching," which is defined as the "living mutual awakening, a mutual give and take and overlaying of each person with the objective sense of the other." See *Cartesianische Meditationen und Pariser Vorträge*, ed. S. Strasser (The Hague: Nijhoff, 1960), 142. Frederick A. Elliston's "Husserl's Phenomenology of Empathy," in *Husserl: Expositions and Appraisals*, ed. Frederick A. Elliston and Peter McCormick (Notre Dame: University of Notre Dame Press, 1977), 213–31, interprets Husserl in a way that validates such a comparison. Lipps shares with Husserl an unreflected rhetoric of presence in the sense defined and analyzed in Derrida's reading of Husserl; see Jacques Derrida, *La voix and le phénomène* (Paris: PUF, 1967).

53. Lukács, *Ästhetik II, Werke*, 12:187; compare also "Kunst und objektive Welt," *Werke*, 4:614–15.

54. "Keine Kunst kann in einen Gegenstand der Freude verwandeln, was naturgemäß Gegenstand unseres inneren Widerstrebens oder gar unseres Abscheues ist. Aber die Kunst kann uns aus alledem Menschliches herausfinden und herausfühlen lassen, nämlich positiv Menschliches, Leben, Kraft, Regsamkeit des Wollens, Arbeit, kurz: Thätigkeit. Und alles Dies, alles Leben kann in uns Widerhall finden oder kann eine Sehnsucht in uns befriedigen. Alle Sehnsucht, die wir fühlen, faßt sich ja doch zusammen in dem Einen: sie ist Sehnsucht zu leben." Lipps, "Einfühlung," 14.

55. Althusser, "Cremonini, Painter of the Abstract," in *Lenin and Philosophy and other Essays* (New York: Monthly Review Press, 1971), 229–42, here 239. This essay contains brilliant insights into the nature of abstract painting. See, further, *Leonardo Cremonini, Nostra antologica 1953–1969* (Bologna: Edizioni Alfa, 1969). A theory of abstraction must avoid the kind of reification afforded it by Worringer (and, for that matter, by discussions such as Richard Brinkmann's survey "'Abstrakte' Lyrik im Expressionismus und die Mög-

lichkeit symbolischer Aussage," in *Der deutsche Expressionismus: Formen und Gestalten*, ed. Hans Steffen [Göttingen: Vandenhoeck and Ruprecht, 1965], 88–114). Surely, in the words of Susanne Langer, "'abstraction' is the recognition of a *relational* structure or form apart from the specific thing (event, fact, image, etc.) in which it is exemplified." See Susanne Langer, *Problems of Art: The Philosophical Lectures* (New York: Charles Scribner's Sons, 1957), 163; my emphasis. The required historical perspective on this issue has been adumbrated by Jonathan Culler. The move at the turn of the century from the concept of the object to one of relation constitutes the major "shift of focus" (and indeed the epistemological break) that *defines* modernism (and much of our current discourse and ideology). Culler alludes to the presence of this shift in the entire series of disciplines: linguistics (Saussure), physics (Heisenberg), philosophy (Ernst Cassirer), philosophy of science (Whitehead), sociology (Durkheim), psychoanalysis (Freud), and literature and painting. George Braque's statement "I do not believe in things; I believe in relationships" may well be "the true modernist credo." See Jonathan Culler, *Ferdinand de Saussure* (Harmondsworth: Penguin, 1977), 51–129, esp. 126–29. It is precisely the definition of abstraction as relational function that is hopelessly obscured by Worringer's text and by so much of its reception. The issue is not merely academic. With regard to Langer (and Culler) the exigent problem remains, however, as to the *kind* and *value* of "relational structure" that obtains. For Althusser, a painter like Cremonini is not an "abstract" painter, but a "painter of abstraction," since he "'paints' the *relations* which bind objects, places and times. . . . Not an abstract painter 'painting' an absent, pure possibility in a new form and matter, but a painter of the real *abstract*, 'painting' . . . real relations (as relations they are necessarily *abstract*) between 'men' and their 'things,' or rather, to give the term its stronger sense, between 'things' and *their* 'men'" (230). Such work "makes us see, not the relations between the painter and his work, which have no *aesthetic* relation between that work and *us*" (231). Finally, such work "'paints' (i.e. 'depicts' by the play of the similarities inscribed in the differences) the history of men as a history *marked* . . . by the abstraction of their sites, spaces, objects, i.e. '*in the last instance*' by the *real abstraction* which determines and sums up these first abstractions: the relations which constitute their *living conditions*" (236).

56. "Wir können uns in etwas 'einfühlen,' dessen objektives Wesen uns völlig unbekannt oder gleichgültig ist, aber der offenbaren Wirklichkeit oder ihrer richtigen Abbildung gegenüber können wir nur zu einem Nacherleben angeleitet werden, in welchem das Bewußtsein, daß es sich nicht um unsere Subjektivität, sondern um eine davon unabhängige 'Welt' handelt, miteingeschlossen ist. Das Spezifische am Erlebnis 'tua res agitur' liegt gerade in dieser Dualität, die eine erlebte Wirklichkeit von der 'Einfühlung,' von der Introjektion unterscheidet." Lukács, *Ästhetik II*, *Werke*, 12:187. Lipps's theory of empathy, Lukács writes in a later essay, "spiegelt treu die ständig wachsende Subjektivierung der künstlerischen Praxis wider, die sich im Übergang vom Naturalismus zum Impressionismus usw., in der wachsenden Subjektivierung der Thematik und der schöpferischen Methode, in der zunehmenden Abwendung der Kunst von den großen Problemen der Gesellschaft äußert." Lukács, "Kunst und objektive Wahrheit," *Werke*, 4:614–15.

A particularly interesting example of the problem empathy poses for an engaged theory of art is provided by Bertolt Brecht. He developed his theory of the *V-Effekt* in direct opposition to the theory of empathy: "Eine völlig freie, kritische, auf rein irdische Lösung von Schwierigkeiten bedachte Haltung des Zuschauers ist keine Basis für eine Katharsis," in his "Kritik der Einfühlung," *Gesammelte Werke* (Frankfurt am Main: Suhrkamp, 1967), 7:240–51, here 241. Yet Brecht came to realize the necessity of a dialectical relation between cognition and empathy ("[sich] hingeben und nicht hingeben können"): "Unsere eigentliche Bewegung wird durch Erkennung und Erfühlung des zwiespaltigen Vorgangs entstehen." See "Gespräch über die Nötigung zur Einfühlung," in *Gesammelte Werke*, 7:899–900, here 900. For Lukács, such a shift for Brecht corresponds to an increased concern for a "revolutionary effect" that the *V-Effekt* tended to cripple. See Lukács, *Ästhetik II*, *Werke*, 12:186–87. For a discussion of the context for the debate between Lukács and Brecht as it evolved, see Henri Arvon, *Marxist Esthetics* (Ithaca: Cornell University Press, 1973), 100–112, esp. 111–12. It is interesting, too, that the school of poetry that most systematically applied Worringer's theory of abstraction to a poetic practice, namely Anglo-American Imagism, could not maintain a consistently "abstract" position. The discrete "image" necessarily dispersed into "montage" and thus admitted the intervention of the readerly expectation (and empathy). See Wolfgang Iser, "Image and Montage: Zur Bildkonzeption in der imagistischen Lyrik und in T. S. Eliots *Waste Land*," in *Immanente Aesthetik: Aesthetische Reflexion: Lyrik als Paradigma der Moderne*, ed. Wolfgang Iser (Munich: Wilhelm Fink, 1966), 361–93.

57. Worringer's racial "argument" flows from the following kind of presupposition: "Each individual people is nationally, in consequence of its innate structure, predisposed more toward the one side than the other, and the observation of whether the urge to abstraction or the urge to empathy prevails in its art provides us, at the same time, with an important psychological characterization" (45 [85]). Worringer here is particularly vulnerable to Lukács's criticism. See the latter's comment:

> Die Bezeichnung "Organik" kann . . . leicht irreführend sein; einerseits drängt sie bei der durchschnittlichen Kunsterziehung und dem allgemeinen Lebensgefühl sehr leicht wieder ein Höherwerten anderen Möglichkeiten gegenüber auf, anderseits muß man ihren Gegensatz zu einseitig (als Abstraktion) fassen, wodurch wie bei Worringer so heterogene Gestaltungen wie Orient und Gothik auf ein Prinzip zurückgeführt werden müssen; dazu kommt, daß Bezeichungen wie "organisch" und "abstrakt" sich noch immer zu sehr auf die inhaltliche, erlebnishafte Erfüllung dieser Strukturdifferenzen und zu wenig auf diese selbst beziehen, wodurch notwendigerweise die hier erreichten Kategorien auf einmalig-historische Komplexe lokalisiert werden müssen und das Stilproblem auf Fragen von Rasse, Milieu, Kultur etc. verschoben wird. ("Heidelberger Philosophie der Kunst," *Werke*, 16:216)

Needless to say, the exact nature of Worringer's participation in the artistic, theoretical, and political activity of Germany from 1907 through the world wars requires a far more nuanced and elaborate discussion than can be offered here. For the early period Brisch's dissertation is helpful, as is, of course, Worringer's own retrospective: *Fragen und Gegenfragen: Schriften zum Kunstproblem* (Munich: Piper, 1956).

58. A few, not atypical examples of this feature of Worringer's discourse are: (47 [85]) on abstraction as the more authentic and originary artistic drive; (46 [85]) on empathy as the "enfeeblement of the world instinct"; (46 [84]) on the "paltriness of rationalistic-sensuous cognition."

59. Vernon Lee, *The Beautiful*, 62.

60. Harold Osborne, *Aesthetics and Art Theory: An Historical Introduction* (London: Longmans, Green, 1968), 58. Further literature on this issue includes: Hermann Pongs, *Das Bild in der Dichtung*, 2d ed. (Marburg: Elwert, 1965), 1:742–47, and brief remarks in René Wellek and Austin Warren, *Theory of Literature*, 3d ed. (New York: Harcourt, Brace and World, 1956), 204–5; also, Karsten Harries, *The Meaning of Modern Art: A Philosophical Interpretation* (Evanston: Northwestern University Press, 1968), 70–71 (on Worringer and Kandinsky's relationship in the light of this problem).

61. Harlow, "Realignment," 127, 130.

62. When Worringer attempts to speak "objectively" as historian-scientist, he uses terms

as neutral as possible. Thus the terms "pole" and "antithesis" (which he takes to describe his binary opposition) are from physics and logic. His psychological terms, "urge" and "drive," were equally "scientific" in his mind. But note that already he has introduced two sets of metaphors: one abstract ("pole") and one empathetic ("urge").

63. Simmel's function in this entire scene is that his was the most ambitious (non-Marxist) attempt (more so than any of the writers mentioned by Worringer and certainly more than Worringer himself) actually to synthesize the products of culture and human experience: form and content. See Rudolf H. Weingartner, "Form and Content in Simmel's Philosophy of Life," in *Georg Simmel: A Collection of Essays, with Translations and a Bibliography*, ed. Kurt H. Wolf (Columbia: Ohio State University Press, 1959), 33–60; and Simmel, *The Philosophy of Money* [1907], ed. David Frisby, trans. Tom Bottomore and David Frisby, from a first draft by Kaethe Mengelberg, 2d enlarged ed. (London and New York: Routledge, 1990).

64. Paul de Man, "Action and Identity in Nietzsche," *Graphesis: Perspectives in Literature and Philosophy, Yale French Studies* 52 (1975), 16–30, here 29.

2

Abstraction and Apathy:
Crystalline Form in Expressionism and
in the Minimalism of Tony Smith

Joseph Masheck

One chief interest—and pleasure—of art history concerns the dialectic of continuity and change. That dialectic has lately flattened out, along with the sense of historicity that makes it possible. Alois Riegl, Wilhelm Worringer and others of the great early modern art historians sustained a kind of stereoptic, or at least bifocal, attention to recent art along with art of the distant, and also the unorthodox, past. At this end of their century, most of the fun seems gone from the game. The barren antiquarian needlepoint of reactionaries persists even as a dreary, quite unspectacular, nihilistic "spectacle" of antihistoricism plays itself out.

If two formally similar works of art, ancient and modern, are juxtaposed—one, say, just nearly classical Greek, and the other, American high abstract[1]—there are still, believe it or not, many who will construe the earlier work as Newtonian cause or "source," direct if possible, of the later work; meanwhile, others will have dismissed the whole setup as hopelessly aestheticizing—as if all I were doing were extending beyond representational art a Winckelmannian sense that the ancient piece in question is still too "early" and, well, chubby, whereas at least the abstract one has the (later antique) *Apollo Belvedere* to thank for its elegant, would-be classical poise. Well, Wilhelm Worringer was not looking for elegant poise, and neither am I, though I do imagine him, too, who in preparing the way for Kandinsky prepared the wider way for abstract art, wondering before my hypothetical comparison about the persistence of an ultimately classical sense of geometric form, now all the more blatant in unalloyed abstraction.

After all, a great deal of abstract painting and sculpture on the geometric or Constructivist, if not the ostensibly Expressionist side, does offer essentially classical form and structure denuded of classical representation: the noble nude stripped down beyond even pose to sheer structural disposition and the undraped forces of pure "composition." So, too, one entire aspect of "abstract" modernist architecture extends essentially classical, preeminently geometric, conceptions of form and composition. This fascinating matter of classical underpinnings in modern architecture arises in such various forms throughout the polemical as well as the historical literature that one might be pardoned the simplification of thinking it the destiny of modern architecture, over and against pedantries old or new, to inherit the most venerable form problems of this only plastic art that has always been "abstract."[2]

Ironically—because we can only see this in a modern light that emanates partly from him—Worringer presents the already convinced *modern* reader with a difficulty. Basically, *he* has to assume that *you* assume (as Jacques Derrida still does) that art is essentially depictive. He wants to convince you otherwise, so his filling in on crucial preclassical, antinaturalistic—I would say, essentially Neolithic[3]—stylization *precisely as abstraction* is supposed to come as a surprise. See: art was already ("abstractly") stylized long before it was classically empathetic-naturalistic. Prehistoric (Neolithic) stylization was itself the antithesis of still earlier, primeval (Paleolithic) *naturalism*. Given the thrust of Worringer's argument, why else would he say "Abstraction" first, and only then "Empathy," especially since the implication is: here comes abstraction *again*. Consequently, those of us who, thanks partly to Worringer, take abstraction as rule, with any naturalism after the Paleolithic (particularly that of the nineteenth century) as fly-by-night exception, can find ourselves stumbling anew over his polemical terms. Looking back over eighty years of abstract art and modern architecture, the higher-level surprise—at least as it strikes me, one who grew up devoted to modernity and seeing the premodern as much as possible in a modern way, every time I read *Abstraction and Empathy* (1908)—is that, okay, the naturalistic Greeks felt at home with the way the world is; but the alternative, a sublimating distancing from nature, is, especially when there is something wrong with the world, supposed to engender *German Expressionism*, not an opposite, geometric Constructivism (including architecture).

All of which concerns me here and now in a Worringerian way because Minimalism, which, despite American desire to be unbegotten, descended in the Constructivist tradition, and which defined itself against the specifically "Expressionist" art, especially painting, of the New York School, was to me and my generation what otherwise antithetical Expressionism was to Worringer and his. While Abstract Expressionism in relation to earlier German Expressionism is a subject unto itself, it is hardly wrongheaded, for instance, to think today of Jackson Pollock where, in that other classic of his, *Problems of Form in the Gothic* (1911), Worringer speaks of "the Gothic line" as "essentially abstract and at the same time of very strong vitality."[4]

Needless to say, there was as yet no such thing as Constructivism when Worringer wrote *Abstraction and Empathy: A Contribution to the Psychology of Style.* Insofar as the absolute debut of Cubism can be dated to 9 November 1908, when Braque exhibited some paintings of the previous year,[5] Worringer could not have seen anything from which Constructivism would derive when he wrote the preface to the book two months before—though his crucial encounter with tribal art at the Trocadéro in the company of Georg Simmel (recalled in his 1948 preface), before he had even settled on this, his dissertation project, must have predated Picasso's equally revelatory visit to the same collection of tribal art in May or June 1907.[6]

Most Western geometric art traces readily back through a great deal of Italianate, classicizing European painting, sculpture, and architecture—confusingly enough, if you try to hold to Worringer on this— to "empathetic" Greek art itself. As Wölfflin puts it, whoever goes from the North to Italy is likely to notice, "How plain and easy to grasp are the planes and cubes!"[7] But that, in a way, is exactly what Worringer is challenging. To understand the original Expressionist frame of mind we must see not only that it embraces the Gothic as "its" own opposite, Germanic analogue, necessarily ad hoc, to codified geometric classicism (a notion that goes back beyond Goethe),[8] building in an affirmative way on the disadvantaged formalist distinction of Northern versus Italianate art that Wöllflin absorbed from his teacher Jakob Burckhardt.[9] We must also see, more problematically, that this alternative system not only *is* a system of sorts, but that as such it also comprehends geometric form, even "classical" geometry.

In critical practice it was possible to stretch the notion of expression far enough to cover a sufficiently updated classicism, at least in architecture. To take a period example: in 1917, the Expressionistically sympathetic art historian Fritz Burger compared two then recent, in one way or another modernist, German buildings: Paul Bonatz and F. E. Scholer's Stuttgart railway station (1911–14; resumed 1919–27), with its loggia of plain, lightly Doricizing square piers, and Peter Behrens's 1911–12 German embassy in St. Petersburg, also known as the Botschafter Palace (of which the young Mies van der Rohe happens to have supervised the construction), having an "'industrially' stylized"[10] engaged Doric order. Faced with the, one might have thought, obvious fact that the great Behrens here seems to fall back on a traditionalist classicism, whereas Bonatz's building makes do with demythologized square piers, Burger opts to count both buildings as expressively astute. The sheer restraint of Bonatz's station he reads empathetic-expressively, while what might have been mere conservatism in Behrens's embassy Burger accommodates as an appropriately different, specifically ambassadorial, expressive statement; namely, a willfully decorous aloofness and an almost femininely elegant sophistication in which even a certain "concession" to classicism finds place.[11] Were rationalization required, I would rather have sought to stress Behrens's Doric order as formally abstract, possibly even as crystalline; but Burger stands by a broad linguistic of expression.

After all, the main argument for geometric abstract form is still the rationalist one, which has a much easier logocentric time laying claim to: the Platonic solids, the Parthenon, Euclid, Vitruvius, Raphael, Poussin, whatever. Today one can easily look, for instance, at two English bridges of the late eighteenth century, built within a few years of each other, and see in the protofunctional geometry of Abraham Darby III's famous Coalbrookdale Bridge (1777–79) a refreshing directness that is not, however, altogether estranged from the classical ornamental geometry of an Adamesque Neoclassical canal bridge at Pulteney (1769–72 or 1797). By now, it would not be wrong to call both bridges "classical" (lower-case), something more than merely "classic."

Nor need one necessarily know the ancient Tower of the Winds, at Athens, so often quoted in post-Renaissance European architecture (especially in steeples), to sense before Tony Smith's sculpture *Tower of the Winds*, 1962, a foursquare and abstractly "classical" structural aplomb. From about the same time, too, dates a sheet, *Untitled (No Stars)*, on which Smith has sketched out simple and complex geometric solids, from "tet," "hex," "oct," and "dodeca" onward.[12] Yet the question, within Expressionism, of crystalline geometry as classicizing or else anticlassical, *anticipates* the question, within latter-day Minimalism, including Tony Smith's, of crystalline geometry as formal or antiformal, antiexpressive or pointedly neutral.

Since Worringer himself was by no means oblivious to the Burckhardtian North-South distinction, it may help in establishing the ambiguous standing of crystalline form in latter-day Minimalism to compare a cube drawn by Dürer (Fig. 1) with a well-known 1962 piece by Tony Smith called *Die* (Fig. 2). Dürer's drawing, from his Dresden sketchbook, dates from the 1520s, after he had spent more than two years in Italy on two visits.[13] It shows a cube like a box with its top lifted off, this transparent enough to show two inter-secting inner diagonals, yet opaque enough, owing to horizontal hatching on the front and diagonal on the side of the cube, to cast a shadow. As transparently crystalline as it presents itself as being, Dürer's drawn cube is also rigid and earthbound, crystalline in the sense, say, of quartz. No one would call Smith's *Die* "light and airy," but as opaque as it looks, Smith's hollow steel cube hovers, slightly propped on two slats, as if definitively demonstrating the academic sculptural distinction—equally doctrinal in the realm of modernist architecture—between volume and mass. Not that the Minimalist ideal of volume without mass was without its poetry; to quote a passage from Joyce, describing a blind man's negotiation of the three-dimensional world, in Tony Smith's beloved *Ulysses:* "How on earth did he know that van was there? Must have felt it. See things in the foreheads perhaps. Kind of sense of volume. Weight. Would he feel it if something was removed? Feel a gap."[14]

Even a natural [!] crystal of iron pyrite seems almost privileged in a quasi-classical way as some marvelous exception to the irregularities (Romantically charming or not) of nature: in its cubicality it might as well have been designed by a cool Neoclassical artist of the late eighteenth century, or equally, I am suggesting, by any cool Mini-malist sculptor of the 1960s or 1970s, not only the Smith of *Die* but also, perhaps, the Ruth Vollmer of *Heptahedron,* cast in acrylic in 1970. That Minimalism was deeply apathetic, in the strict, neutral sense, usually comes down on the classical side as cool—anti-pathetic as the movement was toward the emotional indulgences of Abstract Expressionism, and then, to the embarrassing binge of hedonistic lyrical painting that formalist critics next anointed. The marked in-ertness of Minimalism is widely manifest in recourse to crystalline forms as generated systematically and without inflection, hence sup-posedly affect-free as well as formally self-evident. So I call Mini-malism apathetic with cordial neutrality, much as the critic Charles Henry mobilized the then new concept of "anaesthesia" as the oppo-site of the *aesthetically* enervated state, on behalf of a new anti-Impressionist art in the 1880s.[15] If any of this seems remote from Worringer, who anyway would surely have preferred the art of the Abstract Expressionists, it could probably not have been said, at least this way, but for *Abstraction and Empathy.*

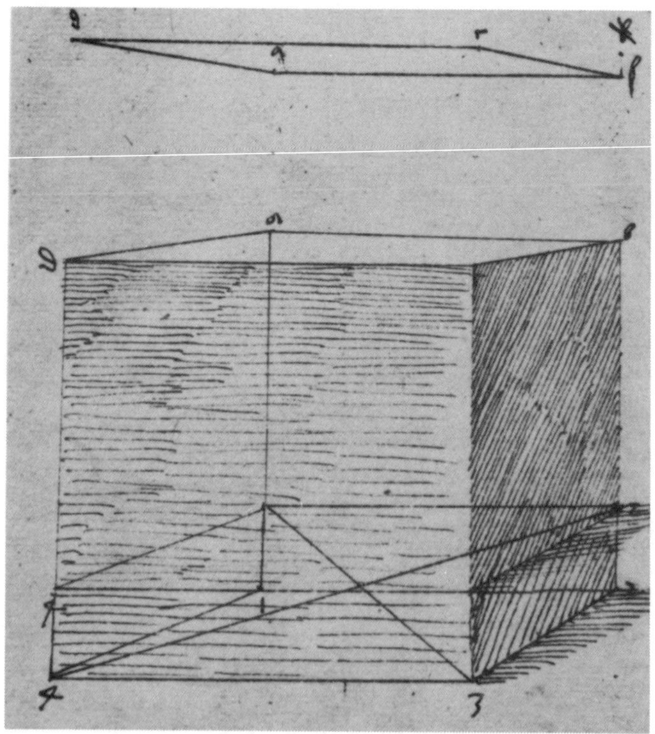

Fig. 1.   Albrecht Dürer, drawing of a cube in his so-called
Dresden Sketchbook, ink, 1520s. Dresden, Sächsische
Landesbibliothek, Ms. R-147, fol. 168v. After the album
*Albrecht Dürer in der königlichen öffentlichen Bibliothek zu
Dresden*, ed. Robert Bruck, Studien zur deutschen
Kunstgeschichte (Strasbourg, 1905), reprinted as Dürer's *The
Human Figure: The Complete "Dresden Sketchbook,"* ed.
Walter L. Strauss (New York: Dover, 1972)

Before considering the speculative background to Worringer's, and
also Riegl's, crystalline imagery, let me make two suggestions. First:
in Rieglian terms, Worringer's appeal to the very word "Abstraktion," Latinate as that is, can only confirm an underlying and abiding,
by no means defunct but innately protomodern, late Latinity—like
Riegl's own deeply grounded philosophical appeal to Saint Augustine
as perfectly, vitally late antique, and also rightly spiritual, in the Holy
Roman Empire of Vienna in 1901.[16] This puts the shoe on the other
foot, leaving the etymologically Germanic "Einfühlung" (and the pre-

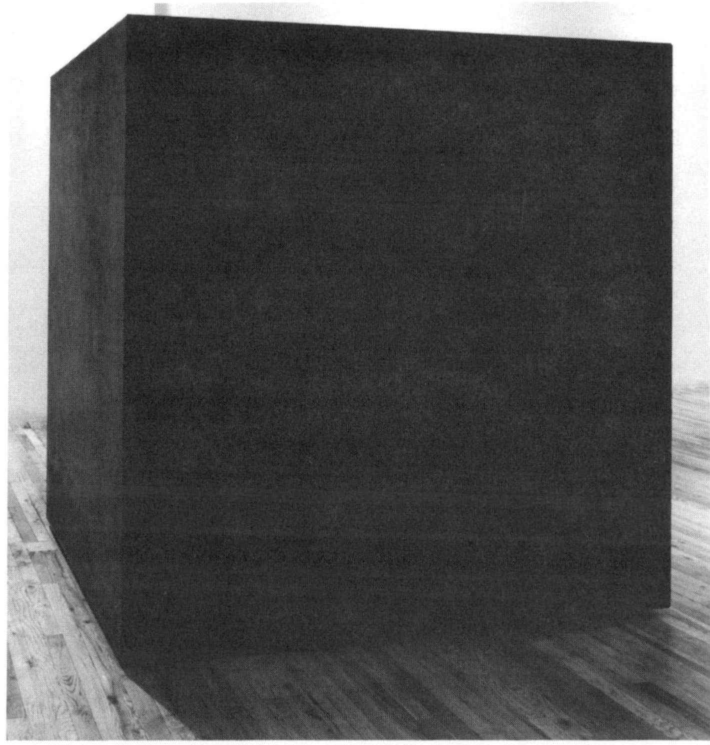

Fig. 2.   Tony Smith, *Die*, steel, 72 × 72 × 72 inches (edition of three), 1962. (Photo by Geoffrey Clements, courtesy of the Paula Cooper Gallery, New York)

vailing contemporary naturalistic aesthetic) in a defensive, by comparison very bodily, roughly physical, even "barbarian," position.

Second: Worringer was so concerned with contemporary psychology—mistakenly, Goldwater thought[17]—that I wonder how concerned he may also have been with other departments of contemporary science. Of course, the legacy of *Naturphilosophie* would remain available even in pre–World War II German culture, almost as if Goethe had still been watching, ever since the summer of 1787 *in Italy*, bursting pine kernels "[throwing] off their hood and reveal[ing] the rudiments of their destined form."[18] But it is worth considering that the understanding of specifically organic structure as crypto-crystalline on even the molecular level was only established with

August Kekulé's hypothetical hexagon of the benzene ring of organic chemistry, in Worringer's childhood. What, after all, in the entire universe, is more literally organic than the metaphorically crystalline benzene ring?

In the very address of 1890 in which Kekulé recounted his *invenzione* of the spatially hexagonal benzene ring, which made modern organic chemistry possible—an address best known, ironically, as a rather Surrealist case of inspiration in dreams—Kekulé testifies that the mind on which the "idea-seed" of this essentially crystalline structural metaphor fell was well prepared: he had discovered in high school special aptitudes for both mathematics and drawing that led his father to encourage him toward architecture even as this flowering of the structural imagination inspired an interest in the historical development of chemistry.[19] In the same spirit, one might even wonder how much subsequent popular comprehension of atomic structure is owed to the children's "Tinker Toys," dating from 1914 and in some sense derivative of Kekuléan thinking about molecules.

In any case, aesthetic speculation concerning regular structure as (finally) *organic*-crystalline-classical, frequent in the nineteenth century, culminated soon after Kekulé in the work of Alois Riegl.

Riegl is referred to at so many points in *Abstraction and Empathy* that I will simply put into extreme closeup, as he himself liked to do in visual description, one or two special passages in his *Spätrömische Kunstindustrie* (1901; 1927) for a fresh sense of what must have attracted Worringer. In one place Riegl considers the faceted antique gemstone as classical and not yet, for his purposes, proto-Impressionistically modern: "classical art did not want to see the stone just for its optical-colorful value, but predominantly for its bodily shape value *(körperlichen Formwert)* and . . . therefore it gave the stone on one side its crystalline shape broken into clearly divided partial planes *(eine kristallinische, in klar geschiedene Teilebenen gebrochene Form)*."[20] In another, however, the crystalline connotes an immobile stasis, as he notes in a late-antique bronze bird "a particular mixture between the observation of . . . animated organic nature and a tendency toward crystalline immotion *(kristallinische Ruhe)*."[21]

Evidently, Riegl's and Worringer's essentially active and sequential, I would say linguistically "asymmetrical," critical polarities owe much to the Apollonian and Dionysian terms of *The Birth of Tragedy* (1872)—just as Nietzsche owes some impetus, and says so, to Schiller's *On Naive and Sentimental Poetry* (1795–96). Again, if Worringer meant simply to shift from a happy Greek classical naturalism to an anxious modern distancing and "stylization," he could have called his book *Empathy and Abstraction*. It is his dialectical sense of filling in with background that reverses the foreground that Worringer owes most profoundly to Nietzsche's great modernist attack on uncritical classicism in *The Birth of Tragedy*.

With Nietzsche the light-cavalry elegance of early nineteenth-century Prussian classicism gives way to a roaring Hellenism that undercuts all classicism of "mere appearance" and proceeds to deepen it. In the "Attempt at Self-Criticism" prefixed to his 1886 reissue of *The Birth of Tragedy* Nietzsche sarcastically regrets not having resorted to "an individual language" of his own, since some readers have obviously missed the point of his having "tried laboriously to express by means of Schopenhauerian and Kantian formulas strange and new valuations that were basically at odds with Kant's and Schopenhauer's spirit and taste"[22]—as if he didn't know!

"It is in Doric art that [the] majestically *rejecting* attitude of Apollo is immortalized," Nietzsche says early on in the *Birth* (sect. 2; p. 39; my emphasis) as he himself begins a great new rejection, it having become "necessary to level the artistic structure of the *Apollinian culture*, as it were, *stone by stone*, till the foundations on which it rests become visible" (sect. 3; p. 41; my emphasis on "stone by stone"). "For to me the *Doric* state and Doric art are explicable only as a permanent military encampment of the Apollinian" (sect. 4; p. 47). Where he says, in a practically crystalline image, "Everything that comes to the surface in the Apollinian part of Greek tragedy, in the dialogue, looks simple, transparent and beautiful" (sect. 9; p. 67), Nietzsche really does mean, only *looks* simple. This is peace only after war. What Worringer owes above all else to Nietzsche is surely this sense that the direct but far from superficial appeal of crystalline form is grounded in and founded upon deep-set, chthonic struggle. (By the time they finish with them, key terms in Worringer and Nietzsche alike take on more adequate senses, if sometimes with apparently opposite valences than they had to begin with.)

An aside: Worringer seems to make something of a historical, as well as Nietzschean, mistake, in making a theoretical point, where he states too simply that "art does not begin with naturalistic constructs *(naturalistischen Gebilden)*, but with ornamental-abstract ones."[23] That could only be maintained by holding off the Old Stone Age as pre-artistic (in a sense, Worringer does still confuse tribal with prehistoric art); but to leave Paleolithic people in the position of *Naturvölker* risks projecting upon them a Romanticism of the Old Stone Age,[24] which would start art history off once more on the wrong foot, winding up yet again with classicism, in an extended sense, as good news. This is only so easy to say because we can understand Paleolithic naturalism as "Dionysian" and Neolithic stylization as (only) subsequently "Apollonian"; Worringer was worried about a later succession anyway. Otherwise, complex enough to count as a tour de force is his more vitally Expressionist argument that whereas the classical Greek temple offers "organic life . . . substituted for matter, . . . in the Gothic cathedral, on the contrary, matter lives solely on its own mechanical laws"—"but these laws," he hastens to add, "despite their fundamentally abstract character, have become living, i.e. they have acquired expression."[25]

At base, this last idea, of Gothic mechanics, has its own protomodern French rationalist history, but for his own Germanic modernist reasons Worringer has to make a point of handling it *his way*. In that his distinctly more "Northerly" way also concerns nineteenth-century Gothicism as erecting itself like an ideological barricade against all further circulation of official classical doctrine, we would do well to turn briefly to two principal midcentury Gothicists, French and English, then back through important Germanic speculations of which Worringer would have been aware.

Eugène Emmanuel Viollet-le-Duc's *Dictionnaire raisonné de l'architecture française du XIe au XVIe siècle* (1854–68) was not so long ago still well known as a kind of old testament to twentieth-century functionalist architectural theory. In it this Gothic-modernist admires the "inflexible logic" of nature at her structural work, extrapolating from an equilateral triangle inscribed in a circle, to a tetrahedron in a sphere, higher and higher crystalline complexities. In one diagram Viollet juxtaposes rhombohedrons of granite crystals with hexagonal crystals of volcanic basalt "derived from the rhombodehral form." I shall resist the temptation to tackle the implied metaphysics by merely pointing out that in selecting this discussion for their analytical edition of selections from the *Dictionnaire*, Viollet's modern editors flag this passage with every appropriate tag: "reason," "geometry," "nature," "epistemology," "crystallization," "system," "organicism," "principles."[26]

In England, between his *Seven Lamps of Architecture* (1849) and his *Stones of Venice* (1853), enthusiasm for the crystalline form on the part of Ruskin, the world's greatest despiser of classical regularity, had detectably increased. In the chapter titled "The Lamp of Beauty" in the *Seven Lamps* even the geologist in Ruskin seems to object that the straight line is at odds with nature, hence with beauty: "to find right lines in nature at all, we may be compelled to do violence to her finished work, break through the sculptured and colored surfaces of her crags, and examine the processes of their crystallization" (IV.vi).[27] But in *The Stones of Venice*, four years after that, under "The Material of Ornament," is a more affirmative paragraph on "*Forms of Earth (Crystals)*": although a sculptor cannot hope to imitate either the scale of mountains or all the "steps of . . . [nature's] fury" in rock and mountain fractures, "crystalline form" now deserves admiration as "the completely systematised natural structure of the earth" (chap. 11).[28]

Germanistically speaking, however, probably nothing is more pressing in this retrospection than Schopenhauer's *World as Will and Representation*, wherein crystalline metaphor of an utterly chemical enthusiasm is consistently prominent in conveying how phenomena snap ever in and out of one or another stable organization only to assume another condition. Of many appropriate passages in the first volume (1819), where the crystalline even has its place in the Platonic musical unity of the organic and inorganic realms (I.lii),[29] two can be singled out. First, as stable aggregate the crystal is taken as the only individuality in inorganic nature, at least provisionally holding its own as thing-in-itself, "just as"—amazing analogy!—"the tree is an aggregate from the individual shooting fibre showing itself in every rib of the leaf, in every leaf, in every branch" (I.xxvi) (1:132). In a later place, Schopenhauer's figure even entails the immortalizing finality of much cubical imagery in memorial art: "the crystal has only one manifestation of life, namely its formation, which afterwards has its fully adequate and exhaustive expression in the coagulated form, in the corpse of that momentary life" (I.xxviii; 1:155).

In Schopenhauer's second volume (1844), an extended and in some sense more Romantic gloss on the first, three passages vie for Worringerian attention. Considering that "our knowledge consists only in the *framing of representations* by means of subjective forms," Schopenhauer's crystal connotes not microsublime simplicity but ultimately inscrutable complication: "For not merely do the highest productions of nature, namely, living beings, or the *complicated* phenomena of the inorganic world remain inscrutable to us, but even every rock-crystal, even iron pyrites, are, by virtue of their crystallographical, optical, chemical and electrical properties, an abyss of incomprehensibilities and mysteries for our searching consideration and investigation" (II.xviii; 2:194–95; emphasis in original). Next, a passage that Riegl would surely have liked: "With the *organic* body . . . its life, in other words its existence as something organic, consists simply in the constant change of the *material* with persistence of the *form;* thus its essence and identity lie in the form alone. Therefore the *inorganic* body has its continued existence through *repose* and isolation from external influences" (II.xxiii; 2:296; emphasis in original). Finally, there is also an extended passage, too long to quote, criticizing Gothic architecture and crystal imagery as applied to it, but which would have concerned Riegl and Worringer for its dubious art history alone (II.xxxv; 2:416–19).

Certainly Schopenhauer knew that to his hated Hegel, in the 1820s, the crystal connoted freedom, insofar as matter assumes its own pure form rather than having form imposed from without; and it is a surprisingly short step—one cannot help thinking, in the German Modernist direction—in the same paragraph, from there to "a similar activity of immanent formation" in the living human body and "its movement and the expression of feelings," whereby "inner activity . . . emerges vitally"[30]—even if, in the regular and symmetrical forms of crystals, "abstractions alone are active as determinants" (1:136). In his treatment of architecture, where the Egyptian pyramids, that a century later would fascinate Worringer and German Expressionist architects, are as yet preclassically "just simple crystals," Hegel takes architecture itself as an "inorganic nature built by human hands" (2:653). But even such "architecture as a mere enclosure and as inorganic nature (nature not in itself individualized and animated by its indwelling spirit) can be shaped only in a way external to itself, though the external form is not organic but abstract and mathematical."[31]

By the time Hegel preached his aesthetics, Friedrich Schiller's "naive and sentimental" distinction was a generation old. Now it is not only when aphoristic ("Our feeling for nature is like the feeling of an invalid for health")[32] or in tone (because the naive poet perceives a "dry truth [*trockene Wahrheit*]" he may seem to deal insensitively with his object)[33] that Schiller adumbrates Nietzsche, who disputes him, but with a firm handshake. There is also a similarly antinomian sense that, dissociated from the "artificial world," the poet can reattain to nature within, "exempt," then, "from all laws by which a corrupted heart is protected against itself."[34] Nietzsche might have disputed the terms of Schiller's distinction between "actual nature *(wirkliche Natur),*" which is commonplace, and "true nature *(wahre Natur),*" to which "belongs an inner necessity of existence *(eine innere Notwendigkeit des Daseins)*";[35] but as for the question of why we "cling" to nature "and embrace even the inanimate world with the warmest sensibility," both Nietzsche and then Worringer too would have applauded Schiller's answer: "It is *because* nature in us has disappeared from humanity and we rediscover her in her truth only outside it, in the inanimate world."[36]

An early point in the *Birth of Tragedy* where Worringer seems to hover very near is also the very point at which Nietzsche most depends on Schiller for purpose of negation: "this harmony which is contemplated with such longing by modern man, in fact this oneness of man with nature (for which Schiller introduced the technical term 'naive'), is by no means a simple condition that comes into being naturally and as if inevitably. . . . Where we encounter the 'naive' in art, we should recognize the highest effect of Apollinian culture—which . . . must have triumphed over an abysmal and terrifying view of the world and the keenest susceptibility to suffering through recourse to the most forceful and pleasurable illusions" (sect. 3; p. 43). Our own later American Abstract Expressionists would only have applauded Schiller's sense that "genius delineates its own thoughts at a single felicitous stroke of the brush (*mit einem einzigen glücklichen Pinselstrich*)," while "to genius, language springs as if by some inner necessity (*durch innere Notwendigkeit*) out of thought, and is so at one with it that even beneath the corporeal frame the spirit appears as if laid bare"—whereas, on the side of all art termed sentimental, meaning worked at, contrived, "the sign (*das Zeichen*) remains forever heterogenous and alien to the thing signified (*dem Bezeichneten*)."[37]

After all this, it will seem like a letdown to quote Kant, against whose sense of the *Ding an sich* Schopenhauer actually sharpened his crystalline imagery. In the *Critique of Judgement* (1790) Kant does sound like an unshakable classicist, maintaining that we admire perfect, regular geometrical figures for their (objective) availability to "all kinds of cognitive uses" rather than for a (subjective) aesthetic, even an "intellectual," beauty (sect. 62).[38] Having done our duty by Kant, we may turn forward toward 1910 and 1960, by way of certain marginal but telling eighteenth-century works of art.

All the more because Worringer was not a rationalist type, and academic classicism was the enemy in 1908, the problem of cubic and crystalline form in the eighteenth century holds Worringerian as well as Minimalist interest. On the very second page of *Abstraction and Empathy*—the Meridian paperback of which appeared during the burgeoning of American Minimalism, in 1967—the new law is laid down: "Just as the urge to empathy as a presumption of aesthetic experience finds its gratification in the beauty of the organic, so the urge to abstraction finds its beauty in the life-denying inorganic, in the crystalline *(im Kristallinischen)* or, in general terms, in all abstract law and necessity" (4; German ed., 4). These are Worringer's own words, even though he sometimes borrows "crystalline" from Riegl (and "cubic" from Hildebrand).

To the annoyance of ahistorically minded artists and others, occasional Neoclassical precedents for Minimalist crystalline form can be found in the eighteenth century. Indeed, sometimes Minimalism begins to look like a replay of eighteenth-century Whiggish nouveau-bourgeois culture, beyond the obvious American attempt to efface historical complexity. One such adumbration I have already entertained, apropos of a supposed stylelessness in Minimalism: a certain Bible illustration by Johann August Corvinus (1683–1738) showing a plain, empty, open-topped cubic box under a loggia, this with a landscape beyond.[39] What can Corvinus's empty cube set in pictorial space have illustrated? The statement in Genesis 18.6 that Abraham told Sarah to run and get specifically *three seahs* of flour, to make rolls (three seahs equalling one *ephah,* or about half a bushel)—in other words, a pure, massless *volume.*

More art-historically relevant is an illustration published by the eighteenth-century classicizing, Neopalladian architect Robert Morris in his *Lectures on Architecture* (1734–36), in which the pure proportions of potentially classical edifices are built up from neutral unit cubes, like children's blocks uniform (except for a half-block) in size. Wittkower, who discussed Morris's essentially proportional thinking in 1944, only to be disputed by Emil Kaufmann in 1955, returned to the matter in a lecture of 1966.[40] To Kaufmann, in Morris's "cubic" method, as he calls it, the Morrisonian "IDEA" was more important than specific proportions[41]—as many a Minimalist has claimed. Now Rykwert adds that the "Ideal Beauty" at which Morris aims in architecture, "is very like what [Francis] Hutcheson describes as 'Original and Absolute Beauty': in which the element of imitation is wholly absent. Yet Hutcheson, explicitly, and Morris, implicitly, recognize their difference from earlier Neoplatonic thinking. The beauty, even the harmony, is not something that is a property of the object: it is an idea in the mind, an idea that relates to the primary qualities of an object" (*First Moderns,* 193). Note that another rubric for Minimalist sculpture, when it first appeared, was "primary forms."

As sparely as he conceived the exteriors of his cubical buildings, typically country houses, this Robert Morris actively allowed for contrastingly ornamented, even quasi-Rococo, interiors (Rykwert, *First Moderns,* 193). Admitting obvious differences (rural versus urban; gentry versus petit-bourgeois), this Morris might thus be said to anticipate by a century Walter Benjamin's claimed origin for the "interior" specifically of the "private citizen" in the age of Louis Philippe.[42] A hundred years after *that,* in the time of Worringer, we encounter the essentially urban, and utterly urbane, domestic architecture of the Viennese Adolf Loos, who sought as early as 1898 to establish "inside the historically determined city . . . a *wohnlichen Raum,*" a closed, "protected" space "in which the individual can find 'shelter,'" this quite the opposite of Expressionist *Glasarchitektur*[43]— and in our time newly appealing in a Minimalist way, like the crystalline Expressionist "glass architecture," mostly of fantasy, itself.[44]

The eighteenth-century Morris's cube clusters would only have been noticed by a sculptor interested in architecture—such as Tony Smith, the author of *Die,* perhaps the single most famous Minimalist cube sculpture. An eighteenth-century sculpturesque work by the poet Goethe was widely noticed when it appeared illustrated, in 1967, in Robert Rosenblum's *Transformations in Late Eighteenth-Century Art.* This is the poet's so-called Altar of Good Fortune, dating from 1777, in the park at Weimar, a symbolic as well as elementally formal work alluding to the sphere of Fortune as resting unstably upon the cube of Virtue. While Rosenblum calls it "more of an exercise in symbolic geometry than a creative work of sculpture or architecture," he also notes that it "was characteristic of the late eighteenth century that these symbolic forms [i.e., sphere and cube] could be pushed to so absolute a reduction that they almost appear unrelated to a particular historical epoch."[45] Even with its funereal tinge, the cubic element of Goethe's monument will remind a modernist of Smith's *Die,* first executed in 1962, then again in 1967 *(Die II),* whose title plays not only on death but on the fateful throw of dice.

The Morris cubes were illustrated in Emil Kaufmann's *Architecture in the Age of Reason* (1955), which was reprinted in paperback and thus widely circulated in 1968,[46] two years after the Minimalist sculptor Carl Andre had begun to exhibit neat low stacks of firebricks in rectilinear disposition on the gallery floor.[47] (The British government purchase of one such piece for the Tate Gallery was to produce a naughty scandal in which the English apparently quite forgot their old Robert Morris.) According to Wittkower, Morris's cube clusters were orthodox classical in their essential proportionality,[48] whereas the art of Andre and other Minimalists stands against composed form per se; but if their placement on the floor is "nonrelational," it is also rectilinear, far from arbitrary, and at least neutrally Constructivistic.

From the eighteenth-century Robert Morris (not the American Minimalist of the same name) through early functionalist interest in the "Taylorism" of the famous American efficiency expert,[49] the cube has served as elemental architectonic unit. Not unlike Morris's stacked cubes, but with an innate severity of cubical massing serving an expressive purpose of spiritual gravity, is Adolf Loos's 1921 project for a black granite mausoleum. Planned to have interior frescoes by the Expressionist Oskar Kokoschka, the mausoleum was to be built to the memory of the great Czech Viennese art historian and friend of the Expressionists, Max Dvôrák; to it, a line from Georg Trakl has been related: "Our silence is a black cavern."[50] Among the antiexpressive American Minimalists, however, Andre's brick stacks make even old Morris's diagram seem nuanced: their stubborn Emersonian plod away from all European "composing" has a stolidity of its own. If cubic and prismatic form is indeed generally counterexpressive, inexpressivity can also amount to expression; impassiveness, to affect.

Beginning in 1911, in Germany, when Worringer's book on the Gothic appeared, Walter Gropius had begun to broadcast an enthusiasm for new American industrial architecture combined with an Egyptian enthusiasm, already influenced by *Abstraction and Empathy,* that in turn would influence Worringer's own *Ägyptische Kunst* (Egyptian Art; 1927). Gropius also praised Peter Behrens's new German industrial buildings as "commanding their surroundings with truly classical grandeur."[51] Ironically, when an "Authorized American Edition" of Worringer's *Form Problems of the Gothic* appeared (in 1918?), "For Which the [anonymous] Translator Has Selected Illustrative Material Chiefly from American Collections" (title page), a photograph of Cass Gilbert's new but neo-Gothic Woolworth Building, of 1913, was included—not one of the more functionalistic industrial structures (pl. xiii, opp. p. 88).

By the time Loos designed the Moller House, in Vienna (1928), where the wall of a stairwell is pierced by a rectangular opening to leave a continuous square-cornered sequence of rising, crossing, descending, and then low right-angled horizontal elements (Fig. 3), he, too, was aware of the type of the American concrete-framed "Daylight" factory with its gridded walls, from 1903 onward. On a visit to this country at the turn of the century the radically restrained, anti-ornamental Loos already, like the more wildly Expressionist Erich Mendelsohn two decades later, found American industrial architecture inspiring.[52] We may tend to think of such forms as belonging to a type of building so utilitarian as to be utterly materialist, but as with later Minimalist sculpture, there was the possibility of a certain chaste ultimacy even in that. Loos would claim in 1932, in the spirit of Le Corbusier's *Vers une architecture,* a decade earlier, that these "Engineers are our Hellenes."[53]

Certainly under the new Minimalist impassiveness Loos looked peculiarly interesting all over again, as a juxtaposition of the Moller House stairway with Tony Smith's *Free Ride,* of 1962, suggests (Fig. 4). And, setting *Free Ride* beside David Smith's *Cubi XXIII,* 1964 (Fig. 5), might only make the rigorous abstraction of the piece by the more famous Smith seem traditionally compositional—what with the syncopated crossing of its twin right angles and its supporting but also formally inflecting pole at one end and footed terminus on the other. Sol LeWitt's Minimal modular lattices are more to the point, even though LeWitt didn't start making them until two years later. Tony Smith's *Free Ride* also predates "our" contemporary Robert Morris's *Untitled (L-Beams),* of 1965, by three years (Fig. 6). Only twelve years after *Free Ride* did LeWitt began his even more similar "Incomplete Open Cubes," in 1974, while *Free Ride* itself relates to experiments in cubical stereotomy in Smith's drawings of around the same time, such as one from 16 December 1962.[54]

With the spatially squared square of *Die,* which at six by six by six feet was designed so that the average person could not look over it, Smith is known to have been inspired by Leonardo da Vinci's famous drawing of the Vitruvian man, of c. 1485–90, this as "reproduced on the cover of a paperback." Recalling that moment, it seems more than likely that the book in question was the then new Anchor paper edition of Geoffrey Scott's antimodernist *The Architecture of Humanism* (1914), in which the Gothic is dismissed under "The Romantic Fallacy." This Scott, a classy Edwardian classical apologist in something of the manner, now, of Prince Charles of England, only intellectual, says that the Gothic "lose[s] architecture in sculpture," and "admits its deep indifference to ordered form."[55] Smith's cube certainly doesn't look Gothic, but in a sense that Scott could not have anticipated it displays its own Minimalist "indifference to ordered form." When Smith reiterated *Die* as *Die II,* in 1967, the sheer interchangeability, if never absolute identity, of the two pieces became a Minimalist statement with modernist architectural overtones of its own (akin to certain modernist architects' demystifying openness to prefabrication).

The whole *Die* project, however, also relates back indirectly to the Worringerian distancing of much geometric Constructivist art, in that fabrication was directed by Smith over the telephone, without even making a drawing. As is by now well known, the Constructivist

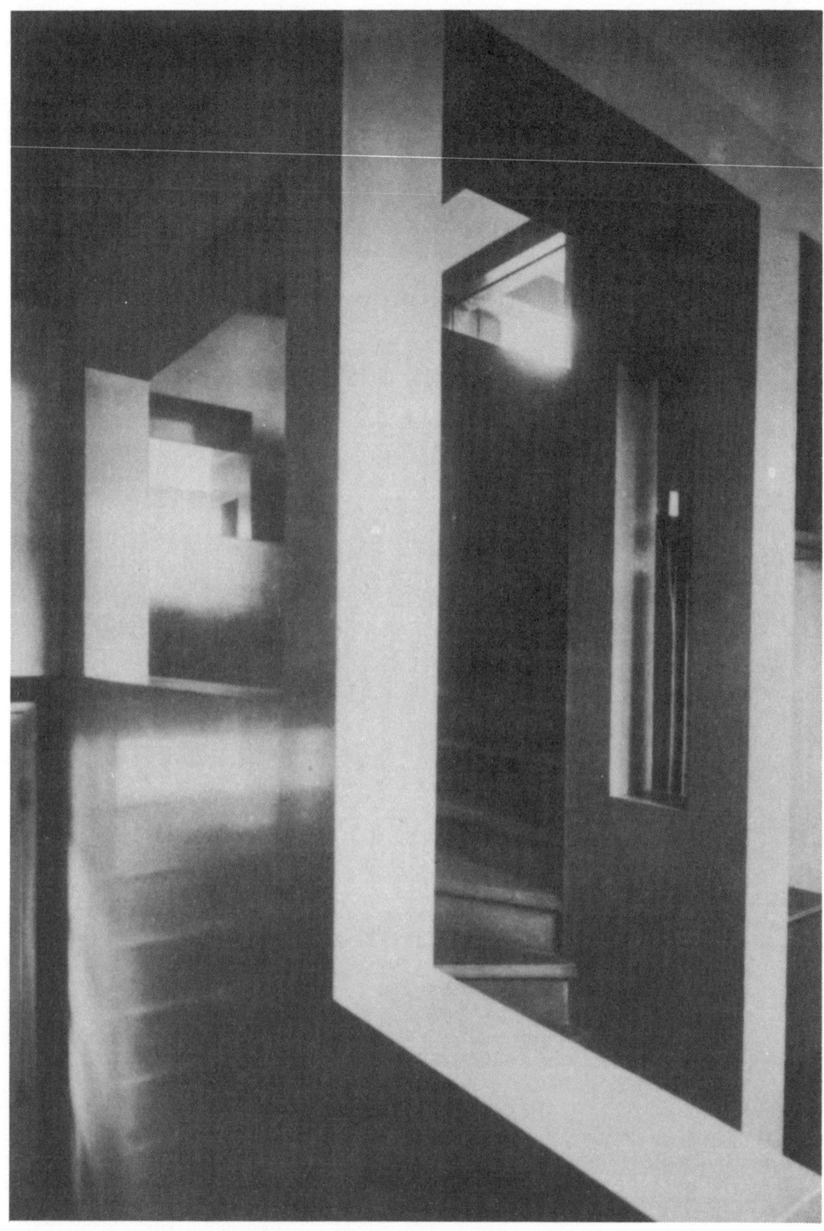

Fig. 3. Adolf Loos, Moller House, Vienna, 1928. Interior staircase. (Photo by Roberto Schezen, courtesy of the photographer)

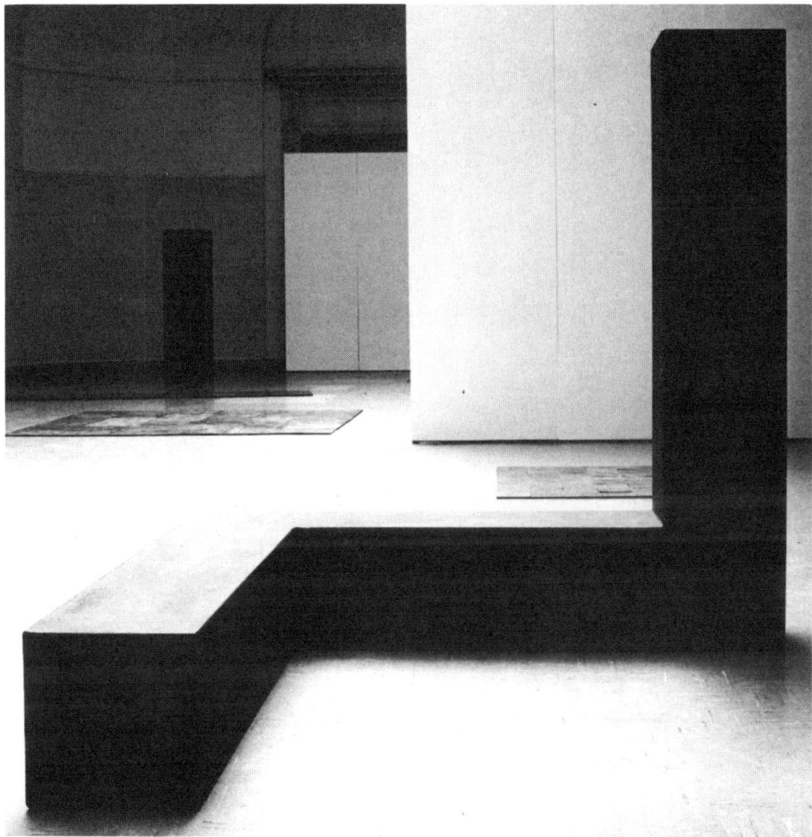

Fig. 4. Tony Smith, *Free Ride*, steel, 104 × 104 × 104 inches, 1962 (edition of three with one artist's proof). (Photo lacking archival data)

artist László Moholy-Nagy had already had a group of five paintings executed by telephone, using graph paper and a commercial paint chart, in 1922, as Smith could easily have learned from a supplement to the second edition of Moholy-Nagy's *The New Vision* (1949), or else from Reyner Banham's classic *Theory and Design in the First Machine Age* (1960), even if he had managed not to hear of this when he studied under Moholy himself at the New Bauhaus in Chicago, in 1937–38.

Born in 1912, Smith went from the Art Students' League of New

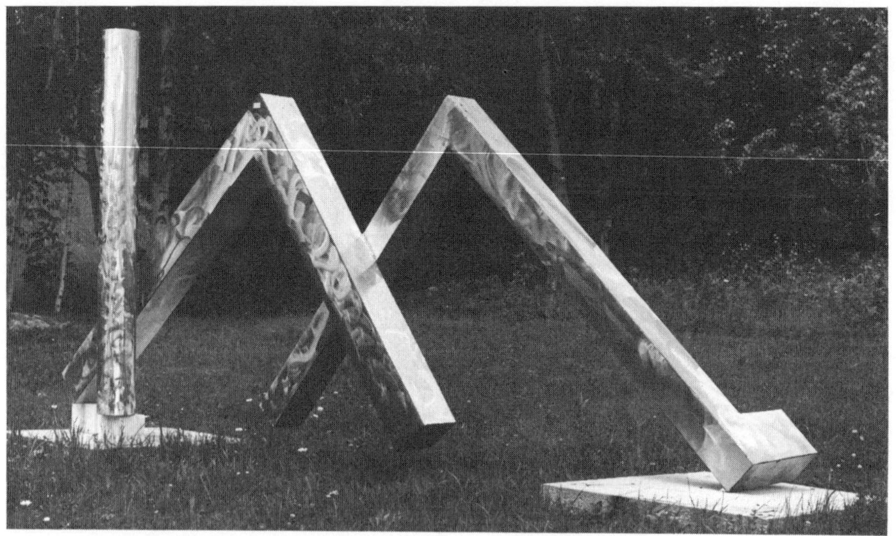

Fig. 5. David Smith, *Cubi XXIII*, steel, 76¼ inches high, 172⅞ inches long, 1964. (Photo lacking archival data)

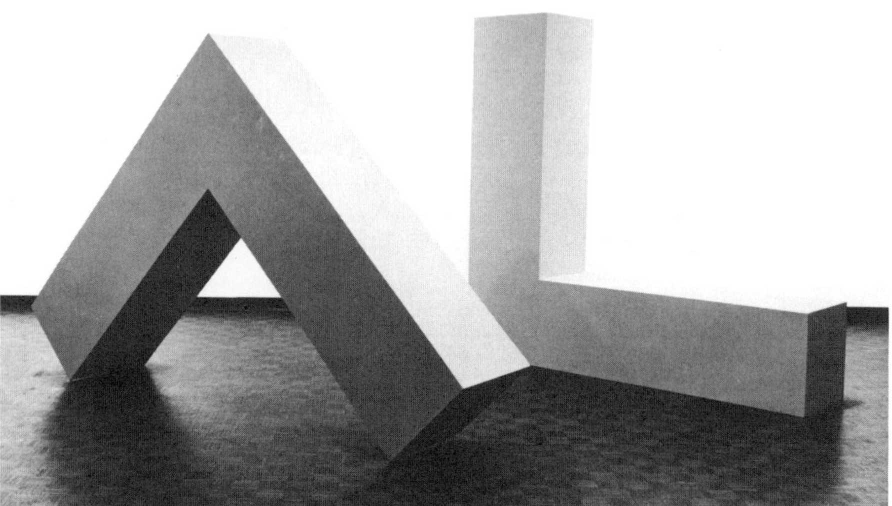

Fig. 6. Robert Morris, *Untitled (L-Beams)*, fiberglass; two units, each 96 × 96 × 24 inches (edition of three), 1965–67. (Photo courtesy of the Leo Castelli Gallery, New York)

York (1931–36) to the "New Bauhaus," in Chicago, with a special interest in architecture. From 1938 to 1940 he worked as a *capomastro* for Frank Lloyd Wright. Architectural practice extended from 1940 into the 1960s, but the years 1953 to 1955 he spent in Germany, where he "began to develop his artwork based [on] modular units," especially in a series of paintings and with architectural projects.[56] Since it was soon after his return that he began to produce his sculptures, one wonders, despite the season in Wright's Thoreauesque all-American entourage, about this Minimalist founding father's exposure to German Modernism. Because he never held an architect's license, Smith's own buildings had to be executed in collaboration with someone else, which function sometimes devolved upon his brother Thomas, who had studied, at Tony's suggestion, under Ludwig Mies van der Rohe in Chicago.[57]

Tony Smith did, however, practice architecture, producing "about two dozen" buildings, "mostly private homes,"[58] between 1940 and the early 1960s. This firsthand architectural work, neither so extensive nor so remarkable as the sculpture that grew out of it, includes a 1943–44 house that extends a clearly Wrightean hexagonal cellular structure along three 60-degree axes of unequal length; an interesting project for a Catholic church on Long Island consisting of irregularly clustered hexagonal cells on *pilotis* that might have had windows directly dripped by his friend Jackson Pollock;[59] and a 1950 house for the Abstract Expressionist painter Theodore Stamos, at East Marion, Long Island, this rectangular in plan but related to the church design by its elevation's expressing the hexagonal unit in vertical wooden trusses (influenced by bridge construction) on stilts.[60] Also prismatic—with a slight torque, and as such quite like such a sculpture by Smith as *For D. C.* (1969), yet at the same time rather Corbusian for its openwork facade—is a model for a small museum. (It is in museum design that Smith has seemed most conspicuously influential upon practicing latter-day architects, especially I. M. Pei, in whose work impassive Minimalist braininess translates too readily into corporate chic.)[61]

Considering his literally architectural activity, I have for years thought that the chamfered, angular faceting of the post and lintel elements of Smith's larger lattice sculptures, such as the enormous plywood mock-up of *Smoke*, erected in the Corcoran Gallery of Art, Washington, in 1967 (and afterward the related works *Smog* [1969], and *Smug* [1973]), shares with such faceting in contemporary "Brutalist" architecture a source in the earlier, so-called Cubist, Central European architecture. I remember how interesting one particular

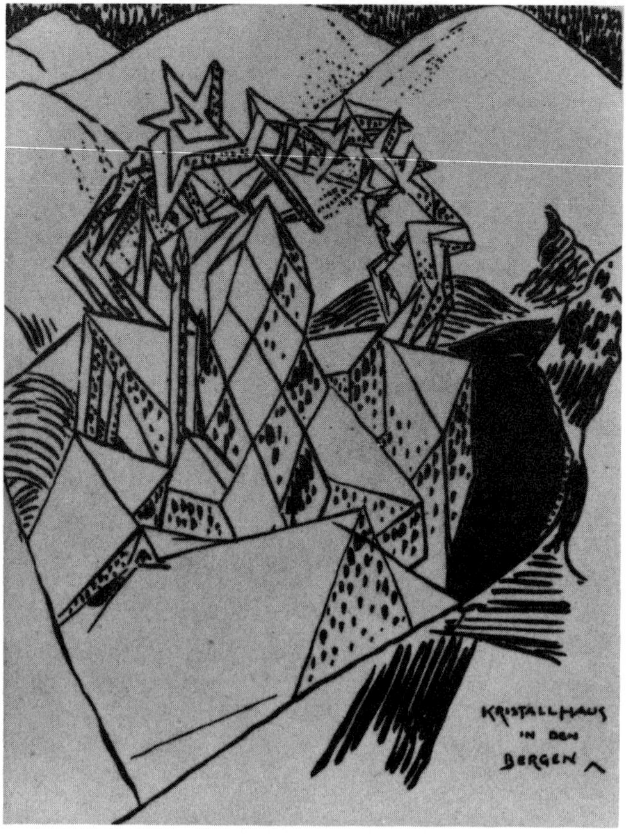

Fig. 7. Bruno Taut, *Crystal House in the Mountains*, ink drawing reproduced in Taut, *Die Auflösung der Städte; oder auch, Die Erde, eine gute Wohnung; oder auch, Der Weg zur alpinen Architektur* (Hagen, 1920)

architectural article looked at the moment of its appearance in 1966: Jaroslav Vokoun's "Czech Cubism." This was not the only publication on the subject at the time, but even the article's dated headline typeface displays a chamfering that looks similar to the memorable illustration of an apartment house in Neklanova Street, Prague, of 1912, by Josef Chochol—who had studied under Otto Wagner in Vienna—as Vokoun published it in *The Architectural Review* for March 1966;[62] that is, less than a year earlier than Smith's *Smoke*, the

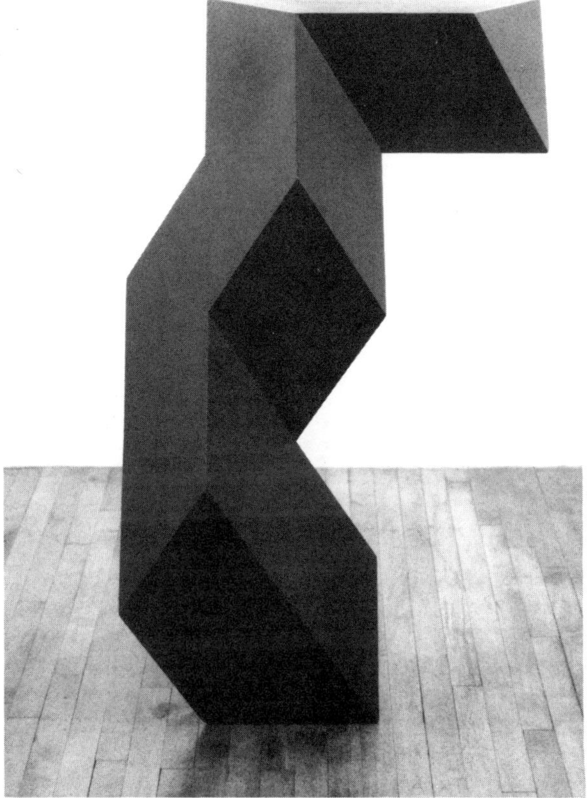

Fig. 8. Tony Smith, *Atlanta*, wooden mockup for bronze (edition of six), 48 × 31 × 24 inches, 1980. (Photo by Geoffrey Clements, courtesy of the Paula Cooper Gallery, New York)

"piers" and "lintels" of which are taperingly chamfered much in the manner of the totally faceted Prague facade.

In her engrossing study of the occult roots of crystal imagery in Expressionist architecture, Rosemarie Bletter makes a point of the inconsistencies, or rather, the freedom, of German Expressionist architects to alternate crystalline and "amorphic" form, and she reproduces two very different designs published by Bruno Taut, in 1919 and 1920, for a "Crystal House in the Mountains," of which the second, published in 1920 (Fig. 7), has "sharp faceted excrescences."[63] Now, with its harlequin diagonal faceting, Smith's sturdily prismatic *Atlanta,* cast in bronze in 1980 (Fig. 8), the year of the artist's death, stands not so far, after all, from such a once hopelessly farfetched Expressionist project in three dimensions as Bruno Taut's mountain house.[64] Before this, one of the last works of Tony Smith, I would add to Bletter's survey of the early spiritual literature something from a dialogue by the seventeenth-century mystic Jacob Boehme: to a student's inquiry, "in what *materia* or form" our bodies are to be resurrected, a master replies that, as with the individual human body, "When the visible world passes away, . . . only a heavenly, crystalline matter and form of the world remains" (6:46–47).[65]

Tony Smith emerged into a latter-day Expressionist context as an architect of essentially prismatic-geometric tendency, and went on to produce freestandingly prismatic or crystalline sculptures. That the origins of his crystalline architectonic structures are rooted, despite superficial stylistics, in the spiritual subsoil of Expressionism itself, is no superficial contradiction. "The evolutionary history of art is as spherical as the universe," Worringer himself says, "and no pole exists that does not have its counter-pole. . . . Only at the moment when we reach the pole itself do our eyes become opened, and we perceive the great beyond, that urges us toward the other pole."[66]

NOTES

1. I have been scrutinizing photographs of a bronze Silenus of the late sixth century B.C. and David Smith's *Albany III* (1959), of painted steel, but countless other comparable examples would serve as well.

2. A pair of critical essays written in the 1950s can be mentioned for their timely, worthy struggle with the ambiguity of "old" classicism versus the classic modernity of the early twentieth century: Colin Rowe, "Neo-'Classicism' and Modern Architecture, I" and "Neo-'Classicism' and Modern Architecture, II" (both 1973), in his *The Mathematics of the Ideal Villa and Other Essays* (Cambridge: MIT Press, 1976), 119–38, 139–58, respectively. William Curtis, "Modern Transformations of Classicism," *Architectural Review* 176, no. 1050 (August 1984), 39–47, understandably critically preoccupied under pressure of Postmodernism, does not itself penetrate to a deeper sense of precedent.

3. See Joseph Masheck, "Neolithic-Modern" (1984) and "On Cycladic Ultramodernity" (1989), in his *Modernities: Art-Matters in the Present* (University Park: Pennsylvania State University Press, 1993), 33–46.

4. Wilhelm Worringer, *Form Problems of the Gothic,* authorized American ed. (unsigned trans. dedicated in 1918), (New York: G. E. Stechert, 1920), 65.

5. William Rubin, ed., *Pablo Picasso: A Retrospective* (New York: The Museum of Modern Art, 1980), 89.

6. Ibid., 87.

7. Heinrich Wölfflin, "Italien und das deutsche Formgefühl," collected in his *Gedanken zur Kunstgeschichte: Gedrucktes und Ungedrucktes* (1940), 4th ed. (Basel: Benno Schwabe, 1947), 119–26, here 120.: "Wie schlicht und leicht fassbar die Flächen und Kuben."

8. Masheck, "Raw Art: 'Primitive' Authenticity and German Expressionism," *Res: Anthropology and Aesthetics*, no. 4 (Autumn 1982), 92–117.

9. Masheck, "A Critical Contribution to Art" (brief comment), *Art-Rite* (New York), no. 1 (15 April 1973), 5.

10. Henry-Russell Hitchcock, *Architecture: Nineteenth and Twentieth Centuries*, 2d ed., Pelican History of Art (Harmondsworth: Penguin, 1963), 341.

11. Fritz Burger, *Einführung in die Moderne Kunst* (Burger et al., *Die Kunst des 19. und 20. Jahrhunderts*, vol. 1), Handbuch der Kunstwissenschaft (Berlin: Akademische Verlagsgesellschaft Athenaion, 1917), 18–19, with illus.

12. In the Westphälisches Landesmuseum catalogue *Tony Smith: Skulpturen und Zeichnungen/Sculptures and Drawings/1961–1969* (Münster, 1988), illus. on 25; hereafter, references to this catalogue as *Tony Smith*.

13. Albrecht Dürer, *The Human Figure: The Complete "Dresden Sketchbook,"* ed. Walter L. Strauss (New York: Dover, 1972), cat. 138 on 280 (illus. on 281).

14. James Joyce, *Ulysses*, Modern Library (New York: Random House, 1961), 181.

15. José A. Argüelles, *Charles Henry and the Formation of a Psychophysical Aesthetic* (Chicago: University of Chicago Press, 1972), 60n–61n. Even though Minimal Art is generally antispiritual in the extreme, one might also think of the passionlessness, or dispassion, of *apatheia*, in mystics.

16. Recall that the great Viennese philosopher Ludwig Wittgenstein's *Philosophical Investigations* (posthumous) opens with an extended quotation from Augustine.

17. Robert Goldwater, *Primitivism in Modern Art*, rev. ed. (New York: Vintage, 1967), 28; my thanks to Marjorie Welish for calling my attention to this.

18. Johann Wolfgang von Goethe, *Italian Journey (1786–1788)*, trans. W. H. Auden and Elizabeth Mayer (New York: Schocken, 1968), 364.

19. Friedrich August Kekulé von Stradonitz, untitled address to the German Chemical Society, *Berichte der Deutschen Chemischen Gesellschaft* (Berlin), 23 (1890), 1302–11, here 1304, 1307.

20. Alois Riegl, *Late Roman Art Industry*, trans. and ed. Rolf Winkes, Archaeologica 36 (Rome: Giorgio Bretschneider, 1985), 194; in the original: *Spätrömische Kunstindustrie*, 2d ed. (Vienna, 1927; repr. Darmstadt: Wissenschaftliche Buchgesellschaft, 1964), 343.

21. Ibid., English ed., 208.

22. Friedrich Nietzsche, *The Birth of Tragedy and The Case of Wagner*, trans. Walter Kaufmann (New York: Vintage, 1967), 24.

23. Worringer, *Abstraction and Empathy: A Contribution to the Psychology of Style*, 3d ed., trans. Michael Bullock (Cleveland: World, 1967), 55; in the original: *Abstraktion und Einfühlung: ein Beitrag zur Stilpsychologie*, 4th ed. (Munich: Piper, 1916), 72.

24. Compare *Nymph and Satyr*, a bronze by Théodore Géricault, with a type of Paleolithic bone carving of wild beasts.

25. *Abstraction and Empathy*, 112–13.

26. *Viollet-le-Duc: Le Dictionnaire d'architecture: Relevés et observations*, ed. Philippe Boudon and Philippe Deshayes (Brussels: Architecture et Recherches, 1979), 271–75, with fig. 5 on p. 275.

27. John Ruskin, *The Seven Lamps of Architecture* (New York: Noonday, 1961), 104–5.

28. Ruskin, *The Stones of Venice*, ed. J. G. Links (New York: Hill and Wang, 1960; repr. New York: Da Capo, n.d.), 106.

29. Arthur Schopenhauer, *The World as Will and Representation*, trans. E. F. J. Payne, 2 vols. (Indian Hills, Colo.: Falcon's Wing, 1958), 1:258–59.

30. Georg Wilhelm Friedrich Hegel, *Aesthetics: Lectures on Fine Art*, trans. T. M. Knox, 2 vols. (Oxford: Clarendon Press, 1975), 1:130.

31. Ibid., 2:654; in the original, Hegel, *Vorlesungen über die Äesthetik* (*Werke*, 14), ed. Eva Moldenhauer and Karl Markus Michel (Frankfurt am Main: Suhrkamp, 1970), 2:295 ("abstrakt und verständig" [= intelligible]).

32. Johann Christoph Friedrich von Schiller, *Naive and Sentimental Poetry and On the Sublime: Two Essays,* trans. and ed. Julius A. Elias (New York: Frederick Ungar, 1966), 105.

33. Ibid., 106; in the original: "Über naive und sentimentalische Dichtung," in *Schillers Sämtliche Werke*, 14 vols. (Berlin and Leipzig, n.d.), 14:118–98, here 135.

34. Ibid., English ed., 142.

35. Ibid., English ed., 158; German ed., 174.

36. Ibid., English ed., 103 (emphasis in original). One might want to excavate still deeper, under Schiller's paired categories, to the rather different opposition proposed in Oliver Goldsmith's "Essay on the Theatre; or, A Comparison Between Sentimental and Laughing Comedy" (1773).

37. Schiller, *Naive and Sentimental Poetry*, English ed., 98; German ed., 129.

38. Immanuel Kant, *Critique of Judgement*, trans. J. H. Bernard, The Hafner Library of Classics (New York: Hafner, 1951), 212.

39. Masheck, "Kuspit's LeWitt: Has He Got Style?" *Art in America* 64, no. 9 (November–December 1976), 107–10, with illus. on 109 (reprint in LeWitt anthology by Editrice Inonia, Rome, forthcoming); Donald Kuspit's response, January–February; reply, March–April.

40. Emil Kaufmann, *Architecture in the Age of Reason: Baroque and Post-Baroque in England, Italy and France* (Cambridge, Mass.: Harvard University Press, 1955; repr. New York: Dover, 1968), esp. 225 n. 213, criticizing Rudolf Wittkower, "Principles of Palladio's Architecture," *Journal of the Warburg Institute* 7 (1944), 102–22; 8 (1945), 68–106, esp. 8:98; this was followed by Wittkower, "English Literature on Architecture" (1966), in his *Palladio and Palladianism*, ed. Margot Wittkower (New York: George Braziller, 1974), 94–112, esp. 104 (not mentioning Kaufmann). Morris's proportional cube plate is now also illustrated in Joseph Rykwert, *The First Moderns: The Architects of the Eighteenth Century* (Cambridge: MIT Press, 1980), on 191.

41. Kaufmann, *Architecture*, 225 n. 213, with ref. to Robert Morris, *Lectures on Architecture* (London, 1734–36), Lecture IX, 147.

42. Walter Benjamin, "Louis-Philippe or the Interior," in his "Paris: The Capital of the Nineteenth Century" (finished 1935), trans. Quintin Hoare, in his *Charles Baudelaire: A Lyric Poet in the Era of High Capitalism*, ed. and trans. Harry Zohn (London: NLB, 1973), 167–69.

43. Benedetto Gravagnuolo, *Adolf Loos: Theory and Works*, trans. C. H. Evans (New York: Rizzoli, 1982), 50.

44. On which see Ian Boyd Whyte, ed. and trans., *The Crystal Chain Letters: Architectural Fantasies by Bruno Taut and His Circle* (Cambridge: MIT Press, 1985); review by Masheck, "Expressionist Fantasias: The Crystal Chain Letters" (1986), in his *Modernities*.

45. Robert Rosenblum, *Transformations in Late Eighteenth-Century Art* (Princeton: Princeton University Press, 1970), 150–51, with pl. 181.

46. Kaufmann, *Architecture*, fig. 14, after p. 118.

47. Angela Westwater and Carl Andre, eds., *Carl Andre: Sculpture 1958–1974* (Bern:

Kunsthalle, 1975), cat. no. 1966-1 (and following), *Equivalent I*, 1966 (destroyed; remade, 1969), on p. 21 with fig. on p. 18.

48. According to Wittkower, the authority of a generation on such matters, Morris was well versed in harmonic proportion theory, in the most orthodox line of Palladio; "English Literature," 94–112, here 104.

49. See the interesting study by Mary McLeod, "'Architecture or Revolution': Taylorism, Technocracy and Social Change," *Art Journal* 43 (1983), 132–47.

50. Gravagnuolo, *Adolf Loos*, 170, with illus.

51. Reyner Banham, *A Concrete Atlantis: U. S. Industrial Building and European Modern Architecture 1900–1925* (Cambridge: MIT Press, 1986), 195, 197, 201; review by Masheck, "Temples to the Dynamo: The 'Daylight' Factory and the Grain Elevator" (1987), in *Modernities.*

52. Banham, *Concrete Atlantis*, 202.

53. Ibid., 258 n. 19.

54. Illus., *Tony Smith*, pl. on p. 38.

55. Geoffrey Scott, *The Architecture of Humanism: A Study in the History of Taste*, 2d ed. (London: Constable, 1924), 243, 244.

56. I rely here and below on Joan H. Pachner, "Tony Smith: Architecture into Sculpture," in *Tony Smith*, 48–71 (German and English on facing pages), here 62 (E) n. 7.

57. Ibid., 62 (E) n. 2.

58. Ibid., 50 (E), with fig. 2.

59. Ibid., with fig. 3 and fig. 7 on p. 52. On the vicissitudes of church design, see Steven Naifeh and Gregory White Smith, *Jackson Pollock: An American Saga* (New York: Potter, 1989), 657, 681, 761–62; also E. A. Carmean, "The Church Project: Pollock's Passion Themes," *Art in America* 70 (Summer 1982), 110–22, the latter disputed furiously, seemingly for daring to entail religious belief (as if abstraction and spirituality were incompatible terms), in Rosalind E. Krauss, "Reading Jackson Pollock, Abstractly" (1982), in her *The Originality of the Avant-Garde and Other Modernist Myths* (Cambridge: MIT Press, 1985), 221–42.

60. Pachner, "Tony Smith," 52 (E), with figs. 4, 5 on p. 51.

61. Pei's 1968 Everson Museum, at Syracuse, N.Y., and his Herbert F. Johnson Museum of Art for Cornell University, at Ithaca, of 1969–73, both carry over the hefty cantilevered blockiness of a Smith sculpture like *Keys to Given!* of which the model dates from 1965 (illus. *Tony Smith*, pls. on pp. 10, 11). As to Pei's later "East Wing" (disjunct from the old building) at the National Gallery, Washington, for which the 1962 *Tower of the Winds* is a likely prototype: it is almost embarrassing to see Smith's *Wandering Rocks*, 1967, placed beside it.

62. Jaroslav Vokoun, "Czech Cubism," *Architectural Review* 139 (March 1966), 229–33, offering, significantly, certain Bohemian Gothic anticipations; there are also Maria Benesova, "Architettura cubista in Boemia," *Casabella*, no. 314 (May 1967), 62–67, and Milos Pistorius, "Kubistická Architektura v Praze," *Staleta Praha* 4 (1969), 135–54 (English summary, "Cubist Prague," 219–20). Illus. of both Chochol's apartment house as shown in Vokoun's article, and T. Smith's *Smoke*, appear in the otherwise less extensively illustrated venue of the present essay: "Crystalline Form, Worringer, and the Minimalism of Tony Smith," in my *Building-Art: Modern Architecture Under Cultural Construction* (Cambridge: Cambridge University Press, 1993), 143–61, esp. figs. 17 on p. 156, 18 on p. 157.

63. Rosemarie Haag Bletter, "The Interpretation of the Glass Dream: Expressionist Architecture and the History of the Crystal Metaphor," *Journal of the Society of Architectural Historians* 40 (1981), 20–43, here 20, with figs. 3 on p. 21 (1919) and 4 on p. 22 (1920).

64. The unexpected similarity is all the more apparent when *Atlanta* is seen obliquely; unfortunately, only the frontal photograph is available.

65. Jacob Boehme, "On the Supersensual Life . . . ; a Conversation of a Teacher and Student" (1622), the "sixth treatise" in *The Way to Christ,* trans. Peter Erb, The Classics of Western Spirituality (New York: Paulist Press, 1978), 186–87.

66. Worringer, *Abstraction and Empathy,* 127.

3

Changing Times, Changing Styles: Wilhelm Worringer and the Art of His Epoch

Magdalena Bushart
Translated by Neil H. Donahue

There are books whose significance results less from their originality or the precision of their arguments than from the point in time of their appearance and their reception. Wilhelm Worringer's successful early publications, *Abstraction and Empathy* (1908) and *Form Problems in the Gothic* (1911), belong to this category of scholarship. In these books, but also in his book on Lukas Cranach (also in 1908), this art historian undertook to establish criteria for evaluating non-classical artistic expressions. The methodological points of orientation for such an undertaking were provided him by, first, Alois Riegl's concept of "artistic volition" *(Kunstwollen)*, whereby art does not depend on the technical ability *(Können)* of the respective stage of culture, but rather from changing psychic needs; and second, the notion of empathy *(Einfühlungslehre)* of the aesthetician Theodor Lipps, upon the basis of which Worringer developed his construct of an "urge to abstraction." In Worringer's psychological system of styles, "abstraction" and "empathy" mark the two poles of artistic sensitivity, whose interchange has determined the development of art since its primeval beginnings: while the "urge to abstraction" represents that need to evade into art an external world perceived as a threat and to capture the multiplicity of phenomena in geometric forms, the "urge to empathy" is understood as a wish to express in the artwork a world-feeling *(Weltgefühl)* of harmony.

In his writings Worringer aimed, according to his own testimony, at animating scholarly discussion. His intention was, so he averred, to open up new areas of research and to reconsider the value of his discipline of "anthropological psychology" *(Menschheitspsychologie)*.[1] In fact, his dissertation *Abstraction and Empathy* and also *Form Prob-*

lems in the Gothic appear, for long stretches, as disputes with the art-historical literature of his time.[2] With that, Worringer found at first, precisely in academic circles, little support or appreciation; there one reacted to his theses with undisguised skepticism. The tenor of reviews ranged from keeping an aloof distance to outright rejection. On top of that, most discussion first appeared several years later, when art historians found themselves forced, as it were, by the popular success of the two books to take a position. In short order, *Abstraction and Empathy* and *Form Problems in the Gothic* were among the most popular art historical texts of the prewar years. While his scholarly colleagues carped that Worringer viewed history from the perspective of the present day and, consequently, could not possibly do justice to historical truth, artists and art critics recognized therein the possibility to interpret the present in a new historical framework.[3]

Especially among the Expressionists, the scholar's theses found a lively resonance. In his works they thought themselves able to discover their own ideas all over again and they welcomed Worringer as a champion of the new art. Thus, Elisabeth Erdmann-Macke, the widow of August Macke, recalls the enthusiastic acceptance of those two texts among the young painters: "I must however add that the books by Worringer that appeared at that time, *Abstraction and Empathy* and *Form Problems in the Gothic*, had an enthusiastic circle of well-informed followers among young artists; most of them bought a copy or lent and borrowed it among themselves. Finally, for once, there was an academic who was receptive to and understanding of these new ideas, who would perhaps step up for them and defend them against so many conservatively inclined art historians, who rejected from the outset everything new and unusual, or didn't even bother with it to begin with."[4] And the art critic Paul Fechter reports in retrospect that he himself at the time recognized at once the epochal significance of Worringer's intellectual construct: "I was pleased, since there it was, what we all had long looked and wished for, and had found nowhere. . . . We received from Wilhelm Worringer . . . finally solid ground beneath our feet for the constant meeting with the modern art that we considered and valued as our art, as the art of our generation of the eighties."[5]

In view of this reception it did not take long before Worringer's books were interpreted as programmatic documents of Expressionism. In 1917, for example, the architectural historian Walter Müller-Wulckow considered *Form Problems* the theoretical justification for the "fundamental transformation that our conception of art has undergone in the present" and attributed to the book a greater importance for contemporary art than for the history of art.[6] Also, probably the harshest critic of Worringer, the art historian Richard Hamann, wanted to grant this work, with due reservations about its methodology, its validity as a theoretical attempt to come to terms with Expressionism:

> And so we appreciate the book and estimate its value: as a document of a new consciousness in search of a style, as intellectual-spiritual [*geistig*] adherent of a new artistic movement, to which the Gothic and primitive art, linearity and surface ornament signify a new value. . . . Just as Worringer describes Gothic structures, so appear the works of Expressionists and Cubists, and as a manifesto of Expressionism, as an artistic product, not as a scholarly achievement, one will have also to give this work its due, which was written by someone who is modern, knowledgeable, extremely impressive and probably only too persuasive with words [*vielleicht der Worte nur zu mächtiger Mensch*]. Time will tell whether [or not] the expressionism of this book will have stood up longer than the art that now already invokes it for legitimation [*die sich schon jetzt auf ihn beruft*].[7]

The assumption that Worringer had actually written his scholarly works with an eye to Expressionism has remained in the secondary literature until the present; for Geoffrey Perkins, Worringer was even the theoretician of the new directions in the arts.[8] Nonetheless, not only does the recollection of Worringer's publisher Reinhard Piper,[9] according to whom this reception was not at all intended by the author, speak against such suppositions, but also the date when the works were written, which makes any direct relation to Expressionism highly dubious: *Abstraction and Empathy* was begun in 1905, the year in which the artist group Die Brücke (The Bridge) was founded, and completed a year later.[10] Worringer signed the contract for the Cranach book in April 1907, and worked on *Form Problems* from September 1908 on. The latter had to have been far enough along by 1909 that the author could submit it for his *Habilitation* (postdoctoral book for tenure and promotion).[11] Only at this point were Wassily Kandinsky, Marianne von Werefkin, Gabriele Münter, Alexej von Jawlensky, and others joining together to form the "New Association of Artists" in Munich, where Worringer lived until May 1909, until his appointment as *Privatdozent* in Bern. Apart from the fact that Worringer's knowledge of modern currents in the arts from

1905 to 1907–8 would not have been all too profound, his concept of art seems, upon closer inspection, surprisingly conservative. Worringer does not in any way argue for the renunciation of obtaining aesthetic norms. Instead, he wanted to limit the "transvaluation of values" that he announced with his investigations, to the area of historical research. For all other realms of inquiry the classical ideal should remain valid, "for the naive appreciation of art must not be expected to hazard in such digressions of powerful cogitation its impulsive and irresponsible feel for artistic matters" (*Form in Gothic*, 9 [8]). Behind this disposition lies less the timidity of the scholar, who knows the small degree of effectiveness of historical research, than an understanding of art that sees in tradition the binding principle guiding the art of the present. His contemporaries were entirely correct when they read Worringer's works as comments on contemporary culture. The slogan under which this commentary stands is, however, not "Expressionism" or even "artistic revolution," but rather "changing times" or "epochal shift" *(Zeitenwende)*. The term represents criticism of the development of culture in the modern period and of modern—impressionistic—society. As ideological premise it informs not only Worringer's art-historical inquiries, but also his essays on contemporary events in the art world. Here, in his critique of modernism, lie then also the actual points of contact between Worringer's understanding of art and the theoretical concept of the Expressionists.

According to the developmental scheme that Worringer designed for the history of art, the desire for abstraction is the result of a religiously determined understanding of the world and marks the beginning of each and every artistic creation. Simultaneously, however, he proposes it as characteristic of the "Germanic race." While the South of Europe has separated itself from the religious determination of art through increasing knowledge of the natural world and its laws, thereby arriving at the classical ideals of harmony and naturalness, for Worringer the North has remained true to a transcendental view of the world. The urge to abstraction, hence an essential element of the "Germanic artistic volition," finds expression in the Nordic ornamental bands just as well as in Gothic cathedrals. Only when the classical ideal, in the development of modern art since the Renaissance, gains entry into German art is this racial disposition suppressed (though also never definitively vanquished). Subsequently, civilization and education *(Bildung)* supplant religious ideals, *ratio* replaces transcendence, modern individualism takes the place of the collective consciousness of prior times, and the art of the North becomes worldly and flat. Now that art begins to resemble the classical art of the South, without ever attaining its life-affirming harmony (*Form in Gothic*, 114–16 [77–79]). Where the Nordic feeling for form has nevertheless managed to assert itself, it arrives there unhesitatingly in conflict with the classical sensitivities of the day. Worringer names Albrecht Dürer and the painter Hans von Marées as prominent examples.

Before the background of this antagonistic model of history, can be seen Worringer's critique of the ideology *(Weltbild)* of modernity. Impressionism becomes the provisional high point, and at the same time, endpoint in the development of modern art. In the course of the nineteenth century, according to Worringer, [empirical] knowledge of the things of the world has reached such an extent that it no longer has an explanatory effect, but rather only creates more confusion. With all the senses and with "female receptivity," the individual has surrendered to the phenomena of life. This manner of increase in knowledge signifies, however, not an enrichment, but rather gives the individual a feeling of spiritual impoverishment. Faced with a multiplicity of impressions, the individual has finally lost perspective, even comes near to losing him- or herself: "This feminine surrender is really equivalent to the will to lose one's self, and it was perhaps the finest instinct of the period that felt that the last and most differentiated stimuli to knowledge were only accessible to whomever remained passive, only to whom dared give up the self."[12] For his own time, nonetheless, Worringer believes himself able to diagnose a transformation in worldview. The reigning cultural values since the Renaissance have begun to sway at the foundation; in their place a perspective opens up upon ideals long believed lost:

> Certainly it seems as if our present psychic constitution brings us closer again, at least indirectly, to Gothic values, since we gradually pronounce the word "personality" with a certain tiredness. The raging pathos of youthful individualism, confident of victory, has shrunk pitifully. And in us something comes to life like the desire for great, necessary values that elevate beyond all the individual noisemaking. Unsettled and tormented by all that is personal, there grows in us slowly an astonished comprehension of the sublime impersonality of the great, old styles.[13]

With the renunciation of a modern sensibility goes also, for Worringer, necessarily, a transformation of values. In the place of passive (womanly) self-surrender is a new activism, a (manly) will to self-assertion; in the place of "analysis" steps "synthesis" ("Architektur," 498). Or as he states elsewhere:

> We stand today in the middle of a crisis, in which the young generation with its unconsumed energies and its restless need for activity breaks through all restraints, as they are ankered in an all too differentiated hyperconsciousness, in an all too sensitive receptivity, and, unconcerned about yesterday's truth, this young generation creates for itself a new truth from its own flesh and blood. It appears that we have matured for a second, other naiveté that will restore to us the happiness and unself-consciousness of an active individual.[14]

Not without pathos Worringer describes the result of this transformation of attitude: "And an art became modern again to which the abstract law stands higher than the subjective" ("Architektur," 497). That this art in each case also presupposed a relation to racialistic and nationalistic precepts is self-evident from Worringer's racial-psychological method.[15]

A similar development, as Worringer describes it, hovered before the eyes of the advocates of "conservative reform." They also considered Impressionism a symptom of cultural decline, whose roots they sought in the Renaissance, "the doom of German culture."[16] They chastised its representatives with charges of hedonistic aestheticism, boundless subjectivism, and a lack of intellectual/spiritual orientation. Impressionism has, so lamented Richard Hamann, "destroyed all values of life in the Beyond of Good and Evil."[17] Instead of cultivating responsibility and feelings of patriotism, one surrendered to individualism, liberalism, and hedonism. The soul has taken the place of reason; psychology the place of philosophy: in brief, the whole culture has become "feminized"[18]—the gender stereotypes under which Worringer operates are already preformulated here. The conservative cultural critics set their hopes for the future on the creation of a new, idealistic worldview: Karl Lamprecht spoke of a "philosophical classicism";[19] Wilhelm Dilthey of a "more masculine, harder and more enlightened manner of thinking about work, duty, love, marriage and religion."[20] From this philosophy (that is, their convictions), a new, uniform style could grow, one that in its suprapersonal dimension would be generally binding and exemplary.[21] This system of coordinates, with its "essential" characteristics, should build up, on the one hand, tradition and, on the other hand, the nation. With that, these cultural reformers maintained throughout a distance to the rabid chauvinism of the Werdandi-Association or the literally understood historicism as practiced by the representatives of the Wilhelminian empire. Finally, they conjured the "spirit" and not the forms of a national past. Adolf Bartels defined this attitude as "conservative, not reactionary," one that "assumes something original and indestructible in each people, [does] not put all of life and being into mere progress, possesses natural piety before the given real national bonds and would like to create out of them, out of their spirit."[22] In reference to Barthel's definition, Worringer also described his own standpoint as "conservatism [. . .], that is not identical to reaction" ("Architektur," 498).

It is as characteristic of the climate of the time as it is for the amorphousness of the concepts that Worringer anticipated the question: In which form then would the transformed "spirit of the times" manifest itself? In these answers can be read not only Worringer's changing personal preferences, but also the change in paradigm that characterized the discussion of art in the prewar years. When in 1905 in an article on the dramatist Frank Wedekind, Worringer first broached the problem of transformed sensitivity *(Weltempfinden),* he still located the desire for abstraction outside of art in the realm of philosophy—in those years, he considered himself, ultimately, more of a literary intellectual with philosophical ambitions than an art historian.[23] Philosophy was to him a "place of refuge" as a "chance to catch one's breath, when we are in danger of getting crushed in the mess of things pressing upon each other tightly in space."[24] In 1909 he came back to that topic again in his reviews of the Marées retrospective in Munich. Now he spoke of a "German classicism." He interpreted the popular interest in Marées as a reaction to the sensual indulgence of Impressionism,[25] which was finally foreign to a natural Germanness *(artfremd):* "We hunger and thirst for an art that does more than delight the eye and stimulate the senses. We stand once again at a point where the ineradicable ideological needs within us have restlessly shifted and wait for fulfillment. We are looking for a sacral art for nonbelievers—to speak with the terminology of the German—we are looking again for a classicism" (64). Indeed, this wish cannot go into fulfillment—according to Worringer's racial-psychological system, since "classicism and Germanness [are] actually a contradiction in terms" (64), classical works for artists of German lineage thus are "only attainable through a powerful exertion of force." Worringer then deemed Marées also a type of artist-personality that had failed in "its tragic heroism" before the conflict of interests between racial disposition and classical world-feeling, related in this tragic sensibility to the "Gothic" artist of the Renaissance, Albrecht Dürer:

> For our sublime insufficiency we have found in him [Marées] a new formula. . . . And if there is a German classicism, then it lies exactly in this restless transforming, so difficult to the Nordic individualist, of ethical moments into artistic values. It has to replace in the dualistically bound German, that which is attainable to other nations as an unconstrained expression of instinct without any problematics.[26]

This eulogy of Marées, who died in 1887, is not exclusively to be understood in retrospective terms. The classical ideal, of which we are speaking here, lived on in the twentieth century in the works of Adolf Hildebrand and Artur Volkmann. Worringer had had for many years an unrestrained admiration for the person of Hildebrand;[27] the title of his famous text about *The Problem of Form in the Plastic Arts* is unmistakably cited in the title of Worringer's *Form Problems in the Gothic,* and the concept Hildebrand develops there of sculptural relief based on "distant perspective" *(Fernsicht)* had served Worringer for his definition of the Nordic desire for abstraction tormented by agoraphobia *(Raumscheu).*[28]

In 1911, only a few months after the publication of *Form Problems,* in two articles that appeared almost simultaneously, Worringer delivered further variations on his understanding of art. The first of the two essays, "The Problem of Modern Architecture," appeared in the *New German Architectural News (Neudeutsche Bauzeitung),* a conservative architectural journal. There Worringer named representatives of *Stilkunst* as executors of the transformed sensitivity of the period: the painter Ferdinand Hodler, the architect Peter Behrens, and, once more, Hans von Marées and Adolf Hildebrand. Their works, created from a new "architectonic" sensibility and bound in equal degree to both the present and to tradition, corresponded to the conflict of modern mankind, "that is tired of its individualism, unable to regain the force of unreservedly universal validity" ("Architektur," 498). The result seems quite violent, and not without reason:

> What is only possible for us today and to which the architectonic sensibility that dominates us now pushes us, is to broaden our general sensitivity. Only such an individual sensitivity, sounded through the feeling for the general necessity, —

no mass sensitivity is possible for us. This sounding will never be completely natural to us; rather it will always represent a strained effort that cannot deny its intentional character. But perhaps exactly that is the decisive feature of our time, that it [the time] cannot support what grows naturally, that it will detect everywhere the strain of overcoming, the effects of conquered inhibitions, the dynamics of the desired synthesis. Therefore we do not strain toward what is self-evident and universally valid anyway, but rather toward the individual element that has consciously constrained itself into the universal. ("Architektur," 498)

This description corresponds to Worringer's thesis according to which the development from abstract "Style" to classical "Naturalism" is irreversible and thus each attempt at a renovation of Nordic (that is, German) expressiveness in art *(Ausdruckskunst)* necessarily remains a compromise—or fails tragically. In this sense can also be explained the series of names. We have already spoken of Marées and Hildebrand as heroes of a modern, "Nordic" classicism. In a comparable way, the art of Ferdinand Hodler can be read as a compromise between the antagonistic principles of creation. His figures combine a pronounced frontality and linearity—according to Worringer's system these are characteristics of Nordic abstraction—with the mannered plasticity of Michelangelo's sculpted bodies. While Marées nevertheless had unmistakably failed with his idealistic conceptions (not by chance did Worringer say to his contemporaries of Marées's paintings: "His works should not be our schooling, but rather his volition and his great attitude"),[29] Hodler could advance to carry the hopes for the future. In 1912, in his *Old German Book Illustration,*[30] Worringer celebrated the painter as renewer of Nordic expressiveness in art *(Ausdruckskunst),* in whose monumental murals for Zürich and Jena the fundamental disposition of the "race" comes finally into its own after several hundred years of foreign domination:

The German is . . . by nature an expressive artist [*Ausdruckskünstler*]. Even if the ground beneath him has been withdrawn since the Renaissance, if he has toiled his way through the centuries, this subterranean force cannot be extinguished. It only waits, as it were, for the word, the cue, to come into its own again. This cue was given at the moment when the problem of monumentality became of moment again. Only a German hears it, only a German understands it, and the world

> can ignore Hodler's compelling frescoes as little as it can ignore Dürer's compelling illustrations. (8)

Worringer's enthusiasm for Hodler certainly had several sources. The painter was considered, ever since his first successful exhibitions in Paris and Munich, the chief representative of a new, idealistic art. The commission for the narrative painting "The Departure of the Jena Students for the War of Liberation in 1813" (1907) for the newly built University of Jena had created a considerable commotion in Germany. More important, however, might have been the influence on Worringer of his teacher Artur Weese, who maintained friendly contact with Hodler and wrote the first monograph about him. In a lecture in 1909 Weese had defined Hodler's art in exactly those categories that Worringer now, in turn, elevated as characteristic features of the new "artistic volition" *(Kunstwollen):* renunciation of the "cult of individuality," typicality, desire for expression, and the return to medieval principles of form.[31] Considered closely, Worringer's definition of the period style can indeed also be extended to other works of *Stilkunst,* to the tormented sculptures of Franz Metzner, for example, or to the paintings of Albin Egger-Lienz.

Worringer ultimately gave a clearly different accent to the second essay (which is far more well known because it was of greater consequence to modern art) that established his renown as a theoretician of Expressionism. Here it is the "young Parisian Syntheticists and Expressionists" (he subsumed all post-Impressionistic painting under this term),[32] who give expression to the new spiritual strivings. This second essay with the title "Remarks on the Historical Developments of Contemporary Art" appeared for the first time in 1911 in the polemical *In Battle over Art (Im Kampf um die Kunst).* That text delivers an answer by art historians, art dealers, and artists to the "Protest of German Artists" that was initiated by the Worpsweder landscape painter Carl Vinnen and published in April of that year. In that pamphlet, Vinnen had criticized the alleged overestimation of French art by gallery owners and museum directors and warned urgently against an "undue estrangement" or "excessive contamination" *(Überfremdung)* of modern German painting because of its orientation on foreign models. The initiative for the counterpublication issued from Franz Marc and Wassily Kandinsky; it was also Kandinsky who turned to Worringer with the request that he collaborate on the book and at first even offered him the position as its editor. Worringer turned down the editorship; he did not feel himself to have sufficient "moral weight" for such a task.[33] Nonetheless he contributed an article to the undertaking.

While most of the other authors of this polemic let it suffice to reject or refute the reproaches raised by Vinnen, Worringer used the opportunity to test his intellectual construct and his ideas about the "volition" of his own epoch on works of French and German avant-garde art. He imputed to them the same objectives that he thought to have already located for the artistic styles of older generations of artists. He also saw in the new direction in the arts primarily a countercurrent to Impressionism; the mainspring of this reaction would be the wish for "overcoming the subjective and arbitrary and what is only individually determined," for the "urge to objectivity," and for "struggling toward synthesis" ("Remarks," 94). The simplifications of form among the new artists, their recourse to "primitive" forms of expression, resulted from the general discontentment with modern culture:

> Today we certainly cannot return ourselves [*zurück-schrauben*], forcefully and artificially, back to the level of primitive mankind, but what arises in us today beneath the surface is ultimately a reaction not only to Impressionism, but also to the entire preceding development in which we find ourselves since the European Renaissance and whose point of departure and direction can be broadly captured by Burckhardt's lapidary term about the discovery of the individual. The great wealth of external knowledge of prior epochs has left us impoverished and from this feeling of poverty we impose today certain demands on art that correspond roughly to those that primitive mankind naively posed. ("Remarks," 95)

For all that, Worringer's defense of the young artists seemed rather subdued. He spoke carefully of "principled partisanship" and of the "will to an understanding" and named their works "experiments, unarticulated sounds," that they have first to work through to a clear formulation. Whereas in the paintings of Ferdinand Hodler or Hans von Marées he found a concrete ideal, he saw in Expressionism a disposition that he accepted only as a "necessity of historical development" ("Remarks," 99). Basically he saw in Expressionism a transitional solution, a "drawing strength out of the concentrated reservoirs of the past." Thereafter, art would have to find its way back, strengthened, to a "more narrow tradition and with that, to itself once again."[34]

Despite his distanced manner of viewing the matter, the art historian entered with this article into the field of vision of the Expressionists, who subsequently also discovered for themselves his other scholarly works. Above all, the authors of the *Blue Rider Almanac (Der Blaue Reiter)* recognized and utilized the opportunities that Worringer's intellectual construct held for the Expressionist movement; his scholarly findings gave their own theoretical efforts much greater weight. The idea that a suprapersonal "artistic volition" *(Kunstwollen)* and not the "capability" *(Können)* of individual artists marked the cultural expressions of an epoch, assured the Expressionist version of modernism an existential justification that had been denied it by contemporary critics. It became a "necessity of historical development" that arose out of the psychic requirements of the epoch and from which the individual could hardly remove him or herself.[35] And the equation of abstract art, a spiritual worldview, and Nordic urge to abstraction not only made this tendency in the arts appealing to a conservatively inclined audience, which could detect here the first step toward a renewal of German art; it also approximated the ideological conceptions of the artists themselves. Thus, Franz Marc and Wassily Kandinsky defined their creative work in antithesis to Impressionism and as a reaction to modern industrial society. Just like Worringer and the conservative cultural reformers, they also hoped for the dawning of a new spiritual period, for which they considered themselves advocates. Also, they preferred the paintings of Hans von Marées, Ferdinand Hodler, and even Hans Thoma, to the art of Max Liebermann, which they felt was merely sensual.[36] By appealing to Worringer's antagonistic model of historical development, Expressionism could establish itself during the First World War as the national movement of opposition to international Impressionism (of mainly French extraction).[37] Already one soon saw, in a mistaken understanding of the historical delineation in Worringer's works, a "theoretical introduction to the most recent artistic strivings," even, moreover, the "productive stimulus to the creativity of numerous young artists."[38]

The attitude of Worringer toward the new art was even then admittedly ambivalent, though he had already long since become the figurehead of the Expressionist movement. He sympathized without reservation only with their anti-Impressionistic, later also their nationalistic, "sentiments" *(Gesinnung)*[39]—not, however, with their own artistic concept. In 1918 he turned down the request by Carl George Heise to review a painting by Conrad Felixmüller, with the reasoning: "Understand me correctly: I affirm the world that resides behind this painting, not the painting."[40] His engagement for Expressionism, as he further clarified, had little to do with aesthetic appreciation in a traditional sense; rather he considered himself more a "believer in a living development": "If I don't believe in an art that goes on eternally in the usual, traditional sense, I do believe in an eternally living, progressively developing humanity that creates for itself ever new forms of expression, whether we call it art or not" (169).

Two years later, in his famous lecture on "Questions about Contemporary Art" (Künstlerische Zeitfragen),[41] Worringer retracted this confession of absolute solidarity with his contemporaries. Now he took definitive distance to Expressionist painting and sculpture, and declared them both a false development into mannerism that only appeared to propel them into a position at the forefront of contemporary sensibility. Works of art, however, do not reveal the worldview of the recent past; rather, it is to be found in philosophy and in scholarship: "Why are we still looking for the creative sensuality of our time in paintings [*Malbildern*] when it resides in works of intellect [*Denkbildern*]? Not in the fine arts, but rather in the spiritual-intellectual extensions of knowledge . . . lie the true artistic achievements of our time" (25). With this polemical turn, Worringer drew a sharp line of separation between his works and the Expressionist artists who cited them for authority. He reproached the artists for having failed utterly with respect to the broader cultural turn toward a new intellectuality *(Geistigkeit)*. In contrast, he counted his own publications among the positive productions of the Expressionist period. Whereas art had produced empty pathos when it claimed to focus spiritual energies, scholarship, and especially art history, with the help of a "suprascholarly ability for intimation and empathy" (26), had done the work of the plastic arts and developed spiritual visions:

> And here there is at work a spiritual urge to expand, which embodies the phenomenon of Expressionism more faithfully and more appropriately for the time than does Expressionism in painting. In these obsolete forms of painterly activity, that [creative] tension of the sovereign spirit has exhausted itself, as it were, upon unsuitable objects and has only been able to produce an unconvincing display of fictions in the airless space of stylistic experimentation; [that (creative) tension of the sovereign spirit] is now really productive and legitimate here, in the area of theoretical knowledge, of scholarly lucidity and vision, and is finally no less stimulating than it was in the

> half-baked commotion of our ungratifying artistic exertions. ("Zeitfragen," 27)

The art historian, who had begun his career as poet and as literary critic with a claim to artistry, has fully reversed himself. Art is dead. Long live art history!

NOTES

1. Wilhelm Worringer, *Formprobleme der Gotik* (Munich: Piper, 1911), 11; *Form Problems in the Gothic*, or in Herbert Read's translation, *Form in Gothic* (London: Alec Tiranti, 1964). Page references are to Read's edition, though the wording has been changed where necessary. The reference to the original German edition follows in brackets. Otherwise, all quotations from Worringer's works are by the present translator and page numbers refer to the original editions as cited. The following discussion is based on the first chapter of my book, *Der Geist der Gotik und die expressionistische Kunst. Kunstgeschichte und Kunsttheorie, 1911–1925* (Munich: Silke Schreiber, 1990).

2. The two-page bibliography that Worringer added to his dissertation, which he edited and published on his own (Wilhelm Worringer, *Abstraktion und Einfühlung: Ein Beitrag zur Stilpsychologie.* Inaugural-Dissertation to achieve the Degree of Doctor of the Philosophical Faculty at the University of Bern, Neuwied, 1907), is missing in the editions published by Piper in Munich from 1908 on.

3. Already the first (and for a long time the only) reviewer of *Abstraction and Empathy*, the poet Paul Ernst, emphasized the topicality of the book for the present: it provided a "historico-philosophical" explanation for the cultural manifestations of the present; review in *Kunst und Künstler* 6 (1908), 529.

4. Elisabeth Erdmann-Macke, *Erinnerung an August Macke* (Stuttgart: Kohlhammer, 1962), 211. Also the painter Gabriele Münter, for many years the companion of Wassily Kandinsky, credited Worringer's works with a decisive significance for Expressionism. In a letter for his birthday in 1951, she wrote: "We know one another now ever since the beginnings of the postimpressionist developments in art, for which you helped prepare the ground. From those early years, I still have my old copy of your book *Abstraction and Empathy*, which had such an animating effect at that time" (Letter of 13 January 1951; GNM–ZR ABK 146/377).

5. Paul Fechter, *Menschen auf meinen Wegen* (Gütersloh: Bertelsmann, 1955), 292.

6. Walter Müller-Wulckow, "Wilhelm Worringers Formprobleme der Gotik," *Das Kunstblatt* 1 (1917), 216–18, here 216.

7. Richard Hamann, "Rezension zu Wilhelm Worringers 'Formproblemen der Gotik,'" *Zeitschrift für Ästhetik und allgemeine Kunstwissenschaft* 10 (1915), 357–61, here 360f.

8. Geoffrey Perkins, *Contemporary Theory of Expressionism* (Bern: Herbert Lang, 1974), 118.

9. Reinhard Piper, *Mein Leben als Verleger: Vormittag–Nachmittag* (Munich: Piper, 1964), 277. Worringer himself characterized the question of how much of an influence his theory had had on the development of modernism, of whether it had served as pacesetter for abstract art, as "inconclusive [*unentscheidbar*] in a historical sense":

> I had at that time a loose personal relationship to Marc and Kandinsky; nonetheless

I recall no conversation that would have brought the matter to a pointed and definite question of either-or. In any case, a direct correlation between the book and artistic practice only emerged later in our historical understanding [of the period]. Whereby one must not forget that my dissertation at that time, which contained the Abstraction and Empathy antinomy, primarily pertained only to historical investigations and interpretations. (Letter to Arnold Gehlen, undated, around 1958. GNM–ZR ABK 146/398; see also Arnold Gehlen, *Zeit-Bilder. Zur Soziologie und Ästhetik der modernen Malerei* [Frankfurt am Main: Klostermann, 1986], 116.)

Worringer first made a claim to have provided an "initial theoretical spark for the fundamental reorientation, . . . that occurred in the artistic practice of our contemporaries" (16) in the foreword to the 1959 edition of *Abstraction and Empathy* (repr., Munich: Piper, 1981).

10. Worringer dates his writing of *Abstraction and Empathy* to "Summer–Fall 1905," after the igniting idea came to him at Easter of the same year in the Trocadéro Museum in Paris (GNM–ZB ABK 146, 7). According to his own recollections, he received his doctorate in June 1906 (according to the resumé in his dissertation, however, only on 12 January 1907) in Bern under the direction of Artur Weese.

11. The detailed chronology of these publications can be found in his estate [*Nachlaß*] (GNM Personalia 1 and ZR ABK 146, 7); cf. further, Worringer's letter of 23 September 1944 to his publisher Reinhard Piper, in Piper, *Briefwechsel mit Autoren und Künstlern, 1903–1953* (Munich: Piper, 1979), 458–61.

12. Wilhelm Worringer, "Zum Problem der modernen Architektur," *Neudeutsche Bauzeitung* 7 (1911), 486–500, here 496.

13. Wilhelm Worringer, *Lukas Cranach* (Munich: Piper, 1908), 36.

14. Wilhelm Worringer, "Moderne Idealisten," *Berner Rundschau* 2 (1907–8), 737–42, 739f.

15. As stated in Worringer's review of the Marées-Exhibition in Munich in 1909: "Yes, this certainty impresses itself upon the viewer as the most surprising and most unmodern: art is not so international as we believed it to be. [Instead] it turns also back to national limitations, if one can call it so, with ultimate and highest effects that cannot be effaced from any general formation" (Worringer, "Die Marées-Ausstellung der Münchner Sezession," *Kunst und Künstler* 7 [1909], 231–32, 231).

16. Compare, for instance, Richard Benz, *Die Renaissance. Das Verhängnis der deutschen Cultur*, Blätter für deutsche Art und Kunst 1 (Jena: Diederichs, 1915).

17. Richard Hamann, *Der Impressionismus in Leben und Kunst* (Marburg: Verlag des Kunstgeschichtlichen Seminars, 1923; 1st ed., 1907), 153. Worringer was most familiar with Hamann's critique of Impressionism; he had reviewed the book in "Moderne Idealisten" in the *Berner Rundschau* (Worringer, see note 14) and also in the *Monatshefte für Kunstwissenschaft* 1 (1908), 338–40.

18. Hamann, *Der Impressionismus*, 150.

19. Karl Lamprecht, *Deutsche Geschichte*. Cited in Worringer, "Moderne Idealisten" (1907–08), 741.

20. Wilhelm Dilthey, "Gotthold Ephraim Lessing," in *Das Erlebnis und die Dichtung* (Leipzig: Teubner, 1906), 1–136, here 136.

21. On the ideas of the conservative reformers, see Richard Hamann and Jost Hermand, *Epochen deutscher Kultur von 1870 bis zur Gegenwart*, 5 vols. (Frankfurt am Main: Fischer, 1977): 4:212–20.

22. Adolf Bartels, "Konservativ, nicht reaktionär!" in *Die Heimat, 1900*, 3–13, 10.

23. At his own admission Worringer had decided relatively late upon an academic career; beforehand he had sought a career as a writer, had written poems, and belonged to a

literary circle in Munich surrounding the philosopher Paul Stern, the poet Karl Schloss, and the art historian, poet, and author of a monograph on Stefan George, Franz Dülberg. Cf. Worringer's letter of 23 September 1944 to Reinhard Piper, in Piper, *Briefwechsel*, 458.

24. Wilhelm Worringer, "Frank Wedekind. Ein Essay," in *Münchener Almanach. Ein Sammelbuch neuer deutscher Dichtung,* ed. Karl Schloss (Munich: Piper, 1905), 55–64; 64.

25. Wilhelm Worringer, "Die Marées-Ausstellung in der Münchener Sezession," *Der Cicerone* 1 (1909), 64–66: "For France, Impressionism was classical, not for Germany. We are indebted to it for a great education in verisimilitude and a lasting enrichment and refinement of our artistic range of expression, but it did not set free the actual expressive forces of our people [*unseres Volkes*]. A more or less strong feeling of discontentedness remains and this feeling makes us ready for Marées, for whose volition [*Wollen*] our eyes are open for the first time" (65).

26. Worringer, "Die Marées-Ausstellung," *Kunst und Künstler* (1909), 231f.

27. Cf. Worringer's review of Adolf Hildebrand's works (Adolf Hildebrand, *Gesammelte Aufsätze* [Straßburg: Heitz, 1909], in *Monatshefte für Kunstwissenschaft* 3 [1910], 212) and his discussion of the exhibition "München 1908" (Wilhelm Worringer, "Die Ausstellung München 1908," *Masken* 4 [1908], 19–24, 21f.).

28. Cf. Bushart, *Der Geist der Gotik*, 40.

29. Worringer, "Marées," *Der Cicerone* (1909), 66. The idea that not the invention of forms, but rather the "attitude" *(Gesinnung)* of contemporary art should serve as a model had been introduced into discussion at the beginning of the century by Julius Langbehn in his highly regarded *Rembrandt als Erzieher: Von einem Deutschen* (Leipzig: Hirschfeld, 1890).

30. Wilhelm Worringer, *Die altdeutsche Buchillustration* (Munich: Piper, 1912), 8.

31. Cf. Artur Weese, *Ferdinand Hodler* (Bern: Francke, 1909), 43–57, and 64. Just how lively was the exchange of ideas between the two scholars is clear from the letter in which Weese reports to his former student of his upcoming lecture:

> Next Monday I will give a lecture in Zürich on Impressionism and eurhythmics. To be exact, —about Amiet, van Gogh and Ferdinand Hodler. A lecture from Hamann to Worringer. I've let myself be carried back and forth in the stream and countercurrent of ideas between the poles of empathy and abstraction, until I've become dizzy. I've been hunting along the border between two worlds and am happy to meet you at each turn; indeed I was also annoyed that you are not here right now. . . . To get over that absence I'll go to visit Hodler in Geneva. I was astonished at what an exact thinker he is. He articulates his ideas like a theoretician, somewhat obscure and rough, but excellent. Everything revolves around unity, parellelism, permanence and symmetry. But I said to him, just as the Parisians have named their new art "Impressionism" after a painting of Monet's, so too I want to call his whole manner, his principle, his style, "Eurhythmics." He was pleased. (Letter of 8 January 1909, reprinted in Artur Weese, *Ausgewählte Briefe, 1905–1934* [Bern: Jahresgabe der Bernischen Kunstgesellschaft für 1935, 1935], IV)

On the relationship between Weese and Worringer, see Hans Christoph von Tavel, "Der Lehrstuhl für Kunstgeschichte an der Universität Bern von den Anfängen bis zum Zweiten Weltkrieg," *Jahrbuch des Schweizerischen Instituts für Kunstwissenschaft* (1972–73), 33–58, 47–50. Possibly, Weese could have also arranged for a meeting between Hodler and Worringer. In his correspondence with Wassily Kandinsky, Worringer mentions an (unsuccessful) attempt to meet Hodler in Geneva; cf. his note from 17 April 1911 and the card from

26 April 1911 (Gabriele Münter-Stiftung and Johannes Eichner-Stiftung, Städtische Galerie im Lenbachhaus, Munich).

32. Worringer, "Entwicklungsgeschichtliches zur modernsten Kunst," in *Im Kampf um die Kunst* (Munich: Piper, 1911), 92–99; here 94.

33. Letter to Kandinsky from 17 April 1911 (Gabriele Münter-Stiftung and Johannes Eichner-Stiftung, Städtische Galerie im Lenbachhaus, Munich).

34. "Remarks," 97. Also: "Since this modern primitivity should not be a definitive stage. . . . This primitivity should rather be a transition, a long respite to catch our breath before speaking the new and decisive word for the future. Out of what, for the time being, are still experiments and unarticulated sounds, will be wrought the clear word, —and how strong can this art of the future become that, which after working out the most elemental and powerful language of forms, will return to a more narrow tradition and thus once again, to itself." That Worringer kept an extreme distance from the "affected primitivity" of modernism is also apparent in his volume *Altdeutsche Buchillustration*. There he warns not only of historical longings ("direct, obvious recourse to past means of artistic expression that are foreign to us"), but also of a new archaism: "Since art is, in both cases, forced back into an abstractly expressive language that it has since lost [*verlernt*]" (7).

35. Cf. Bushart, *Geist der Gotik*, 60f.

36. Marc named Hodler and Marées in one breath with Kandinsky as forerunners of the new art in Germany (Franz Marc, "Zwei Bilder" in *Der Blaue Reiter,* ed. Franz Marc and Wassily Kandinsky [Munich: Piper, 1912], 8f.). And Kandinsky complained in 1912 to Marc about the lack of recognition for Gabriele Münter's paintings with the words: "Today one 'understands' a French brushstroke. A German brushstroke can sound however it wants to, as loudly as it wants—it falls only on deaf ears. . . . Or does it seem too 'unrefined' for the German heart, imbued with French jargon, to hear that German resonance? I posed the same question already to Liebermann with respect to Hans Thoma, whom he, the dear man [i.e., as pun, 'der Liebe Mann'], disdains. Such matters can lead to despair" (Letter from 18 March 1912, quoted from *Wassily Kandinsky–Franz Marc. Briefwechsel,* ed. Klaus Lankheit [Munich: Piper, 1983], 144).

37. Cf. Magdalena Bushart, "Der Expressionismus, ein deutscher Nationstil?" *Merkur* 45 (1991), 455–62.

38. Commentary in the *Frankfurter Zeitung* on the lecture "Bemerkungen zur neuen Kunst" that Worringer held in 1917 in Frankfurt. Quoted in Herwarth Walden, "Bemerkungen zu Worringer," *Der Sturm* 8 (1917–18), 178–79; here 178.

39. Thus Worringer emphasized the separation of the German Expressionists from the "subconsciously binding romanic-classical view of art" and their recourse to national forms of expression (Wilhelm Worringer, "Künstlerische Zukunftsfragen," *Kunst und Künstler* 14 [1916], 259–64, here 262) and later spoke of "a dark new racial and communal feeling" that marked their art (Worringer, "Vorwort," in *Katalog Freie Sezession* [Berlin: Freie Sezession, 1918] 9f., here 10).

40. Letter to Carl Georg Heise, 8 August 1918, as quoted in Jenns E. Howoldt, "Krise des Expressionismus. Anmerkungen zu vier Briefen Wilhelm Worringers an Carl Georg Heise," *Idea* 8 (1989), 159–73, here 169.

41. Wilhelm Worringer, "Künstlerische Zeitfragen." Lecture held on 19 October 1920 in the local chapter of the German Goethe Society. (Munich: Bruckmann, 1921).

4

Against Expressionism: Materialism and Social Theory in Worringer's *Abstraction and Empathy*

Michael W. Jennings

One of the most important trajectories of modern cultural historiography runs from Alois Riegl through Wilhelm Worringer to Walter Benjamin. That trajectory begins with Riegl's epochal—and that is not too strong a word—democratization of the history of culture. Riegl's shift of attention away from periods whose cultural production conformed to classical norms of art-historical evaluation and development and toward the recognition of the full equivalence of what was then held to be "degenerate" or "barbaric" art has begun in the last ten years to receive the kind of critical attention it deserves.[1] Worringer's accomplishment, in contrast, has often been viewed as an attempt to append a taxonomy to Riegl's ideas. And indeed, at first glance, Worringer's assertion of the regular alternation of abstract and empathetic cultural epochs seems to do little more than systematize in a rather rigid manner Riegl's fundamental insights into the character of a people's cultural production. But Worringer in point of fact builds on Riegl at precisely that point where his ideas were vaguest: at the point at which Riegl attempted to describe his famous idea of the *Kunstwollen*, his attempt to describe the complex societal interactions that produced works of art of a particular style.[2]

Worringer's contribution was finally not a kind of systematization, but rather the incorporation of modern social theory into cultural historiography. He adds, in other words, models of mediation to Riegl's system. To continue this line of development, then, it is left to Walter Benjamin to "finish" the work of Riegl and Worringer. Those aspects of Benjamin's complex theory of culture that draw directly upon Riegl and Worringer are organized in two stages: the first in his *Origin of German Tragic Drama*, where Benjamin asserts that the aesthetically problematic German Baroque *Trauerspiel* is not merely coequal to, but in fact is more ethically and historically responsible than the more rounded, organic works of Shakespeare and Calderón; and the second in Benjamin's unfinished magnum opus, *Das Passagen-Werk* (The arcades project), where he fully develops his theory that the key to the understanding of any present age is the historical recovery of a cognate past age through the study of its cultural production. In the remarks that follow I suggest not so much Worringer's exact position on this broadly conceived trajectory as how he marks a site at which a shift of emphasis occurs, however subtly, within the more general approach to cultural interpretation in the early twentieth century. In doing so I shall focus on two aspects of Worringer's work: his historical understanding and, especially, the particular brand of materialist aesthetics that, surprisingly, plays a key role in his two works of 1908, *Abstraction and Empathy* and *Lukas Cranach*.

But first a word about Worringer's reception. Insofar as Worringer's work has attracted attention, it is because *Abstraction and Empathy* has invited reflection not so much upon the material it itself treats—Asian art, primitive art, Gothic spatiality—but upon moments in the history of twentieth-century art that seem in some way its cognates.[3] One need only think here of Joseph Frank and the essay "Spatial Form in Modern Literature," which has spawned a cottage spatial-form industry.[4] But even Frank's brilliant use of Worringer in the service of a certain kind of formalist high Modernism remains an exception. The tendency, instead, has been from the very early stages of Worringer's reception to equate him directly with German Expressionism.

Abstraction and Empathy cannot, of course, be a work *about* Expressionism. Worringer could have had access to very few if any works by the Brücke artists, so that direct access to the formal problems of Expressionism comes into play only if we count the Fauves, who were very often thought of as expressive or Expressionist artists in the early years of the century. Instead, the equation *Worringer equals Expressionism* rests on an assumption in the Worringer literature, now explicit, now implicit, that Worringer's major work represents a parallel exploration of the same problems faced by the Expressionists, that it is Expressionism's cognate in the theory of art history.[5]

We can easily understand the motivation behind such equations. Worringer refers to abstraction as the result of an "immense spiritual dread of space" or "a great inner unrest"; he emphasizes the artist's "feeling about the world"; he is interested in the "psychic state in which, at any given time, mankind found itself in relation to the cosmos." All these suggest quite powerfully his concern to define a theory of artistic production that can account for what he calls either the *Kunstwollen* or the *état d'âme* of an age.[6] And of course Expressionism is that Modernist art that gives the most direct and immediate expression to human interiority in a state of dread or unrest. It is thus no accident that Worringer's work has often been juxtaposed to paintings by the artists of the "Brücke" or by the Kandinsky of the *Blue Rider Almanac.*[7]

But a fundamental confusion is at work here: when he refers to psychic states, Worringer follows Riegl in that he intends neither the *Kunstwollen* itself, nor the art the *Kunstwollen* produces, but rather the generalized psychic state that gives rise to the *Kunstwollen.* The feeling of cosmic homelessness that generates abstraction is not directly "expressed" in art, and certainly not in an art that projects interiority onto phenomena. The *Kunstwollen* is, to quote Riegl, the way "mankind wishes to see the sensual appearance of the world placed before its eyes—according to line and color in plane and space."[8] Any collectivized psychic state must thus necessarily be prior to the volition that is the *Kunstwollen.* And in fact Riegl's claim that the *Kunstwollen* regulates "the manner in which man wishes to see each thing shaped or colored" emphasizes less the psychic states that shape it than the *form* of the objects produced.[9] For Riegl and certainly for Worringer, the *Kunstwollen* is a space of mediation between a collective psyche and the formal properties of the works of art of a specific society. Worringer acknowledges this: he can state that the "contentual element" is "secondary in every artistic representation" (28).

Riegl's theory, furthermore, is all but devoid of any explanation of the mediation that takes place between collective psychic state, *Kunstwollen,* and cultural object. Worringer, too, at first leaves rather vague the exact nature of the links between these three aspects of artistic production. "This psychic state is disclosed in the quality of the psychic needs, i.e. in the constitution of the absolute artistic volition, and bears outward fruit in the work of art, to be exact in the style of the latter, the specific nature of which is simply the specific nature of the psychic needs. Thus the various gradations of the feeling about the world can be gauged from the stylistic evolution of art" (13). At this point it is only necessary that we acknowledge that neither Worringer nor Riegl claims there is a *direct* link between psychic disposition and the form of the art; in fact, both insist on a complex process that "translates," as it were, the inner instability that characterizes eras such as the late Roman era, the Gothic, the Baroque, and the early modern not into objects that give direct, impassioned expression to that unrest, but rather into geometric form. I insist on this point not because everyone else has gotten it wrong, but because, as I hope to show, Worringer's designation as theorist of Expressionism has led to a serious subjectivist bias in his reception, a bias that has ensured that certain aspects of his theory will remain undervalued.

Worringer's text itself points to its genesis within a contemporary artistic context very different from Expressionism. This context suggests itself quite powerfully in the foreword Worringer provided for the 1948 edition of *Abstraction and Empathy*. He recounts there how the first ideas for his dissertation came to him during a visit to Paris. Standing in the Musée de Trocadéro, he saw the great German sociologist Georg Simmel enter the museum. Worringer elaborates in that foreword neither upon the "primitive" ethnographic objects around him in the museum, nor upon the contemporary French artistic context, nor upon the precise meaning for him of Simmel's appearance at the museum. But it is surely no accident that he chose to "correct" the reception of his work through such highly charged references. These references suggest two things: we need to rethink Worringer's relation to Modernist art other than Expressionism; and most particularly, we need to rethink his position on cultural interpretation in social, and not merely aesthetic contexts. The foreword to the 1948 edition points suggestively to the interrelation of "primitivism," French high Modernism, and modern social theory in Worringer's work.

Despite the later fascination with his concepts of space and time, Worringer's text in and of itself, and especially in its reliance on Riegl, is less interested in spatial and temporal relations than in the shape, line, and color of art objects as they represent things; the notion of abstract art as geometric places particular stress upon line and volume. In the book on Cranach written in the same years as *Abstraction and Empathy*, for example, Worringer emphasizes throughout Cranach's anomalous position as a painter of the German "renaissance," not because of any intellectual position or psychic condition that might differentiate him from his contemporaries—Worringer asserts, in fact, that Cranach's art distinguishes itself through the absolute absence of any trace of "inner experience"—but rather because of his continued adherence to the law of the expressive line that he inherited from Gothic art.[10] In rethinking *Abstraction and Empathy* within a French context, then, it would seem that the art that is cognate to

Worringer's text is not so much Expressionism as it is that direction in French art that followed from Cézanne. Any late canvas by Cézanne will do, but the series of paintings of Mount St. Victoire offers an appropriate visual correlative to Worringer's description of the "return to the plane surface, suppression of the organic, and crystalline-geometric composition" (104) in the art he wishes to designate as abstract. Cézanne's concern with volume, with the isolation and analysis of the discrete object, is clearly as important to Worringer's project as is the more proximate discussion of abstracted plant motifs in the decorative arts in Riegl's *Stilfragen*.

I am attempting to contrast Expressionism and Cézanneanism here for one reason: *Abstraction and Empathy* is not a disquisition on the torment of the bourgeois artist, nor is it an examination of the psychic state of the bourgeois subject, yet this is the strong impression lent by the discussion of Expressionism. To put it briefly: Worringer is intensely interested in the question as to how cultural objects are produced. *Abstraction and Empathy* is the elaborate answer to the question as to the mediation through which a collective subjectivity produces art of a particular style. For Worringer, the answer lies in an examination of things in their full materiality. His claim in the central section of the theoretical portion of his book that abstraction is a response to "the spiritual dread of space" does not occur in isolation. Instead, he asserts repeatedly that abstraction is a reaction "to the extended, disconnected, world of phenomena" (16). An insistent emphasis upon the problematic, indeed tortured, relations between the human sensory apparatus and the phenomena of the outer world permeates Worringer's theoretical pronouncements.

> Tormented by the entangled inter-relationships of the phenomena of the outer world, [the civilized peoples of the East] were dominated by an immense need for tranquillity. The happiness they sought from art did not consist in the possibility of projecting themselves into the things of the outer world, of enjoying themselves in them, but in the possibility of taking the individual thing of the external world out of its arbitrariness and seeming fortuitousness, of eternalizing it by approximation to abstract forms and, in this manner, of finding a point of tranquillity and a refuge from appearances. (16)

Cézanne's images, like the cultural objects produced by these "civilized peoples of the East," often perform the same operations described here: the initial focus on the discrete object enables its "eternalization" through the revelation of its inner, abstract form. Why, though, Worringer's insistence upon the role of phenomena in the initial impetus to abstraction?

In seeking an answer, we should recall that Wilhelm Worringer's book is first of all that academic enterprise known as a dissertation. It was undertaken during something like a golden age of the German university. Worringer wrote, as the reference to Simmel makes clear, within the context of German social thought; he knew Simmel and his work, just as he knew Weber's work. The nearest equivalent to Worringer's background in its admixture of social theory and aesthetics is not that of a traditional academic art historian, but rather Georg Lukács, a student of Simmel and Weber during the same period as Worringer. There is to my knowledge no evidence beyond that elliptical remark in Worringer's foreword that could document the "influence" of Simmel and, more generally, German social theory upon *Abstraction and Empathy* and *Lukas Cranach*.[11] But a compelling parallel exists between Worringer's interest in phenomena and the analysis common to Marx, Weber, and Simmel of the role of phenomena in human social life. And for the German social theory of his day, the phenomena most worth examining were precisely money and commodities.

As Marx began to work out in the chapter in *Kapital* on the fetish character of commodities, and as Lukács would later specify in *History and Class Consciousness,* commodities even in their singularity wield an extrasensory power capable of subverting human rational and spiritual capacities.[12] Abstracted from their original context as a product of human labor, such commodities take on, for Marx, a power fully analogous to that of the religious fetish. When they work together in networks, the commodities that arise under industrial capitalism "talk to each other," shaping a totalizing environment that has come to be analyzed under the designation of second nature. That second nature is not nature itself, but a manmade environment that appears to be natural while remaining wholly illusory. Humans move through such networks of commodities as through a phantasmagoria, unable to exert control over themselves or over their environment.

Simmel, in his famous essay "The Metropolis and Mental Life," builds on Marx's ideas as he claims that the individual seeks ways to avoid being swallowed by a "social-technological mechanism" consisting in networks of things.[13] As a defense against the "overstimulation" of life in the new urban environment, humans develop a "blasé" stance; but this very defense mechanism results in an inability to differentiate between things.

This psychic mood is the correct subjective reflection of a complete money economy to the extent that money takes the place of all the manifoldness of things and expresses all qualitative distinctions between them in the distinction of "how much." To the extent that money, with its colorlessness and its indifferent quality, can become a common denominator of all values it becomes the frightful leveler—it hollows out the core of things, their peculiarities, their specific values and their uniqueness and incomparability in a way which is beyond repair.[14]

Simmel, as would Worringer and Walter Benjamin after him, designates as the central feature of the modern experiential condition a failure of the human sensory apparatus when confronted by things, and especially commodities, in their multiplicity. Worringer's argumentation parallels and relies upon this sort of analysis. In describing those eras that give rise to abstract art, he claims that the individual phenomena are relegated to an "arbitrary" and "intuitive" status, with the result that human beings are unable to live properly in what he calls "the extended, disconnected, bewildering world of phenomena." We are "tormented by the entangled inter-relationships of the phenomena of the outer world" (16). The result is something very much like phantasmagoria, the acute disorientation of the sensory and rational capacities described by Walter Benjamin in his great unfinished study of the Parisian arcades.[15]

Abstraction in Modernism results, then, not at all from a psychic unrest that is projected directly onto represented things—Worringer specifically disavows this—but from a general inability of the human sensory and cognitive apparatus to distinguish and evaluate the discrete elements of the lived environment, either individually or in their relationship to one another. Abstraction in art attempts to offer a solution to this dilemma in two ways. First, abstraction does not merely represent things, but attempts through geometrical precision and the analogy to the anorganic to lend to them a materiality, a regularity, and a stability that they cannot attain in their original context. Abstraction renders things "necessary and irrefragable," it helps the object "to approximate it to its *absolute* value" (16). In one of the more remarkable passages in his book, Worringer claims that primitive man seeks abstraction

> because he stands so lost and spiritually helpless amidst the things of the external world, because he experiences only ob-

scurity and caprice in the inter-connection and flux of the phenomena of the external world, that the urge is so strong in him to divest the things of the external world of their caprice and obscurity in the world-picture and to import to them a value of necessity and a value of regularity. To employ an audacious comparison: it is as though the instinct for the "thing in itself" were most powerful in primitive man (18).

This passage pulls together a number of the diverse strands that run out from Worringer's book. First, Worringer implies that primitivism and Modernism—we should certainly think of Cézanne, or as I have suggested, a Cézanne-like Modernism, with its emphasis on volume, regularity, and a kind of necessity—arise from the same sort of reaction to the things of the world that is typical of the "primitive."[16] And second, in the emphasis on the thing itself, we should hear echoes not only of Kant's *Ding-an-sich* but also an anticipation of the notion of reification, *Verdinglichung,* which finds its fullest theoretical elaboration in the central chapter, entitled "Reification and the Consciousness of the Proletariat," of Lukács's *History and Class Consciousness* (1923). Worringer discerns a specific societal malady here: the human lost in the maze of phenomena, unable to lend the requisite specific gravity to any given object. The parallels between the experience of "primitive" humans he describes here and that of the citizen of the modern capitalist metropolis are unmistakable. Worringer here clearly encodes a contemporary societal critique as analysis of art from other times and other cultures.

Abstraction and Empathy makes no overt mention of money or of capitalism. But the situation is very different in *Lukas Cranach.* There, Worringer argues that Cranach's style, which differentiated itself so clearly from that of his contemporaries and especially from that of Dürer, was a direct function of market conditions. "The enormous exploitation of [Cranach's] artistic capabilities, which began with time to resemble a factory, finds its final explanation in the remarkably strong demand awakened by his works." This artistic production, which gradually came to deploy "monopoly practices," resulted in an art that Worringer seeks to anchor not in the empathetic practices of the Renaissance, but in the abstract conception of Gothic art. Cranach's images foreground their own line, which has "a life of its own" and remains resolutely within the domain of the anorganic.[17] While the relationship between abstraction and capitalism is made explicit in *Lukas Cranach,* it functions in *Abstraction and Empathy* as the absent though implied lever that links a particular psychic or sensory state with the form of the cultural objects produced in a given era.

Simmel's description of the effects of this disorientation and depersonalization is astonishingly similar to Worringer's:

> The metropolis is the proper arena for this type of culture that has outgrown every personal element. Here in buildings and in educational institutions, in the wonders and comforts of space-conquering technique, in the formations of social life and in the concrete institutions of the state is to be found such a tremendous richness of *crystallizing*, depersonalized cultural accomplishments that the personality can, so to speak, scarcely maintain itself in the face of it.[18]

Simmel thus not only describes the effects of a money economy as a form of abstraction; he goes so far as to assert that the resultant culture is crystalline and anorganic. Compare this to Worringer's repeated assertion that "the urge to abstraction finds its beauty in the life-denying inorganic, in the crystalline or, in general terms, in all abstract law and necessity" (4). And the particular constellation that *produces* abstraction is the world of modern things, of commodities; the anorganic or crystalline arises in analogy to reified human labor, and not to any inner torment of the bourgeois artist. Taken together, *Abstraction and Empathy* and *Lukas Cranach* constitute a remarkable statement of a socially determined theory of artistic production. Far from an apology for the subjectivist practices of Expressionism, Worringer's texts articulate a theory that mediates between abstract form and human response to life in a given, socially produced environment.

Walter Benjamin's late work represents the full realization of many of Worringer's implications. Benjamin's readers have long known of the general role played by Riegl and Worringer in the great study *Origin of German Tragic Drama*. Benjamin draws and expands on Riegl and Worringer as he turns to the cultural production of eras that produce "degenerate," or, as Benjamin would have it, allegorical art. Rather than Worringer's twinned pair abstract/empathetic, Benjamin opposes cultural epochs that produce symbolic and allegorical works. Certain formal qualities of symbolic works follow from the definition of the symbol itself. At various points in his career Benjamin refers to this kind of work as symbolic, classical, autonomous, or, finally, auratic. Based on its pretensions to a privileged referentiality, the classical work of art claims such attributes as wholeness, completeness, organicism, and integrity. As such, it perpetuates false notions of the structure of history and the nature of human experience. Benjamin opposes to the symbolic work another form, which he generally terms allegorical, although the word *modern* increasingly appears as a synonym. In the third section of the *Trauerspiel* book, Benjamin attempts to rehabilitate allegory, a mode of literature that had fallen into disrepute in the eighteenth century. Allegory has for Benjamin little to do with the traditional understanding of the concept, which treats allegory as a form of narrative, a narrative that constructs an integral relationship of signifying allegorical representation and signified allegorical meaning.[19] Benjamin sees allegory instead as a particular form of writing, a strictly codified series of signifiers that have no *necessary* relationship to a series of signifieds. In allegory the production of meaning breaks down, only to be replaced by the "natural history of meaning":[20] allegory is the concrete and accurate representation of the decay of language. The fundamental characteristic of allegory is its brokenness and, thus, its resistance to a mimetic representation of things as they appear to be. Allegory is never a mirror traveling along a road. Instead of the integral relationship between signifier and signified claimed by the symbolic work, arbitrariness and, often, chaos mark the allegorical text. The allegorical image as "amorphous fragment" stands in stark contrast to the plastic symbol (*Origin*, 176).

Allegory distinguishes itself above all by a peculiar suitability to the representation of history. The haunting images in Benjamin's book on the *Trauerspiel* of a human audience huddled before a stage, clinging desperately to a series of scattered, apparently meaningless yet deeply significant things bear examination for their specific indebtedness to Worringer's thoughts on abstraction and phenomena. Benjamin's book presents a series of apparently aberrant or decadent seventeenth-century dramas as major creations that respond to an important variety of historical experience. In the seventeenth century, the history that was to be experienced was inimical to human life: "The religious man of the baroque holds so fast to the world because he feels himself driven along with it toward a cataract. There is no baroque eschatology; and just because of this a mechanism comes to be which hoards and exalts everything worldly, before it is delivered up to the end of that world. The Beyond is emptied of everything in which even the lightest breath of world still hovers" (66). This stubborn stress upon immanence, the concentrated attention of the *Trauerspiel* to the things of the world, and especially to nature, represents an unmistakable parallel to Worringer's arguments. Benjamin's central analysis of the psychology of the era, in fact, in its stress upon alienation and a resulting anorganicism, echoes the texts of Worringer and Simmel in revealing ways:

> The deadening of the emotions, and the ebbing away of the waves of life which are the source of these emotions in the body, can increase the distance between the self and the surrounding world to the point of alienation from the body. As soon as this symptom of depersonalization was seen as an intense degree of mournfulness, the concept of the pathological state, in which the most simple object appears to be a symbol of some enigmatic wisdom because it lacks any natural, creative relationship to us, was set in an incomparably productive context. (140)

The result was an art form, the *Trauerspiel,* that conforms to the definition Worringer offers of abstraction: in its static quality, in its tendency to turn human actors into puppetlike objects, and in its insistent offering of a series of object-dominated tableaus, the Baroque *Trauerspiel* arises out of a sensory delusion that prefigures that associated with commodity culture two centuries later. The *Trauerspiel* is thus a "contemplative necessity," in fact a "morally responsible" form in its representation of historical conditions and human reaction. "By its very essence classicism was not permitted to behold the lack of freedom, the imperfection, the collapse of the physical, beautiful nature. But beneath its extravagant pomp, this is precisely what Baroque allegory proclaims with unprecedented emphasis." Allegory thus arises as a formal vocabulary that responds to particular historical conditions. Random, esoterically charged allegorical images, in their similarity to natural things, reflect a history that itself has become increasingly analogous to nature's incessant production of shattered, reified objects. In the Baroque *Trauerspiel* this natural history "wanders onto the stage" in the form of props, emblems, and depersonalized, cipherlike human figures, presenting themselves to the viewer in an order supported by neither logic nor significance. It is no accident that the corpse is the ultimate allegorical object (80, 84, 176).

It is important to note here that Benjamin does not conceive of allegory as period-fixed. Benjamin's typology of works as symbolic or allegorical is not the description of a historical progression from one form to the other, not a counterpart to Auerbach's depiction of the Hegelian, seemingly inexorable development toward realism. Allegory is neither limited to the medieval and Baroque periods nor is it in some way a primitive form to be superseded by other, more potent representational strategies. The typical form of the Baroque is allegory, just as it is Baudelaire's most characteristic mode. Benjamin finds allegorical features even in places as unlikely as Russian Naturalism and Cocteau's dramas. And if Benjamin does not label such other modern, technological forms as photography and film allegorical, the parallels he sees between them are too striking to preclude in the typology. Similarly, the symbolic, totalizing work of art occurs in the Renaissance, in all forms of Neoclassicism, and in the twentieth century in a traditional novelist such as Thomas Mann.

For Benjamin, the next great resurgence of allegorical representation after the Baroque is concentrated not in a period but in a single powerful poetic voice: Baudelaire. It is in the analysis of Baudelaire that Benjamin most clearly builds on the modern social implications of Worringer. Benjamin adduces a number of reasons for Baudelaire's recourse to allegory. Historical conditions were, first of all, particularly suited to allegorical representation. Machine production, the division of labor, and above all the ascendancy of the commodity caused a "hollowing out of inner life" identical to that analyzed in the *Trauerspiel* book. Allegory represents, then, the poetic mode best suited to reveal the workings of capitalism. "The allegorical way of seeing is always based on a devalued world of appearances. The specific devaluation of the world of things which occurs in the commodity is the fundament of the allegorical intention in Baudelaire." Benjamin finds in Baudelaire himself an essentially allegorical sensibility called to life by capitalist society. "The devaluation of the human environment by the mercantile economy has a deep-running effect on Baudelaire's historical experience. . . . Spleen is nothing but the quintessence of historical experience."[21] And finally, he points to Baudelaire's own apologies for allegory, the most famous of which is the line from the poem "Le cygne" (The swan) in which the speaker laments, "Tout autour de moi devient allégorie" (Everything around me becomes allegory); he can cite dozens of additional instances.

The power of Baudelaire's images springs from the force of his shock at the experience of modernity. Baudelaire's "frozen horror" leads him to a "flight from images into images [*Bilderflucht*]." Most important, Benjamin adduces Baudelaire's notion that "L'imagination décompose toute la création" as evidence of the poet's awareness of the character of his historical era and the response necessary to it. "Baudelaire's allegory shows the traces of the violence that was necessary to tear through the harmonic façade of the world that surrounded him." Baudelaire's late adoption of allegory was "alien to *all* intimacy with things";[22] allegory alone proved to be a poetic form resistant to what Benjamin called the "sex appeal of the anorganic."[23] The art that was produced under these conditions itself reflects a certain anorganicism and rigidity as it structures itself around tropes of displacement such as allegory.[24] Benjamin finds in Baudelaire's lyrics, again as in Baroque allegory, an uncompromising negativity—"un pessimisme debordant"—that breaks down the fetishized appearances of the commodity, breaks through the mythic, phantasmagorical powers that distort and deflect a true historical experience. In exposing the nature of life under capitalism, Baudelaire's allegory has a positive, political function.

The importance of the anorganic for both Worringer and Benjamin must surely be understood as a reaction against the stress on organicism, vitality, and wholeness that dominates the "philosophy" of the German right from vitalism to Nazism. In his rejection of vitalism, as well as in his positive stress on the crystalline, Worringer's work anticipates not so much Expressionism, which draws upon many of the currents that inform vitalism, as the later work of architects, artists, and writers such as Bruno Taut, Paul Scheerbart, and Robert Musil, not to mention figures such as Mondrian.

Let us return to the second aspect of Worringer's proposal of abstraction as rejoinder to the disorientations of commodity capitalism. Worringer insists repeatedly that there is a kind of violence, even a kind of retribution, involved in removing objects from their denatured and denaturing context. Abstraction's "most powerful urge," Worringer writes, "was, so to speak, to wrest the object of the external world out of its natural context, out of the unending flux of being, to purify it of all its dependence upon life, i.e. of everything about it that was arbitrary" (16). The purification—dare we call it redemption—of objects is thus dependent upon a kind of violent dismemberment of the original, false totality. Walter Benjamin would in 1930 coin a term for precisely this violent action: he would call it citation. "In the quotation, which both saves and destroys, language proves itself to be the matrix of righteousness. It summons the word by its name, wrenches it destructively from its context, but precisely thereby calls it back to its origin. It appears, now with rhyme and reason, sonorously, congruously in the structure of a new text."[25] I mentioned above the possible relation of this implicit materialism to art in the wake of Cézanne. In Paris in 1906, Worringer could of course not have seen any of the canvases of Braque and Picasso that would derive from a Cézannean inheritance the grand, Worringer-like experiment that was Cubism. But he could anticipate it. He could anticipate in an uncanny way the abstraction of high analytic Cubism, he could anticipate the infinitesimal articulation of individual things in the continua of space and time, and he could anticipate that finally very similar materialism that would allow first Braque and then Picasso to integrate the things of the world themselves onto the painted surface. And, in a related fashion, Worringer offers an analysis *avant la lettre* of the various practices of montage and collage, all indebted in important ways to the Cubist project, that dominate the early art of the Weimar Republic.[26] In the photomontages of the Berlin Dadaists, for example, the twinned activities of the purifying destruction of the old and the utopian construction of the new out of its detritus occupy a vexed ground between abstraction and not empathy but figuration. Such violent dismemberments of the real and their integration into a new, politically charged context often figured the overcoming of the old order, the empire, and the construction of a new social space.

In closing, I shall offer a few remarks in the greatest possible abbreviation on Worringer's position within that historiographical trajectory from which I started. His materialism is not his only social contribution; he also offers a path toward, if not a full realization of, an alternative historiography. Riegl, for all his radicalism, still adhered to an understanding of history that was continuous and evolutionary—what we now call a developmental narrative. He was concerned not with overthrowing the metastructure of universal history as with purifying it by removing the need to ignore or dismiss apparently aberrant epochs. With Worringer, we find, to be sure, some talk of historical movement. He speaks, for example, of the "inner developmental necessity" of art (xiv), but he is a German writing after Hegel and we can forgive him that. Especially since this is not at all the dominant moment in Worringer's notion of history. Instead, he proposes a pattern of regular alternation between abstract and empathetic eras; there is in this sense no progress or development but only a repeated return through variation on one of the two dominant modes. We find in Worringer, then, a kind of history at a standstill, or history with a repetition compulsion. This is a marked break from Riegl, who adhered to the dominant tendencies in late nineteenth-century historiography: positivism and a faith in progress. Worringer's notion of repetition offers a powerful counter to the relentless drive forward of nineteenth-century historiography, which emphasized the relentless replacement of the old and obsolete with the new and improved. We should not be surprised at Worringer's failure to adhere to Riegl's model of historical change. In championing those human cultural epochs that produce abstraction—and those eras are clearly privileged in *Abstraction and Empathy*—Worringer offers a model of, if not resistance to the world of commodities described here, then at least a space of retreat from them. But even here Worringer offers only a temporary answer. Such spaces of recuperation through art are, in his theory, always superseded by empathetic eras for whom the world is again perspicuous and livable. In his description of a regular alternation between eras, Worringer occupies a liminal position between "bourgeois" history and Walter Benjamin's wholesale rejection of faith in progress.

Benjamin substitutes a very radical notion of history for a universal or progressive scheme. Riegl's theory was based on a notion of a steady progress of history through the regular alternation of two distinct forms of *Kunstwollen;* Worringer substituted a kind of repetition for Riegl's movement forward. Each of these thinkers based his historical theories on a revolutionary reexamination of cultural products heretofore thought to be decadent or aberrant. Benjamin's theories build upon those of Riegl and Worringer in their emphasis on "decadent" art. But Benjamin's is not merely a democratization of the cultural field; he insists not on equal status for such cultural production as late antiquity, the Baroque, and Modernism, but indeed on its *superiority.* Only art such as this gives us a privileged perception of the true state of history. In its brokenness, its rejection of consolation, and especially its rhetorical fervor, the *Trauerspiel* is a "responsible reflection" of its age. Any integrated, classical form would falsify the historical conditions that gave rise to it; Benjamin underlines this aspect of his thinking when he calls the *Trauerspiel* a "contemplative necessity" (*Origin*, 84, 80).

In addition to its resolute focus on a certain kind of displaced or disfigured art, Benjamin's historical gaze abjures any integrated structure for history. History is for Benjamin (and for his great historical master Nietzsche) a not necessarily continuous stream of discrete moments. There is neither progress nor repetition for Benjamin, only the twinned possibilities of decay (he defines history in the book on the *Trauerspiel* as a *Leidensgeschichte* or history of suffering) and redemption. The importance of history—past moments of human experience, action, achievement—lies primarily in its relation to the immediate present; for Benjamin, a properly dialectical historiography must "become aware of the critical constellation in which precisely this fragment of the past is found with precisely this present."[27] It is only in the construction of such constellations, in fact, that we come to understand the character of our own era. "For we are not concerned to represent works of art in the context of their age but rather to bring to representation the age that recognizes them—and that is our age—in the age in which they arose."[28] Benjamin's much-discussed theory of the dialectical image is finally a theory of the recovery of a hidden history. In fact, Benjamin's understanding of the historical object is never anything so simple as an isolated event, fact, artifact, or person to be found in the past. Historical objects are instead *constituted* in the present as historical writing or as political action. "The dialectical image is, accordingly, the very object constructed in the materialist presentation of history. It is identical with the historical object; it justifies its being blasted out of the continuum of the historical process." Only if the past can be reconstellated with the present can it achieve a "progressive concentration (integration) of reality in which everything in the past can attain a higher degree of contemporary relevance—*Aktualität*—than it had in the moment of its existence.[29] In this knowledge of the past is contained the means of judging—and perhaps of changing—any given present.

If Benjamin's astronomical metaphors, with their rhetoric of constellations and flashes, are wholly appropriate to his ideas, they are finally inappropriate to Worringer's. The historical understanding that is reflected in *Abstraction and Empathy* suggests not breathtaking leaps between astral bodies, but the stubborn movement of a river that inches forward through a broad plain despite its tendency to eddy and turn back on itself. But that river carries boulders with it, the boulders of a new, surprising materialism in cultural historiography.

NOTES

1. The first important statement in this period was Michael Podro's *The Critical Historians of Art* (New Haven: Yale University Press, 1982); despite its considerable limitations, Podro's description of Riegl's work was instrumental in calling attention to Riegl's contribution. See also Margaret Olin, *Forms of Representation in Alois Riegl's Theory of Art* (University Park: Pennsylvania State University Press, 1992).

2. The term *Kunstwollen* has been variously rendered as "will to art" or, in the English translation of Worringer, as the "absolute artistic volition." Since any English equivalent necessarily reduces the term, I have left the German in the text.

3. Exceptions to this pattern exist, of course. See especially Magdalena Bushart, *Der Geist der Gothik und die expressionistische Kunst* (Munich: Silke Schreiber, 1990).

4. See, for example, Jeffrey R. Smitten and Ann Daghistany, eds., *Spatial Form in Narrative* (Ithaca: Cornell University Press, 1981).

5. For recent examples of texts that adduce Worringer within the larger context of Expressionism or of a modernism oriented toward an extreme subjectivity, see Joseph A.

Buttigieg, "Worringer among the Modernists," *Boundary 2* (Fall 1979), 359–66; and Joseph Masheck, "Raw Art: 'Primitive' Authenticity and German Expressionism," *Res* 4 (Autumn 1982), 92–117.

6. Wilhelm Worringer, *Abstraction and Empathy* (New York: International Universities Press, 1953), 13–15; all further references in the text by page number.

7. The standard introduction to German Expressionist art remains Peter Selz, *German Expressionist Painting* (Berkeley and Los Angeles: University of California Press, 1957).

8. Alois Riegl, *Die spätrömische Kunstindustrie nach den Funden in Österreich-Ungarn* (Vienna: Kaiserlich-Königliche Hof- und Staatsdruckerei, 1901), 130. All translations are my own.

9. Ibid., 28.

10. Wilhelm Worringer, *Lukas Cranach* (Munich: Piper, 1908), 28, 34ff.; all translations are my own.

11. For a discussion of one possible nexus between Simmel, Modernism, and Worringer, see Neil H. Donahue, "Fear and Fascination in the Big City: Rainer Maria Rilke's Use of Georg Simmel in *The Notebooks of Malte Laurids Brigge,*" in his *Forms of Disruption: Abstraction in Modern German Prose* (Ann Arbor: The University of Michigan Press, 1993), 75–100.

12. Karl Marx, "On the Fetish-character of Commodities," *Capital,* trans. D. Fernbach (Harmondsworth: Penguin Books, 1976), 85ff.; Georg Lukács, *History and Class Consciousness,* trans. Rodney Livingstone (Cambridge: MIT Press, 1971), 286–95.

13. Georg Simmel, "The Metropolis and Mental Life," in *On Individuality and Social Forms* (Chicago: University of Chicago Press, 1971), 324.

14. Simmel, 329.

15. For an account of the role of commodities and phantasmagoria in Benjamin's cultural theory and especially in the *Arcades project,* see my *Dialectical Images: Walter Benjamin's Theory of Literary Criticism* (Ithaca: Cornell University Press, 1987), 76–79.

16. The exhibition and catalog at the Museum of Modern Art, New York, is only the best known recent exploration of this relationship: *"Primitivism" in Twentieth-Century Art: Affinity of the Tribal and the Modern,* ed. William Rubin (New York: Museum of Modern Art, 1984).

17. Worringer, *Lukas Cranach,* 7–8, 17–18, 34.

18. Simmel, 338; my emphasis.

19. The most sophisticated modern studies of allegory, such as Angus Fletcher's *Allegory: The Theory of a Symbolic Mode* (Ithaca: Cornell University Press, 1964), have continued to stress the narrative and representational aspects of the form. Fletcher seeks to radically expand our understanding of the genre; he emphasizes the "protean" quality of allegory and includes a wide array of examples from literature, film, and the visual arts. It is interesting to note that he closes with a political and historical comment that retrospectively creates a certain parallel to Benjamin's theory: he calls allegories the "natural mirrors of ideology" (368). For a rigorously formalist view that defines allegory as language reflecting upon itself, see Maureen Quilligan, *The Language of Allegory* (Ithaca: Cornell University Press, 1979), esp. 13–24, 33–51. Benjamin's model refuses an easy assimilation to any other theory: it differs from Fletcher's in its assertion of a breakdown of narrative; the involved, self-reflexive qualities of Benjaminian allegory seem to range it closer to Quilligan, but the inextricable ties between historical experience and artistic form prevent any closer resemblance.

20. Walter Benjamin, *Origin of German Tragic Drama,* trans. John Osborne (London: New Left Books, 1977), 166.

21. Benjamin, notes to "Über einige Motive bei Baudelaire," in *Gesammelte Schriften,*

ed. Rolf Tiedemann and Hermann Schweppenhäuser (Frankfurt: Suhrkamp, 1972–85), 1:1151; all translations from this edition are my own.

22. Ibid., *Das Passagen-Werk,* 5:410, 414, 423.

23. Ibid., *Das Passagen-Werk,* 5:130. Terry Eagleton's discussion of Benjamin on the commodity remains the definitive statement; Eagleton, *Walter Benjamin; or, Towards a Revolutionary Criticism* (London, Verso Editions, 1981), 24–42.

24. On Benjamin, Baudelaire, and the function of allegory in commodity culture, see my *Dialectical Images,* 15–41.

25. Benjamin, "Karl Kraus," in *Reflections,* ed. Peter Demetz (New York: Harcourt Brace Jovanovich, 1978), 269.

26. I am indebted to my colleague Dorothea Dietrich for pointing out to me the possible connections between Worringer and the practice of montage in Weimar. For an extended discussion of Worringer and the collages of Kurt Schwitters, see her *Collages of Kurt Schwitters* (New York: Cambridge University Press, 1993).

27. Benjamin, "Eduard Fuchs, the Collector and Historian," in *One Way Street,* trans. E. Jephcott and K. Shorter (London: New Left Books, 1977), 351.

28. Benjamin, "Literaturgeschichte und Literaturwissenschaft," in *Gesammelte Schriften,* 3:290.

29. Benjamin, *Gesammelte Schriften, Das Passagen-Werk,* 5:595.

5

Worringer's Theory of Transcendental Space in Gothic Architecture: A Medievalist's Perspective

*Joanna E. Ziegler**

> Laymen have overestimated Worringer's dissertation and his *Formprobleme,* while scholars of art have underestimated them. . . . [Worringer] touched a deeper layer of the problem of form than many another scholar, and we, too, must seek to delve into this layer without renouncing the task of formulating clear concepts.
>
> —Paul Frankl, 1960

Few words could introduce the problematic of this essay more succinctly than those above of Paul Frankl, one of this century's most distinguished scholars of medieval architecture. This passage appeared more than three decades ago in Frankl's mighty 800-page commentary entitled *The Gothic: Literary Sources and Interpretations through Eight Centuries.*[1] It stood as Frankl's closing remarks on Wilhelm Worringer's two texts—the 1906 dissertation *Abstraction and Empathy,*[2] and *Form Problems of the Gothic* (1911).[3]

*I wish to thank the students in my seminar at Holy Cross College (Spring 1990), Liz Dwyer, Michael Hallett, Elise Hendrikson, Patricia Lawrence, Laura Panzarino, Kristen Pineo, and Patricia Pongracz, for helping me shape my arguments by their challenging comments. I also thank Kermit Champa and Judith Tolnick for reading this text critically and sympathetically. Special thanks is owed to J. Duncan Berry for bibliographical help, and to Mary Gluck for getting me to Hofstra, where I first presented these ideas in a paper. Kathryn Brush deserves special mention for reading the text with a sharp eye; it is, however, her unparalleled command of the German medieval scholarship from this period that stands most perceptibly behind this essay, in concrete detail and as inspiration.

To my knowledge Frankl is the only medievalist—even as arch-critic—to recognize that Worringer's two texts address themselves, in Frankl's words, to "brilliant" problems in the history of Gothic architecture. This will hardly come as news to specialists in early twentieth-century art and cultural history, for Worringer's reputation arose and lives among the Modernists. One need only turn the pages of Geoffrey Waite's first article in this volume on "Worringer's *Abstraction and Empathy:* Remarks on Its Reception and on the Rhetoric of Its Criticism" (originally published 1981) to discover the breadth of Worringer's contemporary reception.[4] As Worringer scholarship richly attests, the literary and artistic circles, where Modernism was breeding, embraced Worringer's ideas zealously.

Interestingly, although Frankl was writing to and about medievalists, it is when seen against Modernist writings that his discussion opens up Worringer's text in intriguing ways. Frankl's text reminds us that what Worringer wrote about Gothic phenomena fell on deaf (or at least unreceptive) ears to virtually all serious practitioners of the medieval branch of art-historical study. Worringer the medievalist had no positive reception![5] In the pages that follow I probe into this situation and explore some of the reasons why it happened.

Frankl opens up several paths of entry to this curious fate of Worringer's reception. Although we may rankle at the authoritarian, hierarchical, and dialectical nature of the terms "laymen versus scholars," Frankl's citation of Worringer's readers is precise: those whose focus is Gothic and those whose focus is not. Moreover, Frankl characterizes the readers' interaction with the texts in ways that Worringer himself, it seems, also recognized. In the foreword to the 1948 edition of *Abstraction* Worringer wrote that its theories "were concerned only with historical interpretation" and that "without knowing, [the author] was the medium of the necessities of the period" (vii). Nine years before his death Worringer wrote in the preface to *Form Problems,* "I ask the reader of this new English edition to imagine the embarrassment of the author in his 75th year . . . whether by the blessing of a special foreword he may newly authorize a publication which hails from the earliest beginnings of his career as a scholar. . . . In fact, under various headings and on many occasions he has published supplements, revisions, corrections, and amendments" (xv). Small wonder these utterances of remorse, for of Worringer's fifteen books, ten are devoted to medieval or pre-modern topics, while of the thirty-four articles, more than one-half treat the same.[6] Worringer's two readers, then, represent complementary but contradictory interpreters. Frankl witnesses this by constructing them as over- and underestimators. There is, then, an irony to Worringer's readership, and it depends on the texts' peculiar and ongoing openness to a considerable range of signals—signals that have thus far received remarkably orderly responses from their readers. I mark these signals as imminence and truism. We turn to imminence first.

Worringer himself perceived the signals of imminence that his work gave off: "The compass of my instinct had pointed in a direction inexorably preordained by the dictate of the spirit of the age."[7] On the surface Worringer looks preoccupied, like many German thinkers of his time, by period themes such as racial types,[8] the Nordic spirit, abstract-geometrical form *versus* organic form, psychology of style, and artistic polarities, among others.[9] So deeply in touch with the times is his discourse that it fits comfortably with institutional ideologies of nearly every medium and philosophical color. Worringer's intellectual roots run deep, for example, in the race theory of Count Arthur de Gobineau (*Essai sur l'inégalité des races humaines*, 1853), the music dramas of Richard Wagner, the aesthetics of Conrad Fiedler,[10] and the empathy theory of Theodor Lipps.[11] He knew Georg Lukács personally, and considered as mentors art historian Alois Riegl and sociologist Georg Simmel. Critics have traced his influence to Britain and to philosopher T. E. Hulme,[12] to leading painters Franz Marc and Wassily Kandinsky,[13] to Belgian art nouveau entrepreneur Henri van de Velde,[14] and into America with D. H. Lawrence.[15] It is small wonder, then, that Worringer has been linked to nearly every important early twentieth-century literary and artistic movement: Imagists,[16] Expressionists (see the essays included in this volume), empathy psychologists (see note 11), literary New Classicists, the *Strukturforschung*-alists, and Bruno Taut's architectural activists.[17] Worringer's ideas and theories have so many reflectors in his Modernist champions and critics (the latter who, as Waite cleverly reveals, did strengthen the privileged and authoritative position of the text ["Worringer's *Abstraction*," 205]) that epithets invoking Worringer as leader and spokesman of the age are warranted.

These relationships—the bulk of Worringer scholarship—are recapitulated and reassessed, in large part, in the essays of this volume, opening a field of inquiry where much further research needs to be done. To say, then, how fully Worringer's discourse contains past and nearly future—in effect, to summarize the one side of Worringer's reception as promised above—I recall the Latin root of the word *imminence*, which means to be near at hand or to jut out over. Nowhere is the phenomenon of imminence more clearly displayed than in the shelf life of *Abstraction and Empathy*, still in print more than eighty years after its first edition. The book has never gone out of print because of its utility in signaling Modernism's imminence, and in all its branches, so concisely.

The signals that fell to truisms are contained not in Worringer's most popular text but in *Form Problems of the Gothic*. In 1910, one year before Reinhard Piper published *Form Problems of the Gothic*, Worringer described it as a "direct sequel" to *Abstraction and Empathy*, an "attempt to apply the questions of *Abstraction and Empathy* to the stylistic phenomena of the Gothic" (*AE*, xv). Although *Form Problems* and *Abstraction* remain his two best-known texts, *Form Problems* never gained the radical chic that *Abstraction* did. Had Hulme's disciple, Herbert Read, not translated the text into English,[18] *Form Problems* would surely have slipped into oblivion along with Worringer's ten other books treating problems of pre-Modernism.

I have isolated for discussion five analytical moments in *Form Problems*. For reasons to be introduced presently, these moments reappeared later in the scholarly discourse under new authorship, disconnected from Worringer totally, whence they found their way into the classroom as truisms of Gothic architecture. In the most curious twist of reception history, once Worringer uttered these statements they went unrecognized as prototruisms.

1. Worringer declared that we must seek predominant types of art and particular means of expression.[19] "We need only utter the word Gothic," Worringer wrote, "to awaken in us immediately the powerfully associated idea of Gothic architecture. This inevitable connection between Gothic and architecture coincides with historical fact, that the stylistic epoch of Gothic was completely dominated by architecture, that all other artistic manifestations were either directly dependent upon it or, at any rate, played a secondary part in comparison with it" (89 [60–61]). Few medieval art historians, even today with their self-proclaimed retrieval of the primacy of the "minor arts," would contest Worringer's point.

Certainly the belief in architecture's supremacy was a Romantic one that predated Worringer by well over a century, and it would be nearly impossible to find a medievalist in Worringer's own time who did not assume architecture's primacy among the media of medieval art. But Worringer's use of this hierarchy differs substantially from that of his predecessors and contemporaries. For them Gothic architecture was an institution, a symbol, and a stylistic gathering point. Gothic architecture *was* its buildings—its specifically identifiable buildings. For Worringer, however, Gothic architecture was an ontology, a meaning rather than a thing. Rather like the Expressionist architects Taut and Scheerbart, for whom the image of the crystal embodied mystical meanings, Gothic for Worringer was a metaphysical and phenomenological metaphor, one that contained and illuminated the intangible, expressive, and spiritual ideas of the Gothic.[20] To frame this within the terms of recent discourse, Worringer saw Gothic architecture as *the* supreme cultural product of the Gothic past and mind. Thus, when we acknowledge that the search for predominant and paradigmatic types of art as cultural reflectors has come to occupy the major part of our scholarly efforts these days, it becomes especially telling to reflect on the fate of Worringer's similar approach. Although he himself described his project as an attempt to reach a deeper understanding of an epoch, medievalists fiercely critiqued and ultimately rejected him (and continue to) because of the "intuitive" nature of his historical research—the part that Worringer believed sought to awaken powerful associations about the essence of Gothic.[21]

2. Worringer held as central to his interpretation the contrast between Classic and Gothic. Although the contrast between Classic and Gothic was certainly a dominant theme in architectural criticism after the middle of the nineteenth century, Worringer alone applied the interpretive paradigm to an analysis of Gothic *space* rather than form.[22] The English critics, John Ruskin and Geoffrey Scott, far more widely acclaimed than Worringer, grounded their analyses in the ideological contrasts of Classic with Gothic. Ruskin thundered often and prolifically about the moral qualities of Italian Gothic over and against what he considered to be the debased forms of Renaissance and Classic styles being built in his own Victorian time. In his *Seven Lamps of Architecture* (1849), Ruskin wrought his theory of visibility via analysis, graphic and textual, of Gothic *forms*: the appearance of labor and workmanship upon the architecture, of perfect finish, and the imitation of natural forms. Gothic for Ruskin was ornament and ornament alone; meaning is the masonry. Ornament preoccupied Worringer's British contemporary, Geoffrey Scott, whose *Architectural Principles in the Age of Humanism*, published in 1914, tried to resuscitate all that Ruskin abhorred by calling for a revival of classical decoration. Neither author, both great of eye and mighty of pen, was interested in *space* or in how Classic and Gothic styles effected the conception of space. This was Worringer's concern alone, a point I will return to shortly.

3. Worringer believed in Gothic as exhibiting the principle of the dematerialization of stone. "All expression to which Greek architecture attained," Worringer declared, "was *through* the stone, *by means*

of the stone; all expression to which Gothic architecture attained, was attained—and this is the full significance of the contrast—*in spite of* the stone" (106 [69]). This is one of Worringer's most brilliant architectural characterizations. That same principle, however, acquired its legitimization not from Worringer but from the French medievalist Henri Focillon (1881–1943), who appropriated the idea and wrote on it more than twenty years after Worringer. Students in America today are still reading Focillon's *Art of the West* (not yet out of print), first published in 1933, for its narrative exposé of the gravity-defying Gothic architect,[23] while *Form Problems* has been out of print in English for nearly two decades.

4. Worringer favored a formal analysis of Gothic architecture that had to do with the dissolution of the solid walls. On this Worringer says that "the solid walls, were dissolved and the construction and aesthetic functions passed to the static individual forces of the structure" (162 [198–90]). This principle was to become singularly associated with Worringer's contemporary, the German architectural historian and medievalist, Hans Jantzen (1881–1967), who published his theory first in article form in 1928; it did not appear until 1957 as a book, *Kunst der Gotik*. This text was to become, and remain, an American classroom classic under the English title, *High Gothic: The Classic Cathedrals of Chartres, Reims and Amiens*.[24] I challenge the reader to find an architectural history textbook that does not in one form or another reference and recognize Jantzen's terms, rather than Worringer's, for the Gothic cathedrals—that is, Gothic architecture more or less as an architecture of diaphanous walls.

5. Scholasticism, Worringer argued, is an analogy of Gothic architecture. "Scholasticism," Worringer observed, "is in the sphere of religion what Gothic architecture is in the sphere of art" (168 [114]). Most art historians know full well that in the early 1950s Erwin Panofsky published an exploration of the analogy under the precise title of *Gothic Architecture and Scholasticism*.[25] Ever since, this analogy has been singularly identified with Panofsky and, moreover, viewed as a historical interrelationship to be taken for granted. The analogy did, of course, predate both Worringer and Panofsky. The German critic and theoretician, Gottfried Semper, for instance, coined the term "Scholasticism in stone" *(steinerne Scholastik)* in the 1870s (cited in Frankl, *The Gothic*, 488). Other French and German scholars of medieval art and history routinely applied the analogy. By the latter half of the twentieth century, however, the analogy between Gothic architecture and Scholasticism had reached a nonspecialized audience. It was Worringer who attempted to reach

that broader readership early on—more than three decades before Panofsky had.

Why did Worringer's five stunning moments of Gothic architectural theory become truisms rather than Worringerisms? Although to answer this would require a study dedicated to this topic alone, a few ideas can be offered here nonetheless. In the first place, the emigration of the German-Jewish art historians, like Panofsky, needs to be much more fully understood than it is at present.[26] There was, on the one hand, the geographical migration to America in which Worringer, who stayed in Germany during the Second World War, did not participate.[27] Scholars also migrated ideologically, as it were, into a new positivism. On our shores a hardy commitment to the "science" of art historical research took root with the emigrés, a position nourished and renourished by a disdain for the seemingly soft and subjective intellectual ground from which Worringer's method sprang.[28] The result was that all that Modernists found imminent in Worringer, medievalists ultimately and systematically dismantled from acceptable interpretations treating Gothic as a historical phenomenon. The interaction between these two groups of interpreters (the moderns and the medievalists) has not yet been featured, however, in the vast enterprise that constitutes the history of Worringer's reception.

What, then, did Frankl mean when he said, with uncharacteristic ambiguity, that "we"—we, I stress, to Frankl means medievalists— "must seek to delve into this [deeper] layer [of the problem of form] without renouncing the task of formulating clear concepts"? In response we finally turn to the concept announced by the title of this essay—transcendental space. Worringer's treatment of transcendental space in Gothic architecture signals his profoundly original thought— thought that if I may be permitted to pursue the imagery of my own discourse remains captured between imminence and truism: thought that has been rendered invisible by those two powerfully positive signals in the text as identified above. Overestimators and underestimators have not read what is *not* imminent or *not* truistic in the text: that being Worringer's discussion of the least tangible of all artistic properties, Gothic space.

When we dismantle the signals of imminence from the text we find ourselves face to face first (and surprisingly) with rationalism. For Worringer the phenomenon of Gothic space originates in constructional principles. In fact, he argued that "the constructive element . . . is an end in itself, for it coincides with artistic intentions of expression" (107 [69–70]). He treats at length the significance of the pointed arch. For example, he states "that it cannot be looked upon as a Gothic discovery. But Gothic alone connected it and its constructive significance into an element of an entire system carried through with utmost consistency" (154 [100]). The pointed arch—this is the very language of analysis that we, together with Worringer, identify with the nineteenth-century rationalists, Viollet-le-Duc (1814–79) in France and Georg Dehio (1850–1932) in Germany. It was its introduction, as all three scholars see it, that allowed the Gothic architect to achieve his aim.[29] Recognizing such aims, Worringer goes beyond the rationalists to postulate that construction is an expressive vehicle. This teleology arose because of Worringer's view that the history of architecture is "not a history of technical developments but the history of changing expressive aims" (90 [62]). Sharpening this notion, he likens Gothic to modern architecture, also taken over by the "medium of construction" (109 [72]), but *contends that Gothic ideas were attained, "not by means of the material (as they were in modern architecture) but in spite of the material"* (my emphasis). Stone is released from its material weight in Gothic architecture. This "weightless, wallless, massless elimination of gravity" (106 [68–69]) that is Gothic—hardly debatable even to the most card-carrying technocrat—is Worringer's springboard to interpretation: "Spirit is the opposite of matter. To dematerialize stone is to spiritualize it" (106 [68–69]).

Several images emerge in Worringer's attempt to describe the true character of Gothic space as an "expressive activity" (157 [104]). Consider Worringer's statement that "[i]t is as if, with the introduction of the pointed arch, the building were permeated by a great wave of self-awareness" (156 [103]). And then contemplate how closely this concept of self-awareness approximates the American architect Louis Kahn's indelible dictum of "what the building wants to be."[30] Out of this phenomenological angle the first image emerges; and it does so when Worringer says that the Gothic is the "mechanically articulated building" (110 [73]) and that "its preference for that abstract mechanical activity was due to its vast superiority in strength of expression to organic activity . . . just as a mechanically controlled marionette is more strongly expressive than a living, acting human being" (157 [104]). This vivid image Worringer used to describe how rational principles control the movements of the actual facts of the Gothic architectural being. Yet, despite being formulated rationally in the details, as an architectural conception, the Gothic architectural achievement is a spatial one. The Gothic architect, Worringer argues, is a fashioner of interiors, a space-former. But we can only comprehend space (the least tangible of architectural elements), Worringer claims, "when we take from it its abstract character . . . in short, when we turn experience of space into an experience of the senses, abstract space into real atmospheric space" (158 [105]). The mechanically controlled marionette is thus a metaphor for the constructionally expressive premises of atmospheric space.[31]

This introduces Worringer's second image—real atmospheric space. Worringer in turn attempts to develop ways to image rhetorically, perceptually, and metaphorically the experience of that space. This he does as he contrasts Roman architecture and its "clarification" of space with Gothic. Anyone who enters a Gothic cathedral, Worringer claims, "encounters an intoxication of the senses" (159 [106]). Music, soon to be joined by spiritual ecstasy, Worringer now introduces as the metaphor for the experience of Gothic space. "To be deafened by the *fortissimo* of the music of space"—this is how Worringer describes Gothic architecture meeting the needs of medieval religion. This experience is elaborated as Worringer postulates that the senses are the primary vehicle of the Gothic experience, such as they are when hearing "atmospheric life . . . as if with an audible roar . . . break against the vaulted roof" (160 [106–7]). This aural experience—itself conducted by the abstract being of sound—is thus Worringer's metaphor for abstract Gothic space as it turns into atmospheric space.[32] The experience of Gothic space, however, ultimately supersedes its point of entry into the senses by uniting with the abstractness that is space. This is what Worringer means when he calls the Gothic experience a "super-sensuous" one or, to recall its more dated early twentieth-century concept, transcendental space (see note 22).

This, then, I would argue, is the deeper layer of the problem of form to which Frankl alluded so many years ago. Worringer attempted to reveal the true nature of Gothic space *and* to reveal it as transcendental; the experience of it as spiritual, as ecstatic, to be precise. He, like many other great thinkers before the First World War, sought to disclose the essence of artistic experience (Gothic cathedral space) in these terms: as that which originates in the senses but rises above them, by nature of the properties of the medium, to a higher level. That is what Worringer means to do when he likens the experience of Gothic space to a spiritual or ecstatic one—a mystery—that begins in the senses and ends in unity with the infinite abstraction that is god.

Images of marionettes, atmosphere, and music pervade Worringer's language as he struggles to understand the Gothic world of cathedral form and space *and* the rational principles that control it (Bushart,

Der Geist der Gotik, 30). Like many of his contemporaries Worringer believed broadly and deeply in the phenomenon—and here we need to stress the point—that the senses alone could set free that nearly unfathomable and unique category of ineffable experience roughly called inner feeling. In this connection, philosopher and psychologist William James (1842–1910) comes swiftly to mind. His vivid exposition of the mental and emotional states characteristic of religious conversion and "knowledge," published in 1902 as *The Varieties of Religious Experience*, offers a number of hypotheses that correspond remarkably to Worringer's. These have to do with James's likening of inner feeling—whose only point of access he claims is the five senses—to being in love, listening to music, and uniting ecstatically with the godhead.[33] Where Worringer is absolutely distinct, however, is that he uses spiritual experience to engage and reveal *spatial* experience: "[But] spiritual experience, like spatial experience," Worringer wrote, "is something apart from everything intellectual and abstract, something that is directly fed by our senses" (172 [118]). Space to Worringer is immaterial, apart from all natural things, abstract but rendered into being by definite constructional properties; it is accessed through the senses and yet not synonymous with personal or random subjective sensibility.

Herbert Read's translation into English of *Formprobleme der Gotik* as *Form in Gothic* is a telling gesture. By giving priority to form as a material attribute over the Germanic abstractness of form as a phenomenological concept, Read reminds us that Worringer has been deconstructed—read for what is *not* there—for a very long time. In returning to Worringer's theory of transcendental space I have undertaken, it is true, to perform something of a reverse operation. My aim has been *not* to open a reading of *Form Problems* (in Derrida's sense) but to protect it[34]—to capture between imminence and truism Worringer's unique vision of Gothic *as space*.

Frankl was right: Worringer alone dared to delve into that deeper layer of Gothic form. Indeed, of all that I have read as a medievalist and of all that I know of the scholarship of Gothic architecture, Worringer alone stands forth in admitting (and remarkably early on in the twentieth century) that Gothic architecture is about *Gothic space*—that it "lifted him above his earthly limitations and his inner wretchedness . . . that he could experience the awe of eternity" (159 [106]).

NOTES

1. Paul Frankl, *The Gothic: Literary Sources and Interpretations through Eight Centuries* (Princeton: Princeton University Press, 1960), 679.

2. *Abstraktion und Einfühlung* (Munich: Piper, 1908). I have consulted *Abstraction and Empathy: A Contribution to the Psychology of Style,* trans. Michael Bullock (New York: International Universities Press, 1980). The English edition is hereafter cited as *AE.*

3. *Formprobleme der Gotik* (Munich: Piper, 1911). I have used the 3d edition, published by Piper in 1912, hereafter referred to as *FdG.* I have also used the Herbert Read translation, *Form in Gothic,* trans. Herbert Read (New York: Schocken Books, 1964), hereafter referred to as *Form.* To facilitate comparison of Read's translation with the original German I have cited the page numbers of both editions. The page numbers in the text that refer to *Form,* the English translation, are in parentheses while the page numbers for *FdG* follow in brackets. For a review of the publication history of *Formprobleme,* see Ann Stieglitz, "The Reproduction of Agony: Toward a Reception-History of Grünewald's Isenheim Altar after the First World War," *Oxford Art Journal* 12, no. 2 (1989), 87–103.

4. Geoffrey Waite, "Worringer's *Abstraction and Empathy:* Remarks on Its Reception and on the Rhetoric of Criticism," in *The Turn of the Century: German Literature and Art, 1890–1915,* ed. Gerald Chapple and Hans H. Schulte, McMaster Colloquium on German Literature 2 (Bonn: Bouvier, 1981), 197–223.

5. I would place emphases elsewhere than Waite does regarding the "function of the Gothic in Worringer's text . . . [as] some figure for [his] own abstracting attempt to impose order on an alienated view of history and on a deep confusion within the order of discourse within which he writes" (219). I see it equally as a *scholarly* problem for Worringer. For discussion of Worringer's reception as a Gothic specialist, see Magdalena Bushart, *Der Geist der Gotik und die expressionistische Kunst: Kunstgeschichte und Kunsttheorie, 1911–1925* (Munich: Silke Schreiber, 1990). Bushart's approach is quite different than mine as a medievalist. This makes sense, given her objective to explore the Expressionist Worringer.

6. Erich Fidder, ed., *Wilhelm Worringer: Fragen und Gegenfragen, Schriften zum Kunstproblem* (Munich: Piper, 1956), with Worringer's bibliography prepared by Wulf Schadendorf, 189–92.

7. *AE,* vii–viii. For a different reading of this statement, see Waite, 217.

8. On Worringer and race theory, see Stieglitz, "Reproduction"; and Jolanda Nigro Covre, "Wilhelm Worringer prima e dopo: Da un equivoco a un 'tramonto,'" *Ricerche de storia dell'arte* 12 (1980), 65–76.

9. Waite comprehensively covers Worringer's relations with Modernist ideologies, movements, and intellectuals mentioned here.

10. For the link of Worringer to Fiedler (1841–95), see Lionello Venturi, *History of Art Criticism* (1936), trans. Charles Marriott, rev. ed. (New York: Dutton, 1964), 274–78.

11. Routinely Worringer has been placed squarely within the branch of psychological aesthetics called Empathy (Ger., *Einfühlung*) theory, practiced notably by Theodor Lipps and Vernon Lee [Violet Paget]. For general introductions to Worringer's place in empathy theory, see Melvin Rader, *A Modern Book of Esthetics* (1st ed., 1935; New York: Holt, Rinehart, and Winston, 1960); and Rudolf Arnheim, "Wilhelm Worringer on Abstraction and Empathy," in his *New Essays on the Psychology of Art* (Berkeley and Los Angeles: University of California Press, 1986), 50–62. A more rigorous account, with bibliography, is found in Waite, 206–7. The importance of empathy theory and of Worringer's comparison with Lipps has, in my view however, been altogether overestimated; Simmel was far more influential than Lipps. To what extent empathy theory is central to Worringer's ideas remains open to debate.

12. On Hulme and Worringer, see Waite, "Worringer's *Abstraction*," 203–4. Hulme said that he heard Worringer lecture at the Berlin Congress of Aesthetics before World War I [1913], in his *Speculations: Essays on Humanism and the Philosophy of Art,* ed. Herbert Read (London: Routledge and Kegan Paul, 1924), 82. Read, who in 1927 made the standard translation of *FdG* used here, said that it was because of his being asked to edit Hulme's posthumous papers that he learned about Worringer. See Read's obituary of Worringer in *Encounter* 25, no. 5 (November 1965), 58–60.

13. Arnheim, 52; Peg Weiss, *Kandinsky in Munich: The Formative Jugendstil Years* (Princeton: Princeton University Press, 1979), 158–59; Rose-Carol Washton Long, "Expressionism, Abstraction, and the Search for Utopia in Germany," in *The Spiritual in Art: Abstract Painting, 1890–1985,* exh. cat., ed. Maurice Tuchman (New York: Abbeville, 1986), 201–17; and Bushart, *Der Geist der Gotik,* 20.

14. Iain Boyd Whyte, ed. and trans., *The Crystal Chain Letters* (Cambridge: MIT Press, 1985).

15. Gregory L. Ulmer, "D.H. Lawrence, Wilhelm Worringer, and the Aesthetics of Modernism," *D. H. Lawrence Review* 10 (1977), 165–81.

16. Worringer came into the Imagist circle with Hulme. On this, see Malcom Bradbury, "London 1890–1920," in *Modernism,* ed. Malcom Bradbury and James McFarlane (London: Penguin, 1976), 172–90; and Natan Zach, "Imagism and Vorticism," ibid., 228–42.

17. The latter two movements' relation (architecture generally) to Worringer has been less well studied than other Modernist ones, especially those concerning painting and literature. See Sheldon Nodelman, "Structural Analysis in Art and Anthropology," in *Structuralism,* ed. Jacques Ehrmann (Garden City, N.Y.: Anchor Books, 1970), 79–93; Iain Boyd Whyte, *Bruno Taut and the Architecture of Activism* (Cambridge: Cambridge University Press, 1982), with an excellent bibliography; and Whyte, *The Crystal Chain Letters.* Covre, "Wilhelm Worringer" (69–70), even goes so far as to trace Worringer's influence to geometrical abstractness in Chicago architecture of the early twentieth century.

18. *AE* was translated into seven languages, *Formprobleme* into one. See Stieglitz, "Reproduction," and also note 12.

19. See especially *Form,* 88; *FdG,* 59.

20. On the crystal and Expressionist architecture, see Rosemarie Haag Bletter, "The Interpretation of the Glass Dream—Expressionist Architecture and the History of the Crystal Metaphor," *Journal of the Society of Architectural Historians* 40, no. 1 (1981), 20–43; and Rose-Carol Washton Long, "Expressionism, Abstraction," 201–17, esp. 206. See also note 19 above.

21. Bushart, *Der Geist der Gotik,* 18–20. The problem (then as now) is that speculative inquiry is considered to be subjective, and therefore lacking in "scientific" value. This is the basic thrust of Julius Baum's review of *FdG* in *Kunstchronik,* n.s. 29, no. 14 (January 1918 [1917/1918]), cols. 145–50.

22. Although his analysis begins in northern ornament, with its life-giving form blood, space for Worringer is the ultimate expression of Gothic. Worringer further developed his analysis of the experience of Gothic space and its analogies with music, mystery, and the transcendental in "Zur Frage der gotischen Monumentalität," in *Vom Geiste neuer Literaturforschung, Festschrift für Oskar Walzel,* ed. Julius Wahle and Victor Klemperer (Wildpark-Potsdam: Akademische Verlagsgesellschaft Athenaion, 1924), 211–23. Susanne Vivian Cloeren has worked on this article at length and I am grateful to her for sharing with me her unpublished study, "Kenneth Noland and Monumentality," where she applies Worringer's ideas to 1960s painting.

23. Henri Focillon, *Les Mouvements Artistiques,* in *Histoire du Moyen Age,* ed. Henri Pirenne, Gustave Cohen, and Henri Focillon (Paris: Les Presses Universitaires de France,

1933), 419–663. This essay was later translated by Jean Bony and appeared as *The Art of the West in the Middle Ages,* 2 vols. (Leicester: Phaidon Press, 1963).

24. H. Jantzen, "Über den gotischen Kirchenraum," *Freiburger Wissenschaftliche Gesell-schaft* (1928) and later as *Kunst der Gotik* (Hamburg: Rowohlt, 1957), now as *High Gothic: The Classic Cathedrals of Chartres, Reims, Amiens,* trans. James Palmes (New York: Pantheon Press, Minerva Books, 1962).

25. *Gothic Architecture and Scholasticism: An Inquiry into the Analogy of the Arts, Philosophy, and Religion in the Middle Ages* (1st ed., 1951; New York: Meridian, 1957). I am preparing a reassessment of how Scholasticism has been read in relation to Gothic architecture and shall trace its nineteenth-century roots.

26. Colin Eisler, "Kunstgeschichte American Style," in *The Intellectual Migration: Europe and America, 1930–1960,* ed. Donald Fleming and Bernard Bailyn (Cambridge: Belknap Press, 1969), 544–629. A monumental study of the emigration of art historians of Jewish background from Germany is currently in preparation at the art history institute of the University of Hamburg. This project will be of great value in tracing the effects of mass emigration on the subsequent development of art history in Germany and America.

27. Much of Worringer's biography remains a mystery, especially his whereabouts between the two World Wars and the crucial question of whether he was Jewish. It seems that he taught in the art history institute at the University of Bonn during the 1920s, having been called there from the University in Bern. After the Second World War, in 1946, he held the chair at Halle University that Frankl had abandoned in 1933 to emigrate to the United States. Some intriguing suggestions about this period in Worringer's life may be found in Covre, "Wilhelm Worringer."

28. For an analytical account of the pioneering German medieval scholarship and its impact on the development of medieval art history in North America, see Kathryn Brush, *Excavating Medieval Art History: Adolph Goldschmidt, Wilhelm Vöge and Shapes of Discourse, 1885–1914* (Cambridge University Press; forthcoming); and Brush, "Integration or Segregation Among Disciplines? The Historiography of Gothic Sculpture as Case Study," in *Artistic Integration in Gothic Churches: An Interrogation,* ed. K. Brush, P. Draper, and V. Raguin (Toronto: University of Toronto Press, forthcoming). In the years immediately following its publication, *Formprobleme* received relatively little positive reception among medieval art historians. Indeed, one of the few works published at this time that embraced Worringer's ideas is Karl Scheffler's *Der Geist der Gotik* (1917). However, I would date the beginning of the medievalist's large-scale rejection of Worringer to 1920 with the publication of Erwin Panofsky's "Der Begriff des Kunstwollens," *Zeitschrift für Ästhetik und allgemeine Kunstwissenschaft* 14 (1920), 321–39. This was Panofsky's attack on Riegl and the unscientific (because ahistorical) approach of psychological analysis of form. As we know, Panofsky emigrated, as did many of the Germans, to the United States around the time of the Second World War; see Eisler, "Kunstgeschichte." Panofsky is among the most prominent "fathers" of American studies of medieval art. For an English translation, see Erwin Panofsky, "The Concept of Artistic Volition," trans. Kenneth J. Northcott and Joel Snyder, *Critical Inquiry* 8 (Autumn 1981), 17–33. For a critique of Worringer, more or less contemporary with Panofsky's, on the basis of the weak intellectual grounding of psychological aesthetics, see Heinrich G. Lempertz, *Wesen der Gotik* (Leipzig: Karl W. Hiersemann, 1926).

29. *Form,* 156; *FdG,* 103 ("Der ganze Bau scheint nur um ihretwillen zu existieren").

30. Kahn (1901–74) shares with Worringer more than this one fundamental defintion of architecture. Both men, for example, place emphasis on space, both believe that architecture cannot be "read" with intelligence alone, and both attempted to form a program of humane values out of the abstractions of architecture. See Romaldo Giurgola, with Pamela Berg,

"Louis I. Kahn," *MacMillan Encyclopedia of Architects* (New York: Free Press, 1982), 2:537–46.

31. The period role and derivation of Worringer's marionette image deserve further investigation but certainly one could cite as an influence the important essay by the German Romantic, Heinrich von Kleist, "Über das Marionettentheater." I am preparing a study of the marionette theme in twentieth-century dance—what I see as meaning the semblance of alien control (for example, Petrouska and Coppelia)—as a metaphor for women's spiritually expressive experience and its relations to analogous descriptions of medieval women mystics. It might also be useful to include in this investigation Ludwig Kirchner's sculpture of a female figure, now in the Kunsthalle, Bremen.

32. I wish to thank Robert Norton (Vassar College) for his intriguing suggestion that music might also for Worringer be constructional and rational. Although the point needs to be developed further, it seems, however, that Worringer was more concerned with music as a metaphor for the "spatial mystery" of Gothic architecture, an idea he elaborated in his "Zur Frage der gotischen Monumentalität."

33. For a discussion of William James, related theories of the senses, and the sensory experience of art, see chap. 2 of my *Sculpture of Compassion: The Pietà and the Beguines in the Southern Low Countries, c. 1300–c. 1600*, Studies on Kunstgeschiedenis, Belgian Historical Institute of Rome 6 (Brussels and Rome, 1992).

34. Waite's "Worringer's *Abstraction*" discussion of Derrida (201) challenged me to adopt Derrida's quote this way, as an opposite reading to Waite's.

6

Modern Art After "The End of Expressionism": Worringer in the 1920s

Charles W. Haxthausen

"In October 1920, a deeply shattered Wilhelm Worringer, one of Expressionism's theoretical forerunners and founders, pronounced a funeral oration [*Grabrede*] over the movement." With these words Georg Lukács opened his essay of 1934, "Greatness and Decline of Expressionism" ("Größe und Verfall des Expressionismus"), which provoked the now-celebrated "Expressionism debate" of the thirties.[1] The "funeral oration" to which he referred was Worringer's text, "Questions about Contemporary Art" ("Künstlerische Zeitfragen"), first delivered as a lecture in Munich and published as a book in 1921; Lukács, who quoted the text at length, attributed to it a particular diagnostic significance that has been neither questioned nor critically examined since. "In Worringer's eyes," explained Lukács, "the collapse of Expressionism is far more than just the business of art. It is the collapse of the attempt by bourgeois intellectuals to master the 'new reality' (the reality of imperialism, the epoch of World War and world revolution), in thought and in art."[2] Because of that failure, he argued, Expressionism had helped pave the way for fascism; it had become part of the "legacy" of National Socialism.

Given the canonical status that Lukács's text has enjoyed in the reception history of Expressionism, it is surprising that until now no one appears to have noticed that he seriously misrepresented the substance of Worringer's text. Worringer did not in fact claim, as Lukács attested, that the collapse of Expressionism extended beyond the practice of art: on the contrary, he asserted that his lugubrious obituary applied, "it should be well noted, *only to visual art. It alone do I have in mind*" (my emphasis).[3] Moreover, it was not just *Expressionist* art that was the issue for Worringer, but all modern plastic art. Expressionist art had in his view demonstrated beyond all doubt that the art forms of painting, sculpture, and architecture were no longer capable of giving expression to the spirit of the time, that they had become marginal to modern existence. Artists had become "refined specialists on the margin of what is necessary and immediate to life for us today. Let us not confuse these marginalia of our culture with its proper text. Art once stood within the text—in the very middle of it—today it stands irretrievably at the margins, and any assertions to the contrary are based on an unconscious fiction" (119). Expressionist art, according to Worringer, had been merely the final revolt against the growing sociological irrelevance of visual art; it was a last desperate attempt to pretend that things were otherwise, to pretend that painting and sculpture still served some essential social purpose. The tragedy of Expressionism arose from its overweening ambition and striving in a situation in which visual art had ceased to have a genuine social function. "A tragic situation," Worringer summed it up, "in no other time has there consciously been so much demanded of visual art when it is doubtful whether we any longer have a meaningful, creative visual art in the deeper sense of the word" (110).

This bleak assessment Worringer presented in a carefully crafted text whose rhetorical effects are skillfully calculated. Through the greater part of his essay Worringer does indeed seem "shattered," as Lukács would later characterize him; his text reads like a cathartic outburst of despair. But in the final third of the essay, which Lukács ignored, Worringer's tone shifts dramatically. Far from conceding, as Lukács had claimed, the failure of intellectuals to master the "new reality," Worringer declared that intellectuals, specifically the critics and art historians, had succeeded precisely where painters, sculptors, and architects had failed: one needed only to compare what had been written and theorized about art during the previous decade with what had been painted during that same period to see where the real creative energies of the time lay, where the "greater artistic clairvoyance" was to be found.

> Yes, what has been written in the last decade alone on visual art . . . has told us more about the nature of art than the pictures of this same period have revealed. . . . Books are written that are disciplined scholarly visions, nourished by a sensuousness of historical perception that is the purest incarnation of our times. . . . No, art has not been replaced by scholarship, rather scholarship itself is becoming art, is beginning to carry out its work with an élan that is artistic. And here there

is a spiritual impulse at work that embodies the phenomenon of Expressionism more authentically, in a manner more appropriate to our time, than does Expressionist painting. The true Expressionism of our time lives not in the new optics of our eye, but in that of our minds. (123–25)

Creativity, the artistic impulse, has flown, Worringer explained, "into our intellectuality. . . . In short, mind as art, as the most vital and most sensuous organ of our existence" (122).

The most compelling evidence for this development, in Worringer's view, was Oswald Spengler's *Decline of the West,* the first volume of which appeared in 1918, and which had been the catalyst for Worringer's pronouncements concerning the marginalization of painting and sculpture.[4] He granted that one might find Spengler's argumentation flawed, one might reject his conclusions, but his book was nevertheless indisputably "an indigenous manifestation of the times"; its success, declared Worringer, was a sign

> that the instinct of the times finds realized here in the form of thought something of that which in painting it never found credibly achieved: here there is indeed that Expressionist straining beyond horizons, that widening of intellectual and sensuous perspectives, that intoxicating spiritual panorama . . . which were only ostensibly present in Expressionist painting, yet remained without proper gravity and therefore without persuasive power. The drive for spiritual expansion, whether one wants to call it Expressionism or whatever, has migrated from paintings into books. (127–28)

Because the Expressionism of these books had been more easily and lucidly realized, declared Worringer, it was more serene, more intense and impressive than the noisy, convulsive, sham Expressionism of pictures.

If one strips away the refulgent cloak of Worringer's rhetoric, his position comes down to this: If art had not fulfilled his prophecies, if it had not conformed to his prognosis, then that proved only that painting and sculpture were finished, not that his historicist paradigm was flawed. He had erred only in neglecting to recognize that these art forms had become historically irrelevant anachronisms. He and the other apologists for Expressionism had merely been too modest: they had failed to see that their discourse was the true artistic expression of their time. Lukács, by conveniently truncating Worringer's text for his own purposes, thus distorted its essential point and consequently misrepresented the nature of his reassessment of Expressionism. For the message of Worringer's so-called funeral oration was not, as Lukács claimed, that Expressionism as a cultural phenomenon had died, but that artistic expression had migrated from painting and sculpture into the critical discourse on these media. Succinctly stated, the point of Worringer's "funeral oration" is: "art is dead; long live art criticism."

Alois Riegl, whom Worringer acknowledged as the most important influence on his early books, wrote in the introduction to his *Die spätrömische Kunstindustrie* (Late Roman art industry, 1901) of the "fact that can no longer be ignored, that even scholarship, in spite of its ostensible independence and objectivity, ultimately takes its direction from the intellectual inclinations of the day and the art historian, too, cannot really transcend the characteristic artistic proclivities of his contemporaries."[5] Although this was fully consistent with his historiographical position, Riegl made this concession with a tone almost of regret. Worringer, however, now exulted in this very limitation of scholarly and critical discourse, he relished its embeddedness in the culture of its time; for him the aestheticized discourse on art now supplanted art itself as the most intense and effective expression of the *Kunstwollen,* of the will-to-art, of the modern epoch. And "Questions about Contemporary Art," so poignant in its portrayal of the "tragedy" of Expressionism, so skillful in its manipulation of the reader's emotions, with its unexpected shift to a major key after pages of unmitigated gloom, was itself doubtlessly conceived and crafted by Worringer as an exemplary document of this new criticism—of criticism as art. Interestingly, six years before the appearance of "Questions about Contemporary Art," Richard Hamann had anticipated Worringer's self-assessment in a sharply critical review of *Formprobleme der Gotik (Form Problems in the Gothic).* It is "as a manifestation of Expressionism," wrote Hamann, "not as a scholarly achievement, that this book must be considered. . . . Time will tell whether the Expressionism of this book will last longer than the art inspired by it."[6] Now, Worringer embraced and glorified the very limitations that Hamann had used to criticize his earlier work.

The scholarly examination of Worringer has up to now focused on his prewar writings, particularly *Abstraction and Empathy* and *Form Problems in the Gothic.* After "Questions about Contemporary Art," Worringer's subsequent writings had no discernible resonance within the world of contemporary art, from which he now felt estranged. During this period he published nine books, some of them, to be sure, consisting only of short introductions, such as his commentaries on the Passion woodcuts of the Renaissance artist Urs Graf and on the Cologne Bible; but there are more substantial publications as well, on the beginnings of panel painting, on Egyptian art in 1927, and a book in which he undertook a reevaluation of the dichotomy he had earlier posited between the Hellenic and Gothic views of the world.[7] The focus of this essay, however, is not this considerable body of work but Worringer's sparse writings on modern art in the decade following his famous obituary on it. My purpose here is to point out some aspects of Worringer's writing that merit more detailed investigation in the context not only of his own corpus but of the historiographic developments of the 1920s.

Four years after the publication of "Questions about Contemporary Art," Worringer took up the question of Expressionism anew in an essay entitled "The Late Gothic and Expressionist System of Form" ("Spätgotisches und expressionistisches Formsystem"), published in the *Wallraf-Richartz Jahrbuch*. Here he turned once more to the theme that had permeated Expressionist criticism—the alleged affinity between the Gothic and Expressionism, a discourse for which his *Form Problems in the Gothic* (1911) had been the catalyst. The Gothic, he had declared at the conclusion of that book, was "not a phenomenon bound to any single period or style, but (reveals) itself continually through all the centuries in ever new disguises: . . . an ageless racial phenomenon, deeply rooted in the innermost constitution of Northern man, and for this reason, not to be uprooted by the leveling action of the European Renaissance."[8] As Magdalena Bushart has written, Worringer's book sparked a renewed fascination with the Gothic in the German art world.[9] By 1912, critics were already seeing parallels between the Gothic and the new art, and because in this deeply historicist discourse most confidently believed they understood the laws governing cultural development, critics like Ludwig Coellen, Paul Fechter, Wilhelm Hausenstein, and Adolf Behne predicted the emergence of a culture that would be both collective and religious: subjectivity and individualism, associated with Impressionism, would give way to a new objectivity, a new anonymity of the artist in the service of renewed religious faith.[10] At first Worringer did not make explicit this connection between the Gothic and contemporary art, but the implication was clearly there, and he himself made the link in an essay of December 1915, "Questions About the Future of Art" ("Künstlerische Zukunftsfragen"), published in the *Frankfurter Zeitung* and a few months later in the monthly magazine *Kunst und Künstler.* There the journal's editor Karl Scheffler—no friend of the new art—introduced it with the words: "the program of the new generation has in all likelihood never before been so well and clearly articulated as here." Just as Gothic architecture had been developed in the more sensual culture of France but could realize its proper historical development only in the more spiritually oriented culture of Germany, Worringer wrote, so it was with contemporary art: France had initiated the new art of expression and Germany was destined to bring it to its fullest fruition.[11]

Worringer further developed his thesis on this Gothic-Expressionist historical axis in an essay of 1919, "Critical Thoughts on the New Art" ("Kritische Gedanken zur Neuen Kunst"). "What is historically exciting about Expressionism," he wrote, is

> that it is the first unreserved attempt within our narrower European postmedieval art to carry through the experiment of a complete spiritualization of expression. For the phenomenon of a thoroughly spiritualized art was up to now known to us only outside of the modern European cultural context. It was known to us above all only as an expression of the masses, as the collective artistic expression of unified multitudes, bound together in their consciousness by a unified religious and spiritual structure. And we know that such a living collectivity has not existed in Europe since the Renaissance. Correspondingly, art since the Renaissance has been emphatically an art of individuals.[12]

Expressionism was a revolt against the sensualist, individualistic aesthetics of natural beauty that had dominated Western culture; it was a reminder that there was another axis of artistic development alongside the sensuous, earthbound, immanent aesthetic of the Mediterranean peoples. But in "Questions about Contemporary Art," Worringer, who had done so much to nurture the myth of a "spiritualization" of art, now declared that earlier position to have been a *Zeitirrtum,* a self-delusion of the Expressionist generation: "Certainly, there was a spiritual art," he declared, "the mistake was to believe that there could be such an art today. For such an art requires the precondition of a spiritual dependency that we have irretrievably lost, and for that reason it lives for us only in programs, not in souls."[13] By looking only at the formal resemblances between the old "Expressionism" and the new they had deceived themselves into believing that such an art was possible today (109–10):

> But as we became gradually aware of the content within these old forms, with what tensions and energies they were suffused, as we . . . glimpsed for a few seconds the power of their metaphysical bonds, which gave these forms their great Expressionist elementarity, then we were inescapably exposed to the crippling tragedy of self-knowledge, and we knew at once with an unequivocal certainty that all of our Expressionist efforts were but a mournful philosophical fiction [*traurige Philosophie Als-Ob*].[14]

As remarked above, in "The Late Gothic and Expressionist System of Form" Worringer returned again to the affinity of the Gothic and Expressionism. Having earlier discredited the presumed mutual spiritual identity of these two cultural moments, he now offered an entirely new argument for their kinship and historical parallelism: their character as formal systems. Both the late Gothic (under which he considered only painting and sculpture) and Expressionism are distinguished by a unity of style, by a stylistic system. "The will to system is in both cases seen as the most distinctive characteristic of the German artistic spirit," declared Worringer.[15] "System," he explained, "is an escape from our solitariness and therefore stands under a reactive impulse" ("SuEF," 66–67). But the system is taken over from other peoples; it is merely adapted by the Germans, who, ironically, of all peoples are the one with the deepest faith in system. But systems can originate only among peoples with a true collective feeling. The German subjects himself to a system as a voluntary slave, because it is his only possibility to feign collectivism. Because of his individualistic incapacity to create form he becomes an unconditional believer in a system transmitted from without. Thus no people is more individualistic than the German and simultaneously none more fanatically devoted to system ("SuEF," 67). Consequently, Germany does not invent form, for that can be achieved only by a true community, of which the individualistic Germans are incapable. Instead Germany adopts formal systems like the Gothic and Expressionism from without and stylizes them into a rigid formalism ("SuEF," 70–71).

Reading this essay, one wonders what on earth Worringer has in mind. Clearly he believes in a unified Expressionist style, but he does not discuss its concrete qualities beyond generalities about abstraction, stylization, formalism, etc. Precisely whom or what could he

be referring to? The reader remains in the dark, since Worringer
mentions not one Expressionist, not one work of art, whether Gothic
or "Expressionist." He offers not one shred of evidence in support
of his assertions. Moreover, in arguing that Expressionism is a stylistic
system, that there is an Expressionist unity of style, he takes a position
that sets him apart from every other major German critic of his era.
Hans von Hildebrandt conceded, in a study of 1919, that the term
"Expressionism," which for him as for most critics was synonymous
with the art of the European avant-garde, did not do justice to the
diversity of the art, and Expressionism was nowhere more diverse,
less unified than in Germany.[16] Eckart von Sydow, in a book published the same year, divided German Expressionism into four different schools.[17] In 1922 Adolf Behne characterized Expressionism as a
"mixtum compositum" of every possible tendency.[18] And precisely
this diversity within Expressionism was a major factor in Wilhelm
Hausenstein's loss of faith in the ostensible movement, as he expressed it in his own, slightly earlier "funeral oration," "Art at This
Moment" ("Die Kunst in diesem Augenblick"). Hausenstein, who
as recently as 1918 had labored strenuously to show the unity of
Expressionism, gave up the struggle soon thereafter. "What is Expressionism, who is an Expressionist?" he asked. "One could just as well
maintain that no one is an Expressionist as claim that all are, or a
few: because it is not certain what Expressionism is. . . . It is a con-
vulsion that comes just as close to the all as to the void. Thus the
diversity of the attempts; the elusiveness of the concept; the immeas-
urable span between Picasso and Nolde, Kandinsky and Rousseau,
Klee and Meidner, Seewald and Kokoschka. The common denominator vanishes."[19] Paul Westheim, reviewing Hausenstein, argued that
it was precisely because "Expressionism" had brought forth so many
independent, strongly individual talents, precisely because it did not
configure itself into a stylistically homogeneous school, that there
was no ground for despair.[20]

To be sure, before 1914 most critics had believed in the imminent
emergence of a collective unified Expressionist style. But after 1919
no one seriously claimed that this had been achieved; all of the major
critics now recognized the diversity of German art—all of them, that
is, except Worringer, who, in spite of the eccentricity of his claim,
felt no need to support it by any particularity, by any concrete example, by any evidence whatsoever. Since the spiritual affinity of the
Gothic and Expressionism had proved to be a fiction, it is as if Worringer, rather than abandon the myth that had helped to build his
reputation, felt compelled to ground that affinity on some other basis.

He now wove a new historiographic fiction in the face of overwhelming evidence and a critical consensus to the contrary. We recall his words: "The system is for us an escape from our solitariness and stands under a reactive impulse." Indeed. Worringer's claim for the Germans' radical bent for systematizing *(Systemwut)* seems valid above all as a self-characterization.

Ernst Bloch, in a 1938 critique of Lukács's "Greatness and Decline of Expressionism," observed that

> in not a single line [of Lukács's text] does the name of an Expressionist painter appear. Marc, Klee, Kokoschka, Nolde, Kandinsky, Grosz, Dix, Chagall are not mentioned. . . . What now is the material through which Lukács acquaints us with his concept of Expressionism? It is not the thing itself, with its concrete imprint at a given place, with its reality that presents itself to be experienced, but the material itself is already something secondhand, it is literature on Expressionism, which becomes the basis for yet more literature, theory, and criticism.[21]

This applies equally to Worringer. Not only in "The Late Gothic and Expressionist System of Form" did Worringer avoid even the mention of individual artists. So far as I have been able to determine, not once in the criticism he wrote on the modern movement between 1911 and 1925 did he mention the name of a single German artist, of a single avant-garde group; not once did he name, let alone discuss, a single German work.[22]

In 1925, however, Worringer broke this long pattern of abstract generalization, in an essay he published in the *Neue Schweizer Rundschau* and devoted to a single modern artist and a single work. It is an important essay for our understanding of Worringer, four years after he had pronounced plastic art clinically dead. The discovery of this particular painting, he declared, became for him "an unhoped-for event." He had no longer expected any "living revelations" from the painting of his time, because, he explained, he had seen the "development peter out in a dead end of convulsive studio experiment and had forgotten how to believe that a living future might be possible." But that changed when he encountered the work in question.

> Profoundly taken aback I remained standing before it and savored the now rare happiness of being totally under the spell

of a contemporary picture, I savored the unexpected happiness
of believing once more in the newest painting. There hung a
square meter of painting on the wall that . . . revealed the full
dimensions of existence, that compactness of the lived experience of being, whose realization in painting I had no longer
believed possible. The last one who had given me something
of this experience had been Cézanne. Thereafter modern
painting had become for me dimensionless in the deeper sense
of the word. . . . And [now] for the first time I responded to
the breath . . . of a modern painting with *my* breath, with the
breath of my entire being.[23]

The artist who was able to work this spell on Worringer, to succeed
where the "convulsive studio experiments" of Picasso and Matisse,
Léger and Gris, Kirchner and Beckmann, Klee and Kandinsky, had
failed, was the Italian painter Carlo Carrà, a former Futurist, and the
work that Worringer received like a gift from heaven, that restored
his faith in the potential of modern painting, was *Pine by the Sea*, of
1921, a pallid and classicizing coastal scene, executed after the painter
himself had retreated from the heady experimentation of Futurism
and *pittura metafisica*.[24]

"Why so many grand words for such a simple picture?" asked
Worringer rhetorically: because Carrà's painting offered proof that
out of the unavoidable complexity of modernity there was "still a
path that led to such a simple and for that reason universally understandable beauty" ("CC," 88). But for him Carrà's picture, painted
in the year in which Worringer published his so-called funeral oration,
represented a new phase in the development of Expressionism, what
he, in an apparent paradox, called a "quiet Expressionism" ("CC,"
90). In 1919, Worringer had described Expressionism as an art in
which spirit had reasserted itself over against the experience of nature.
"The cry of redemption of the Veni creator spiritus sounded out of
artistic necessity."[25] It was an attempt to break through to the divine.
An art informed not by the laws of nature but by the laws of the
spirit. Now, however, Worringer regarded the earlier Expressionist
attitude as a "dictatorship of the spirit," and "it is the virtue of Carrà's
picture to have rediscovered the innermost elective affinity between
the law of the spirit and the law of nature." That "violation of nature"
by the spirit was now, without contradiction, reconciled with the
most profound *devotion* to nature. The domination and the service
of nature became again as one ("CC," 88).
Earlier Expressionism had torn spirit and nature apart and "spirit

highhandedly triumphed." Now what Expressionism had torn asunder could be found fused into a new unity, and "this meant nothing else than that feeling for life that we designate with the term classicism," which is always capable of renewal. "There is an eternal classicism of a full and ripened feeling for life" ("CC," 88). There had been a lot of talk about the metaphysical dimension of Expressionism, Worringer observed, probably "because in its spiritual obsessiveness it knew so little of the metaphysical immanence of all things. This metaphysical immanence defined the soul of the quiet Expressionism," which he believed to see in Carrà's *Pine by the Sea* ("CC," 88).

The terms "Nazarene" or "Nazarenertum" do not appear in Worringer's essay on Carrà; that term, taken from the school of nineteenth-century German painters who painted religious subjects in the style of the fifteenth-century Italians, had a pejorative ring to it, and he had used it in that sense in his own work up to now. In 1919 he characterized this phenomenon as a bloodless art that was only ostensibly spiritual and that was based on a long digested, smoothly stylized nature. And yet that description would seem to fit Carrà's picture. "The *true* spiritual art," Worringer had argued in 1919 in his role as an Expressionist apologist, "scorns this spirituality achieved through the grace of a spiritually pretentious subjection to the laws of nature, [the true spiritual art] knows only the spirituality that draws its nourishment from shocks *prior to* and *beyond* the laws of nature."[26] In 1921 Worringer used the term again, but now acceptingly, with an air of resignation: "The elegiac classicism with a Nazarene coloration, which today in post-Expressionist Europe is unmistakenly emerging, is seemingly already the result of the state of affairs I have indicated." It was a sign that "art wanted to rest from its strenuous ambition, it was the beginning of a new self-contentment. A postlude of long familiar sounds begins. A postlude, fading away, growing dimmer on the edge of our culture, no longer at its center. Let us say yes to it."[27]

Worringer's admiration of Carrà is therefore understandable; he admired him in part because Carrà embodied what Worringer believed to be historically necessary—anything other than what he had predicted to be the historical destiny of art had to be a self-deception. As he put it, in the midst of the decade dominated by Beckmann, Klee, Picasso, Mondrian, Kandinsky, Otto Dix, "he expected no more living revelations" from painting ("CC," 88).

To underline his point about the vitality of Carrà's traditionalism, to confirm it as a sign of the confluence of the *Zeitgeist* and *Volksgeist*, Worringer linked it with another contemporary Italian phenomenon—Benito Mussolini. Germans misunderstood Mussolini's theatrics, his appeal to tradition, Worringer claimed, they saw it as a masquerade. But

> Mussolini may dare to use the grand rhetorical words and gestures, because the air around him is so filled with historical-sensuous vitality that it can bear these words and gestures. In Germany they would necessarily fall into a void and sound comically hollow, because . . . we have never been a national community of such full historical-sensuous resonance and because for these same reasons our historical consciousness of tradition has never achieved that inner unity and logic of formation, which alone makes possible a natural continuity between the oldest and the newest. Only in a Latin country can a person of the most modern consciousness simultaneously be naively immersed in tradition. ("CC," 90–91)

Thus, with this allusion to Mussolini, Worringer's text on Carrà's *Pine by the Sea* suggests that even if Lukács had indeed misread "Questions about Contemporary Art," he may have been essentially correct in judging the larger and darker implications of Worringer's thought.

In his melancholy pronouncements on the marginalization of plastic art as an effective embodiment of the spirit of the modern epoch, Worringer may have left the impression of merely returning to the position taken by Hegel nearly a century earlier in his lectures on aesthetics. Hegel had declared that art "no longer affords that satisfaction of spiritual needs that earlier epochs and peoples sought and found only in it" when it was intimately connected with religion. In terms of this, its highest mission, art belonged to the past, and "has thereby also lost for us its genuine truth and life and has shifted to the realm of *ideas* [*Vorstellung*] rather than maintaining its former necessity or assuming its higher place in reality." Accordingly, Hegel considered inquiry into the nature of art to be a more timely form of spiritual activity than the creation of new works of art.[28]
Then again, there is much in Worringer's approach, both before and after his "funeral oration," that recalls his contemporary, Spengler. Just as Spengler pronounced the *history* of philosophy, encompassing a comparative morphology of cultures, to be the last topic of Western philosophy,[29] Worringer, who believed that "scholarship itself is becoming art," seems to have seen in the morphological history

of art the supreme artistic expression of his time. His books of the twenties, such as *Ägyptische Kunst* (Egyptian art, 1927) and *Griechentum und Gotik* (Hellenism and the Gothic, 1928), are very consistent with such a conception. Yet, even if one concedes that factual representation in history is a positivist delusion, and acknowledges the purely literary and mythic dimensions of all historical writing,[30] most of Worringer's texts remained too schematic in their racial, national, and historicist generalizations, too solipsistic in his disdain for the concrete, to merit the designation "history," even within the strongly historicist German culture within which he worked. The totalizing schemas of Riegl and Wölfflin, to cite only the two best-known and most influential examples, are grounded in abundantly detailed comparative analyses of individual artists and works of art. Worringer, by contrast, always seems uninterested in the factual basis of art's history; as with his discussion of the "Expressionist system of form" cited above, the reader is usually left guessing as to how he has arrived at his interpretation.

Ultimately, because of the solipsistic, self-indulgent character of Worringer's writings on modern art, the model they bring to mind is, perhaps, not Hegel or Spengler or Riegl or Lamprecht, but Oscar Wilde, in his dialogue, "The Critic as Artist." For Wilde, too, criticism had become the supreme art form within modern culture. "Criticism," Wilde's mouthpiece Gilbert explains to his partner in conversation Ernest, is more creative than conventional art forms, unimpeded as it is by verisimilitude or by anything else external to itself. Purely subjective, it is concerned not with external objects and events but with "the spiritual moods and imaginative passions of the mind" of the critic.[31] Wilde, like Worringer, regarded contemporary artistic production with disdain, but considered its poverty no impediment to the potential creations of the critic, whose work was to be valued as the highest form of art. For the critic, the work of art was simply a "suggestion for a new work of his own, that need not necessarily bear any obvious resemblance to the thing it criticizes"("Soul of Man," 29). "Who cares," Gilbert asks rhetorically,

> whether Mr. Ruskin's views on Turner are sound or not? What does it matter? That mighty and majestic prose of his, so fervid and so coloured in its noble eloquence, so rich in its elaborate symphonic music, so sure and certain, at its best, in subtle choice of words and epithet, is at least as great a work of art as any of the wonderful sunsets that bleach or rot in their corrupted canvases in England's Gallery; greater indeed . . .

> on account of the fuller variety of its appeal, soul speaking to
> soul in those long-cadenced lines, not through form and color
> alone, . . . but with intellectual and emotional utterance, with
> lofty passion and with loftier thought, with imaginative in-
> sight, and with poetic aim. (26–27)

"It is Criticism that leads us," declares Gilbert in a Hegelian perora-
tion worthy of Worringer himself: "The Critical Spirit and the World
Spirit are one" (64). Yet, as the example of Ruskin shows, even
Wilde's conception seems to presuppose an attention to individual
art objects that is rarely in evidence in Worringer's criticism.

What Worringer offered was not so much criticism as *theory* in the
guise of history, a theory of art's historical development that, in his
own view at least, supplanted art as a major locus of creative ferment.
There is a parallel here, in this discourse of the "Modernist" era, to a
salient tendency of our own "postmodern" one, in which, as Andreas
Huyssen has observed, while "skepticism about the feasibility of an
artistic avantgarde was on the rise . . . the vitality of theory . . . was
never in serious doubt. To some, indeed, it appeared as if the cultural
energies that had fueled the art movements of the 1960s were flowing
during the 1970s into the body of theory, leaving the artistic enterprise high and dry."[32] Any verdict on our own time is premature,
but since Worringer's time posterity has so far shown a more intense
and sustained interest in the "convulsive studio experiments" of Beckmann, Matisse, Picasso, Klee, Mondrian, and their contemporaries
than it has in his own writings.

NOTES

1. Published in English translation as Georg Lukács, "Expressionism: Its Significance
and Decline," in *Essays on Realism*, ed. R. Livingstone, trans. David Fernbach (Cambridge:
MIT Press, 1981), 76 (slightly altered translation). First published in *Internationale Li-
teratur* 1, no. 1 (1934), 153–73. For the major texts of the "Expressionism debate," see
Hans-Jürgen Schmitt, ed., *Die Expressionismusdebatte. Materialien zu einer marxistischen
Realismuskonzeption*, 3d ed. (Frankfurt: Suhrkamp, 1978).

2. Lukács, "Expressionism," 76.

3. Wilhelm Worringer, "Künstlerische Zeitfragen," in *Fragen und Gegenfragen: Schriften zum Kunstproblem* (Munich: Piper, 1957), 121. All subsequent references in the text
are to this edition.

4. See Oswald Spengler, *Der Untergang des Abendlandes* (Munich, 1972), 375–80. On
the impact of Spengler's book on German art criticism, see Charles W. Haxthausen, "A
Critical Illusion: 'Expressionism' in the Writings of Wilhelm Hausenstein," in *The Ideological Crisis of Expressionism: The Literary and Artistic German War Colony in Belgium,*

1914–1918, ed. Rainer Rumold and O. K. Werckmeister (Columbia, S.C.: Camden House, 1990), 186–88.

5. Alois Riegl, *Die spätrömische Kunstindustrie*, 2d ed. (Vienna: Druck und Verlag der Österreichischen Staatsdruckerei, 1927), 3.

6. Richard Hamann, "Besprechung: Wilhelm Worringer, *Formprobleme der Gotik*," *Zeitschrift für Ästhetik und allgemeine Kunstwissenschaft* 10 (1915), 360–61.

7. Wilhelm Worringer, *Die Anfänge der Tafelmalerei* (Leipzig: Insel-Verlag, 1924); *Ägyptische Kunst: Probleme ihrer Wertung* (Munich: Piper, 1927); and *Griechentum und Gotik: Vom Weltreich des Hellenismus* (Munich: Piper, 1928).

8. Wilhelm Worringer, *Form in Gothic*, ed. Herbert Read (New York: Schocken Books, 1957), 179.

9. Magdalena Bushart, *Der Geist der Gotik und die expressionistische Kunst: Kunstgeschichte und Kunsttheorie, 1911–1925* (Munich: Silke Schreiber, 1990), 20–25.

10. See Haxthausen, "A Critical Illusion," 173.

11. Wilhelm Worringer, "Künstlerische Zukunftsfragen," *Kunst and Künstler* 14 (1916): 259, 263.

12. Wilhelm Worringer, "Kritische Gedanken zur neuen Kunst," in *Fragen und Gegenfragen*, 96.

13. Worringer, "Künstlerische Zeitfragen," 107, 115.

14. Ibid., 110. The expression "Philosophie Als-Ob" comes from Hans Vaihinger's *Philosophie des 'Als ob'*, published in 1911.

15. "Spätgotisches und Expressionistisches Formsystem," in *Fragen und Gegenfragen*, 66. All subsequent references to this source are abbreviated "SuEF."

16. Hans Hildebrandt, *Der Expressionismus in der Malerei* (Stuttgart: Deutsche Verlags-Anstalt, 1919), 3.

17. Eckart von Sydow, *Die deutsche expressionistische Kultur und Malerei* (Berlin: Furche, 1919, 73–75 and passim).

18. Adolf Behne, "Expressionismus als Selbstzweck," *Sozialistische Monatshefte* 28 (24 June 1922), 580.

19. Wilhelm Hausenstein, "Die Kunst in diesem Augenblick," *Der neue Merkur* 3 (special issue, undated [late 1919]), 120.

20. Paul Westheim, "Umschau: Das 'Ende des Expressionismus,'" *Kunstblatt* 4, no. 6 (1920), 187.

21. Ernst Bloch, "Diskussionen über Expressionismus," in Schmitt, *Die Expressionismusdebatte*, 181–82.

22. Indeed, as far as I have been able to determine, before 1925 the only contemporary artist that Worringer mentions by name is Picasso—and even then only once—in a 1919 article on Cubism. There, too, Worringer generalizes about Cubist aims and Cubist style without discussing a single work or date. See "Bemerkungen zum Kubismus," *Jahrbuch der Kestner-Gesellschaft* (1919), 150.

23. Wilhelm Worringer, "Carlo Carrà's 'Pinie am Meer,'" reprinted in and quoted from *Realismus: Zwischen Revolution und Reaktion, 1919–1939* (Munich: Prestel, 1981), 88. All subsequent quotations from this source are abbreviated "CC."

24. Along with Giorgio de Chirico, Carrà had exerted a major influence on German painting in the late teens and early twenties—Ernst, Schlemmer, Grosz et al.—through his *pittura metafisica* works. For a color illustration of *Pinie am Meer*, see the exhibition catalogue *Realismus* (note 23 above), 89.

25. Wilhelm Worringer, "Kritische Gedanken zur neuen Kunst," 88.

26. Ibid., 90–91.

27. "Künstlerische Zeitfragen," 128–29. See also Worringer's essay, "Nazarener," written around 1924, in *Fragen und Gegenfragen*, 130–37.

28. "Art no longer affords that satisfaction of spiritual needs that earlier epochs and peoples sought and found only in it—a satisfaction that, at least on the religious side, was most intimately connected with art. . . . In all these respects art is and remains for us in terms of its highest mission a thing of the past. It has thereby also lost for us its genuine truth and life and has shifted to the realm of our *ideas* [*Vorstellung*] rather than maintaining its former necessity or assuming its higher place in reality. . . . Therefore, the *scholarly study* of art [*die* Wissenschaft *der Kunst*] is a much more pressing need in our day than it was in times in which art in itself purely as art furnished complete satisfaction. Art invites us to a consideration of it by means of thought, and indeed not for the purposes of again creating art, but in order to know, by mean of scholarship, what art is." G. W. F. Hegel, *Vorlesungen über die Ästhetik* (Frankfurt am Main: Suhrkamp, 1970), 1:24–26 (my translation).

29. Spengler, *Der Untergang*, 64.

30. See Hayden White, "The Fictions of Factual Representation," in *Tropics of Discourse: Essays in Cultural Criticism* (Baltimore: Johns Hopkins University Press, 1978), 121–34.

31. Oscar Wilde, "The Soul of Man under Socialism," in *Plays, Prose Writings and Poems* (London: Dent, 1930), 25–26. All subsequent references are to this edition.

32. Andreas Huyssen, "Mapping the Postmodern," in *After the Great Divide: Modernism, Mass Culture, Postmodernism* (Bloomington, Ind.: Indiana University Press, 1986), 184.

7

From Worringer to Baudrillard and Back: Ancient Americans and (Post) Modern Culture in Weimar Germany

Neil H. Donahue

In Wilhelm Worringer's study *Egyptian Art* (1927), he reverses the position on primitive art he had staked out famously in his most well-known and influential study *Abstraction and Empathy* (1908).[1] There, Egyptian art figured as the most representative articulation of abstraction in the art of "primitive" (i.e., non-Western, non-technological) cultures. In his later work Worringer views Egyptian art in an entirely different light. Whereas *Abstraction and Empathy* had been read with enthusiasm and embraced by the artists of the avant-garde as a scholarly manifesto for their own movement, *Egyptian Art* appears, surprisingly, as a polemic against modernism, a document of irrationalism and cartoon of *Geistesgeschichte*[2] in the service of German nationalism in the late Weimar period. Despite its superficial concern with ancient Egypt and its dubious thesis about both the art and the culture, Worringer's study retains interest precisely for its "one-sidedness and exaggerations" (18 [22]);[3] that is, for the peculiar anxieties it reveals about Weimar Germany and its place among other nations.

Anxiety surfaces in his language. Unlike most scholars, who were suspicious of his popularity outside the narrow ranks of the academy, Worringer has always departed from the norms of scholarly, "scientific" writing, evincing instead a lively, supple style and dramatic sense of phrase. Yet in *Egyptian Art* those same qualities, that earlier felicity of formulation and fluidity of style, appear to have congealed and been reduced to an almost mechanically periphrastic, and often pejorative, glibness. That strained quality of both his thesis and his style reveals, however, the very contemporary motivations for a scholarly exercise well outside his areas of expertise. In his essay

"Critical Thoughts on Contemporary Art" (1919), Worringer had asked, "What is then art . . . other than the most sensitive seismograph [that registers] the most delicate tremblings of our cultural organism" (94). The same might be said of his scholarship,[4] which, in the case of *Egyptian Art*, registers the disorientation, the fears and anxieties, of Weimar culture in general.

Yet his rhetorical excesses link his work not only to the particular conditions of his own time, but also anticipate the rhetoric of some recent postmodern cultural theory, such as the work of the French social philosopher Jean Baudrillard. After first situating Worringer's work in the context of Weimar culture, I shall then describe a trajectory in intellectual history from Worringer's *Egyptian Art* (1927) to Baudrillard's *America* (1986). This trajectory of six decades in midcentury links Worringer's Weimar to Baudrillard's America and suggests an affinity between post-Expressionist and post-Modernist theory of culture. Thereafter, this essay returns to Worringer's text to complete the examination of its embeddedness in Weimar culture. The movement from modernity to postmodernity, from Worringer to Baudrillard, *and back* underscores the need to view both writers historically, in light of each other, in order to frame speculation about the uses and abuses of *Geistesgeschichte.*

Foremost among the anxieties that dominate Worringer's study is a suspicion of the rising role of American culture in the world. Fear of Americanization appears in Worringer's text in the surprising parallel he draws between ancient Egypt and modern, twentieth-century America in order to denounce in one breath what he considers long-standing pieties about Egyptian art and, more urgently, the threatening forces of urban-technological modernity. Worringer's discussion of Egyptian art provides him with a forum to denounce under the rubric of Americanization Germany's rapid rise to modernity in the Weimar period.[5] Yet the traits of modernity in all areas reflect for Worringer mere symptoms of a more fundamental concern about the integrity of German culture.

For Worringer, both societies, ancient Egypt and modern America, constitute "anything but a unified and autochthonous product; it is rather a region of deposits composed of ethnic elements from all points of the compass" (2 [2]); yet despite that diversity of ethnic origins, both have given rise to a particularly uniform type of people and society. Here Worringer situates himself in a long-standing debate in Germany, especially in art criticism since the late 1890s, between the reactionary defenders of a supposedly organic German *Kultur* and the advocates of a European (French), social-democratic *Zivilisation,* whereby the latter term is heavily pejorative.[6] That debate figures most prominently in the feud between the brothers, Thomas and Heinrich Mann, and has its last gasp, however long-winded, in Thomas Mann's ranting *Reflections of a Nonpolitical Man* (1918).[7] Nonetheless, Worringer avails himself of that vocabulary and applies the terms of that debate directly to ancient Egypt and, indirectly, to modern America.

Both societies appear to Worringer as artificial, false cultures that are in fact held together by a resistance to depth, an ontological emptiness and absence of gravity that is not passive, but instead exerts a force of superficial uniformity, of "this levelling Egyptian artificialization of existence [*Kunstformung des Daseins*] . . . that levelling power of transformation" (3 [4]). Neither society can sustain real "culture"; both seem to Worringer merely a "hothouse culture/cultivation" (*Treibhauskultur*); that is, an overdeveloped, mostly ornamental superstructure cut off from its roots. Both exhibit instead a decided "estrangement from nature by ultra-refined cultivation of [the habits and structures of] civilization" *(zivilisatorischen Hochzucht)* (7 [8]). That trait gives both societies the same position in their different epochs: "Egypt in certain respects plays in antiquity the part played in modern times by America" (3 [4]). Oddly, in order to execute this unlikely comparison, Worringer reverses his earlier distinction between the ancient Egyptian and modern man in a classification of psychological types.

In *Abstraction and Empathy* the Egyptian, as with other "primitive" cultures, appears in paroxysms of existential uncertainty and "spiritual agoraphobia" (*Platzangst* or *geistige Raumscheu*):

> Agonized by the confusing disorder and flux of external phenomena, such peoples were dominated by an immense need for tranquillity. The possibility for pleasure that they looked for in art did not consist in projecting themselves into the things of the outer world, of enjoying themselves in them, but rather in taking the particular thing of the external world out of its arbitrariness and apparent fortuitousness, in making it eternal by approximation to abstract forms and, in this way, finding a point of tranquillity in the flux of phenomena. (16– 17 [50])

However questionable his psychological typology, Worringer's earlier presentation of non-Western "primitive" cultures argued for the independent and separate validity of their arts as self-expressions on their own terms, apart from Western aesthetic standards. His later work, in contrast, applies his own Weimar anxieties to Egyptian culture and attributes to the Egyptian not *Platzangst* but a superior rationality and technical ability to control his environment, as we see in the following metaphor:

> The Egyptian converts the catastrophic phenomenon of the inundations [of the Nile, that is] into an element of the highest fertility in just the same manner as [no differently than] a modern motor engineer utilizes explosions so as to convert them by clever calculation into highly advantageous production of power. . . . Clever human calculation outwits the destructive force of nature. (6)

In language that resonates with censure (clever, outwits), Worringer now conflates modern technological man and the ancient Egyptian and implies the moral bankruptcy of both cultures.[8] Both are equally detached from any organic harmony with nature, which they simply dominate through hypertrophic rationality.

That one-sided technological intelligence reflects a larger "technicalization of life" (6 [8]) that has multiple correlates. The first is perhaps the most fundamental and concerns the sexuality of the culture, which Worringer describes as "manly" because it is predicated upon action rather than passivity, which he deems feminine. Yet that Egyptian manliness is spurious since it is dictated by technical rationality and is thus "without the least tinge of the heroic and primordial" (6 [8]). The activity it generates is merely mechanical function, a "compulsion" *(Unternehmungszwang)* instead of a "pleasure of enterprise" *(Unternehmungslust)*, which "does not go one step beyond the dictates of utility" (6 [8]). The detachment of ancient Egyptian culture from its organic roots through technical intelligence has resulted for Worringer in the effectual emasculation of that culture, which parallels a rise of femininity, or the status and rights of women, as in modern America: "America again presents itself for comparison. It is correct for the American case as well as the Egyptian to say that this type of masculine development is connected with a high regard for women and the family" (7 [8]), though what goes unstated here is the emergence of women in Weimar culture as a more immediate threat to established gender roles in the patriarchal culture that elected Hindenburg in his dotage to the presidency.[9] Worringer employs the terms of *Kultur* versus *Zivilisation* to defend an exclusive male eros and to chastize any threatening deviations from the patriarchal standard: "Every culture which keeps close to nature is permeated with eroticism; a culture diluted by civilization, however, loses touch with this cosmic native soil [*Mutterboden*, mother earth] and only sexuality is left to it. Thus we find obscenities on the margins of Egyptian culture but no Eros in its midst" (7 [8]). Oddly, Worringer invokes a "mother earth" in defense of patriarchal culture and reduces other forms of sexuality, including female sexuality in general, to just so many obscenities![10]

Likewise, to note a further symptom of cultural decline as a result of overweening rationality, Worringer cites disapprovingly the failing military spirit of Egyptian culture, where the soldier has been displaced by the writer: "The exponent of Egyptian ideas of life is not the soldier but the scribe" (7 [9]). Here Worringer echoes Thomas Mann's diatribes against what he called, with his brother in mind, the "literati of civilization" *(Zivilisationsliteraten).* The eros of battle has succumbed, not only to feminine sexuality, but also to the privileging of reason in literature and scholarship, again, devoid of visceral urgency: "The erudition of the Egyptians [*Gelehrsamkeit*] is a mastery of formulas, but not an urge to learning with a theoretical purpose of its own" *(Wissensdrang mit theoretischem Selbstzweck)* (7 [9]). In matters of both sexuality and war, ancient Egypt appears to Worringer dominated by an anemic rationality ("etiolation [*Blutverkümmerung*] . . . thin-blooded ideology") that elevates to primacy women, children, writing, and values of mere quantifiable utility, "in short, utilitarianism and pragmatism instead of ethics" (8 [9]). The former terms are associated, of course, with Anglo-American thinking, as in John Stuart Mill and William James, and behavior; the latter term *(Ethik)* seems, however, intended to preserve unquestioned the mystery of patriarchal privilege rather than to prescribe modes of communal and humane behavior. The lack of ontological depth that Worringer perceives in ancient Egypt leads that culture to exhibit a sort of opportunistic practical behavior he finds typical of American culture: "This highly elaborate technique of conventional good behavior also reminds us sociologically of America" (8 [9]). In effect, Worringer reduces Egyptian culture to a prototype of America as Disneyland, and all the values it has represented, in particular, to European observers. Worringer on Egypt, self-stylized as "the critical observer" (9 [10]), recalls Baudrillard's recent vision of America as a stylized chronicle of the observer's own preconceptions, though Worringer's misconceptions do not rely on a *familiar* stereotype, as do Baudrillard's.[11]

Baudrillard's *America* (1986) represents the now common mode of writing in postmodern discourse, commonly known as the "rhetorical sublime" or what Steven Connor calls the "postmodern stylistics of the sublime" (220),[12] which reveals some affinities to Expressionist scholarship and the German *Geistesgeschichte* of that period in general.[13] In his attempt to write a popular text with theoretical verve, Baudrillard's *America* constitutes a particularly felicitous (or egregious) example of some of the distinguishing traits of postmodern discourse: *America* is a self-consciously rhetorical embellishment of its object in terms of pathos-filled conceptual language that is mostly empty of concept. Rather than to demonstrate successive points in the development of a thesis, Baudrillard's evocation of his America seems designed, through non-sequitur riffs of rhetorical escalation, to induce awe before an unfathomable phenomenon that, indeed, for Baudrillard surpasses understanding: *"the mystery of American reality* exceeds our fictions and interpretations" (emphasis in original, 98 [96]).[14] If Worringer's depiction of Egypt and polemical swipes at America call to mind Disneyland in advance of the fact, Baudrillard finds in Disneyland the quintessence of all of Western culture: "If one considers that the whole of the Western world is hypostatized in America, the whole of America in California, and California in MGM and Disneyland, then this is the microcosm of the West" (55 [56]).[15] If Worringer derives the characteristics of ancient Egyptian culture from the necessities imposed by the desert, Baudrillard remarks that "American culture is heir to the deserts" (63 [63]).

Unlike Worringer, Baudrillard is not directly critical of America, but celebratory, yet his exaltations of American culture are willful and Romantic. Baudrillard appears in *America* as a sort of postmodern Chateaubriand creating (yet another) mythic landscape of the New World for French consumption. Like Worringer on Egypt-America, and betraying an equal debt to Nietzsche's Apollonian-Dionysian dichotomy, Baudrillard divides his America into two opposing traits: "growing abstractness" *(l'abstraction grandissante)* versus "a primary, visceral, uncoercible vitality" (7 [12]). Of course, the term "abstraction" recalls Worringer, who first gave the term wide currency in aesthetics, and underscores immediately the affinity between the two writers. Abstraction in Baudrillard's America reflects both "its technological refinement" (7 [12]), which produces its material artificiality but also, in the desert, a natural barrenness that defies that artificiality: "a mineralogy, a geology, a sidereality [or constellatedness], an inhuman facticity, an aridity that drives out the artificial scruples of culture, a silence that exists nowhere else" (6 [11]). Whereas Worringer retains his dichotomy but reverses the valorization of his terms, from his early *Abstraction and Empathy* (1908) to *Egyptian Art* (1927), Baudrillard seems, in his praise of America, to conflate, then sublate, the two. Baudrillard gives his Americans the positive, expressive qualities of Worringer's primitives from *Abstraction and Empathy* and also, positive qualities of Worringer's ancient Egyptian technocrats from *Egyptian Art*. That is, both aspects lead in *America* to a transcendent enigma.[16] For Baudrillard, America is not a real culture, but rather "an entire (un)culture" (8 [13]), whose sheer dimensions, on both sides of that dichotomy, catapult it into the realm of "hyperreality."

Like Worringer, Baudrillard's language, in sketching out his dichotomy, revolves around a limited set of terms and likewise, soon becomes mechanically periphrastic. For Baudrillard, as for Worringer, what allows that development into an artificial culture, or culture of simulacra, is detachment from original roots, its "lack of roots" *(déracinement)* (7 [12]). In a virtual echo of Worringer, Baudrillard describes America as *"the only remaining primitive society"* (emphasis in original, 7 [13]), both futuristic and primitive, at once an amazing amalgam, "of complexity, hybridity, and the greatest intermingling [*promiscuité*], of a ritualism that is ferocious but whose superficial diversity lends it beauty" (7 [13]), and a "miracle of obscenity that is genuinely American" (8 [13]). Yet America appears also as "the most conformist society that exists" (9 [14]) of "empty signs, functional gestures" (10 [15]) where "[e]verything . . . is real and pragmatic" (28 [32]). Here, we see a virtual reiteration of Worringer's terms, which culminates in the observation that a clash of burgeoning contradictions produces in America a "violent expressionism" (22 [26]).

Baudrillard's discussion turns upon the paradoxical coincidence of these apparently contrary characteristics, as in the following remark: "This country is naive, so you have to be naive. Everything here still bears the marks of a primitive society: technologies, the media, total simulation (bio-, socio-, stereo-, video-,) are developing in a wild state, in their original state" (63 [63]). Everywhere he looks in America, Baudrillard finds "the same mythical and analytical exaltation" (29 [32]). Baudrillard subsumes all aspects of American culture to his vision of roving cybernetic troglodytes; his dichotomy remains, necessarily, static and ahistorical, neither analytical or dialectical in assigning America a position as the endpoint of history: "the same paradox faces us today: *we shall never resolve the enigma of the relation between the negative foundations of greatness and that greatness itself.* America is powerful and original; America is violent and abominable. We should not try to deny either of these aspects, nor to reconcile them" (emphasis in original, 88 [87]). Baudrillard does not enter into the object of his description, but rather remains point-edly uncritical in order to elevate his vision.[17]

Thus, the allusion to Disneyland in discussing Worringer's *Egyptian Art* is, though anachronistic, not absurd. Founded in 1955 in California (DisneyWorld in Florida in 1971), Disneyland has come to appear as the *pars pro toto* of a ubiquitous and friendly American superficiality. As such, Disneyland captures the values that Worringer perceives in both ancient Egypt and modern America. In effect, Disneyland is a monument to the values that produced it as are the pyramids in Egypt. Briefly, Worringer regards the ancient Egyptian people as an "artificial people" *(Kunstvolk)* (8 [10]), incapable of depth of emotion, of neither vision nor tragedy. What he finds missing is "the mighty breathing of a deeper feeling for life" (8 [10]) because "the feeling for the ultimate tension of all being has been lost" (9 [10]). That ontological tension would produce apocalyptic visions of world demise *and* utopian renewal ("World-decline means world-renewal" 9; "Weltuntergang heißt Welterneuerung" [11]), both foreign to ancient Egyptian and modern American culture. In short, Worringer faults Egypt because he finds there no ancient Egyptian Expressionism! He criticizes both cultures for lacking the tortured ecstasies of Expressionism, or what he called in his *Form Problems in the Gothic* (1911) "sublime hysteria" *(erhabene Hysterie)*—whereas Baudrillard calls his America "an *hysterical* land" (Terre *hystérique*) (102 [100]).

Instead, for Worringer, the "Disneyland" cultures of modern America and ancient Egypt are organized around cheap "craving for sensation" (8 [10]) and "one-sided artificiality" (12 [14]) and are therefore hollow of any redemptive urges: "Egypt—in this again resembling America—has an outward history but not an inward" (9 [11]). Both cultures are essentially only a "superstructure [*Hochbau;* skyscraper] of artificial conventions . . . maintaining its formative impulse out of the rationality of institutions and not out of the irrationality and individuality of their exponents" (11 [14]). Each culture is in effect an edifice of empty conventions, artificial and not organic, and therefore, essentially a park like Disneyland; Worringer reminds us, with prescient anticipation of Disneyland, "that it is no accident that the modern idea of protected natural parks originated in America" (13 [16]).[18] Worringer finds in ancient Egypt and modern America the same paradoxically repulsive appeal in what he calls, anticipating Baudrillard, "the fascinating power of the senseless" (15 [18]). That "hyperreality" (to use Baudrillard's term) of advanced science and empty artifice makes ancient Egypt, like modern

America, into a "wonderland of ultimate, most secret wisdom" (16 [19]).

Such an orgy of senseless sensation combined with rational structure conceals an absence of both depth of reflection and higher yearning for transcendance. Even in matters of religion, elemental forces of pagan belief survive only as empty forms of ritual superstition void of immediate urgency and cut off from their original function. In terms recalling contemporary discussions of postmodernism, Worringer suggests that these empty forms are thus free to conjoin in counterfeit accretions: "Thus the whole resembles a syncretism" (14 [17]). In all aspects of life in Worringer's Disneyland-Egypt the same tendency obtains: "Primitive forces [*Urkräfte*] are domesticated" (15 [17]) with the same contemporary implication: "Here again we find everywhere in parentheses the word 'America'" (15 [18]). Worringer continues to return to the real object of his discourse and to what he considers the most immediate threat to Germany in the Weimar period; the ontological emptiness he decries and the hollow superstructure of material proliferation he perceives carry always the same signifier: the Egyptian people "absolutely no longer encompasses, in the stratum of its existence, the depths in which subterranean life-tensions find relief in metaphysical sadness. Once again the word America suggests itself" (20 [24]). Worringer's overwrought rhetoric, at times demagogic, focuses ultimately upon the central paradox, in his view, of ancient Egyptian and modern American culture: "that the highest sense of material culture could combine with the utmost senselessness of ideal culture" (16 [19]).

That paradox takes on visible form in the architectural monuments of each culture. Worringer reviews certain types of practical American architecture, such as industrial buildings, factories, and grain silos, to praise their "sureness and absoluteness of form" (23 [28]), yet since that quality does not arise out of inner conflicts, Worringer draws the conclusion: "To put it bluntly: the American power of formation is lack of imagination. For this reason its form is the highest form of objective rationality" (24 [28]). In Worringer's argument this objective rationality links American culture and architecture to ancient Egypt, where the same qualities are equally in evidence: "The characteristic which speaks out most clearly in it as a phenomenon in general is that naked, abstract absoluteness of the constructive spirit in its cold grandeur, its terse decidedness, its renunciation of every superfluous articulation" (24 [28]). Though he recognizes in these works an advanced stage of development, of its kind, the term "abstract" has now become pejorative, even derisory, of that kind, entirely the opposite of its earlier, famous usage. Here, in fact, Worringer equates what he calls "architectonic Americanism" with the "dictatorship of the abstract" *(Diktatur des Abstrakten)* (24 [29]), suggesting a threat and form of oppression imposed from without, implicitly of course, onto the post-Versailles "impotence" (15 [18]) of Weimar Germany.

Interestingly, however, Worringer's own earlier evocation of abstraction, which he now abjures, in both *Abstraction and Empathy* and in *Form Problems in the Gothic,* did in fact influence the actual development of German modernist architecture. As the architectural historian Reyner Banham has convincingly and fascinatingly demonstrated,[19] Walter Gropius's "close, perceptive and rather ingenious reading of *Abstraction and Empathy*" (204) allows him to derive from Worringer his ideas about the affinity between Egyptian architecture and American concrete industrial buildings. Although Europe had architects, such as Adolf Loos,[20] already at the work of stripping away ornament and tradition, American engineers of monumental industrial buildings exemplified an unselfconscious, modern-primitive "artistic volition" *(Kunstwollen).* The powerful aesthetic-expressive affect was not their design, though the buildings were na-ively designed by them for practical purposes. In a lecture of 1913 Gropius even cites for authority both Worringer and Riegl. Gropius's essay of the same year "The Development of Modern Industrial Architecture" ("Die Entwicklung moderner Industriebaukunst") appeared in the *Jahrbuch des deutschen Werkbundes* (1913) preceded without introduction by seven pages of photographs of grain elevators and factory buildings in North and South America. Banham notes that this essay and especially the photographs prepared for "the legitimization . . . of industrial forms as the basic vocabulary of modernism" (215). Worringer would have seen the images there as well. Through these photographs, Worringer was, so to speak, influenced, in turn, by his own influence on Gropius. With some of the images from Gropius's essay reprinted in his own book,[21] Worringer is then the first to execute a comparison between ancient Egyptian and modern American industrial architecture, though now in order to denounce those forms of Americanization in German architecture for which he, through Gropius, was largely responsible.

In sequence Worringer also reviews other forms of Egyptian art in order to demonstrate further that equation to American culture and he thereby engineers the full reversal of his terminology in *Abstraction and Empathy.* In works of low relief-wall sculpture Worringer notes that "no unrest born of depth finds its way into it. It is entirely without tension and conflict. The third dimension, the actual dimension of depth in experience, this dimension from which all that is more profound in the drama of artistic creation draws its inspiration, is not present at all as resistance in the artistic consciousness of the Egyptian" (25 [30]). The existential depth of anxiety and suffering that comprised the crux of his argument in *Abstraction and Empathy* is now a mere vacuity; the elimination of three-dimensional perspective in "primitive" art, which subdued anxiety and created abstraction, is now the object of his criticism. Instead of maintaining his original duality of terms, dividing the history of art into "naturalism" and "abstraction," or simply dismissing the duality as invalid, Worringer retains the terms but uses both to condemn Egyptian/American culture. In Egyptian art he now finds "combined in the absurdest manner two diametrically opposed artistic elements, or elements of form, namely the crudest naturalism and the ultimate degree of purely abstract formal logic" (26 [31]).

Worringer reverses himself in his understanding of abstraction, but maintains the structure of binary opposition in his argument in order now to apply both terms negatively to the cultures of ancient Egypt and modern America. Both are characterized by a "welding together of opposites" (29 [34]), a "twofold aspect [*Doppelgesicht*] of immediate nearness to nature and of abstraction as far removed as possible from nature" (30 [36]), and "hybrid intellectual character" *(geistige Zwitterhaftigkeit)* (31 [37]). That schizophrenic, hybrid character, with its condemnatory overtones in the word *Zwitter* of unnatural miscegenation and hermaphroditism or androgyny, indicates to Worringer an absence of organic, unified *Kultur*; the different manifestations of Egyptian art betray "not an evolution into an organic and integrated *interfusion* [*Ineinander*], but into a logically opaque *juxtaposition* [*Nebeneinander*]" (33 [39]). That juxtaposition of irreconcilables, that internal contradiction of an artificial culture, finds full expression in both the sphinx and the hieroglyph, whose renowned inscrutability Worringer pointedly dismisses as a product of the logical inconsistency in the culture as a whole.

The most representative instances of that perverse paradox are the monumental structures of stone in a landscape of sand. What Worringer calls the "petrified absoluteness" (30 [36]) of these structures contradicts the fleeting, shifting undulations of the surrounding sand to exert "the force of absolute contrast" (38 [47]), which for Worringer is the source of its spurious and unmediated visual power and the sign of the culture's failure. The breach between structure and environment reveals the inorganic and artificial nature of ancient Egyptian culture; in their disconnectedness to the terrain, Egyptian monuments only manifest the "dictate of a cold will to power" (38–39 [47]). Here Worringer adopts again the vocabulary of political domination in order to adumbrate his contemporary concerns about Germany in the decade after its defeat in World War I.

Worringer's Egypt lacks a middle dimension of organic cultural development and, instead, reveals two separate stages of development that contradict one another: "primitive atavism and the claims of civilized high culture" (39 [47]). The latter, as "dictate of a cold will to power," has been superimposed onto the former, highlighting the gap, the internal contradiction between the two. In fact, the latter negates the primordial mythic potential of the former, which in Egyptian culture figures only as a vestigial reminder of that culture's essential superficiality: "it is the primitive ideas of the monumental in architecture that are carried on from this myth-creating early age into the oasislike high culture of Egyptian life" (46 [56]). That refined Egyptian culture cannot do justice to its past, to which it has lost all inner relation, and which it thus can only preserve in its external forms.

The same disjunction from its mythic past could happen to Germany. Worringer's use of the pejoratively loaded term "civilized" (*zivilisatorisch*) calls to mind, for his readers, the French and their European Allies, who dictated the terms of postwar reparations and sought to impose European republican forms of governance onto German culture. Worringer's nationalistic argument emerges in the lessons he draws out of his tendentious (mis)representation of Egyptian culture:

> For this fact must be kept steadily in view—only a myth-creating people [*Volk*] is also capable of creating architecture in the grand sense. Colossal utilitarian architecture of great form may also come into existence in spheres of civilization poor in myths, but a trueborn and free monumental style can only grow up under the pressure of a tremendous idea dominating the whole of life. (46 [56]).

The monitory tone here is ominous, as is Worringer's appeal to *Volk* and his use of adjectives that have no meaning in an architectural context ("trueborn," "free"), but which in Weimar Germany would be a clear appeal to native Germans to reject foreign tutelage in democracy. The thought of "a tremendous idea dominating the whole of life" seems to anticipate the propagandistic fervor of Germanic mythmaking, and the "coordination" *(Gleichschaltung)* of policymaking for all aspects of life, under Nazi totalitarianism.

However, Egyptian monuments are only in part devoted to preserving that primordial past:

> But the gigantic character of Egyptian architecture as a phenomenon is not exclusively a mummification of the grandeur of early times, but is partly made up also of a craving for the colossal, of which the first symptoms are to be found in quite another direction. I am referring to what we designate sociologically as Americanism. . . . If this primitive, strongly rooted, colossal quality is a natural product of vital feeling at its highest tension, a tension finding organic relief in the utmost exertion of physical effort outwards, the late form of this quality is on the contrary a substitute [*Ersatzproduct*] for a tension of vital feeling which has been lost. Civilization without a great idea at its core [*inneren Großgedanken*] stupefies itself in a display of external greatness, and is supported in doing so by the mass-activity of existence under civilized conditions [*Massenbetrieb des zivilisatorischen Daseins*]. (47 [57])

Not only must Germany protect itself against the direct imposition of French *Zivilisation*, but also against the indirect, though more pernicious, encroachment of Americanization in the form of a "craving for the colossal." Whereas ancient Egypt had at least a "primitive, strongly rooted, colossal quality" to preserve, America does not; yet both ancient Egypt and modern America constitute a "late form" of cultures in decline, having lost or having never acquired the "tension of vital feeling" and "great idea" within necessary to produce real culture. Again, that ontological emptiness covers itself through external "display" characteristic of a mass society seeking to compensate through outward extension for its lack of intensity and inner cohesion.

As we have already seen, that extension is apparent in the similarity of monumental Egyptian and American industrial edifices. Yet that combination of inner emptiness and rigidity of form, the strict "linear framework of the sociological structure" (58), manifests itself throughout both cultures. With a military metaphor Worringer describes what occurred in ancient Egypt and, implicitly, what threatens to take place in Weimar Germany: "the unqualified victory, as regards construction, of the rationalism of civilization over all the attributes of natural growth" (50 [60]). Worringer's protostructuralist approach

finds the same symptomatic traits in all cultural forms from hiero-
glyphics to building complexes. In both he sees "the artificiality of
the orthogonal system" (50 [60]) alien to organic culture. Worringer
reads Egyptian hieroglyphs as architectural forms and reads Egyptian
architecture as hieroglyphs; in both he discovers "an emptiness of
ideas under material achievements of 'record' proportions" (48 [58])
that relates Egyptian to modern American culture and, typically, reveals itself in the distinct urban profile in both cultures.[22]
The modern city is the paragon instance of rational artificiality
triumphing over organic development, as in the New York grid plan
since 1811. Predictably, Worringer finds "artificial cities" (52 [62]) in
Egypt, that is, planned complexes built by pharaonic fiat in the desert;
the parallel of urban construction provides him with resounding and
conclusive evidence for his argument: "This fact must be given three-
fold emphasis, for the Americanism of this Egyptian high culture
could not possibly be demonstrated more clearly than by this proof
of the creation of ready-made artificial cities. It is a case of the city
not as a living entity of natural upgrowth, but as a constructed arte-
fact!" (52 [63]). Here, Worringer militates against Spengler's "attempt
to give profundity" *(Vertiefsinnlichung)* (55 [66]) to Egyptian architecture as a "'metaphysics in stone'" (55 [67]) and shows instead that
"the abstract schematism of this conventionalized mass-activity"
(Massenbetrieb) (58 [70]) has broken the organic, epic wholeness of
the culture, forcing the intimate and emotional "female" side of Egyptian life into a "world of its own apart" *(abgetrennte Sonderwelt)* (58
[70]), where it proliferates in artificial excesses, as in a hothouse.
Thus, opposite the colossality of "male" Egyptian schematism in the
city, Worringer sees an "entire atmosphere of lyricism due to the
most graceful refinement of taste, full of played-out dalliance, senti-
mentality, and pampered tender-heartedness" (59 [71]), and evokes,
as above, a whole series of traits associated, primarily, with French
Symbolism.[23] These traits, expressed in Egyptian wall reliefs, evoke
a world of "effete metropolitan overcultivation of luxury" (59 [71])
and "refinements of civilization" antithetic to healthy Germanic culture, in Worringer's eyes. His reiterations of the schizophrenic divi-
sions in ancient Egyptian culture culminate in his denunciation of
the metropolis as a center of decadence; the "world metropolis,"
anticipating Baudrillard, appears as a "hyper-civilization with all its
accompanying phenomena" (59 [72]). The metropolis is the point
where the fatal contradictions of the culture emerge most virulently:

Once again we are confronted with this juxtaposition, to us incomprehensible and abrupt, of the macroscopic and the microscopic, of massiveness and refinement, loud cubic tones and the whisper of bas-relief, of the sublimity of the desert and the delicacy of the oasis, the gigantic and the child-like. . . . [M]odern metropolitan culture [*Großstadtkultur*], the meaningless juxtapositions of which we have indeed long lost the habit of testing by the logic of artistic sensibility. (67–68 [81–82])

His descriptions of metropolitan life in ancient Egypt, and his vocabulary of denunciation, again carry ominous overtones. Three times he uses the word "degeneracy" *(Entartung)* to describe the arts, the science, and the civilization of ancient Egypt.[24]

In the above quotation, talking about ancient Egypt and talking about modern America, Worringer invokes the same principle of juxtaposition and parataxis *(Nebeneinander)* by which he had characterized abstract art ("primitive" and modern) in his *Abstraction and Empathy.* Then, the disjunctions of juxtaposition signaled both the individual's existential discomfort in the world *and* a straining to get beyond the natural world to higher truth; the interstices of juxtaposition or *Nebeneinander* were abrupt openings of transcendent longing, for which a whole generation of Expressionist artists felt sympathy and solidarity. Now, in his *Egyptian Art* (1927), Worringer reviews at once two cultures and, assuming consensus and complicity among his readers, finds in both "to *us* incomprehensible and abrupt juxtapositions" (my emphasis) concentrated in the modern metropolis, "the meaningless juxtapositions of which *we* have indeed long lost the habit of testing by the logic of artistic sensibility" (my emphasis). Unlike in his early works, Worringer now writes for a conservative consensus and has turned full circle in the trajectory of his career; he now finds in those interstices of *Nebeneinander* the fault lines of these cultures and the sure signs of their "degeneracy."

In conclusion, Worringer's text about ancient Egyptian art, outside his areas of expertise, is dominated by anxieties that were common in the cultural establishment of Weimar Germany: the loss of essential German cultural identity to French *Zivilisation* after the Treaty of Versailles, and to forms of American rationalization in industry and metropolitan life; the military "impotence" of Germany, reflected on the home front in the rise of literary culture, both in general and in particular in government ("not the soldier, but the writer"); and the threat to patriarchal traditions by the rise of women's rights and the androgyny of Weimar fashions. These multiple anxieties emerge in his comparison between ancient Egyptian and modern American culture. Further, my comparison of Worringer's America to Baudrillard's *America* suggests an affinity between Worringer's Expressionist mode of scholarship (even after Expressionism) and contemporary modes of theoretical discourse; it suggests as well the troubling nature of ecstatic *Geistesgeschichte*, then and now, that submits its putative object to the force of personal vision, or collective ideology.

NOTES

1. See the Bibliography to this volume for editions in the original and translation. As a convenience to the reader, I refer to the published translations, when they exist, though in all cases, I have made alterations, in some cases substantial, where I felt them necessary. The page number in the German edition follows in brackets. In the English edition, the subtitle of that work, *Problems in its Evaluation (Probleme ihrer Wertung)*, has been dropped. For quotations from Worringer's essays, when no published translations exist, translations are my own.

2. This term refers to the "intellectual history" approach prevalent in German scholarship at the time.

3. Compare his programmatic statement on method in his introduction to *Formprobleme der Gotik* (Munich: Piper, 1911). There he advocates attempts to grasp intuitively the "inner preconditions of bygone ages" (1 [1]) through what he calls the historian's "faculty for divination" (2 [2]). This intuitive, hypothetical method requires also, however, a system, "an ideal auxiliary construction of purely antithetical application" (2 [3]); that dialectical system "as an heuristic principle is the nearest approach to a possible overcoming of historical realism and its pretentious shortsightedness" (3 [3]). By 1927 that confident intuitive freedom from historical objectivity, that Expressionist headiness, had devolved into mere tendentiousness.

4. Worringer's essays are collected in *Fragen und Gegenfragen: Schriften zum Kunstproblem* (Munich: Piper, 1956). In his 1921 essay "Questions about Contemporary Art," Worringer in fact maintains that Expressionism has not died away, as Georg Lukács would have it, but has simply found a new medium commensurate with an age when art itself no longer has expressive validity and only manages to subsist on the margins of society; for Worringer, that new medium is scholarship, works of historical inquiry: "And this sensuous refinement of perception in our historical and scholarly forms of inquiry and interpretation creates a new atmosphere in our intellectual life. Art has not been replaced by scholarship, no, scholarship has begun itself to become an art and to work with artistic élan" (124).

5. Walter Laqueur, *Weimar: A Cultural History* (New York: G. P. Putnam's Sons, 1974), notes that the surprisingly strong economic recovery in Germany after the Great Inflation in 1923 "was made possible by the existence of a skilled labour force unique in Europe and by the adoption of modern (American) production methods; 'rationalization' became the great slogan of the 1920s. . . . Above all the expansion was the result of foreign capital, first and foremost from America" (22–23). This is important to keep in mind when reading Worringer's *Egyptian Art* in order to hear the inflammatory resonance of his

vocabulary, and the whole set of traits he associates with American "rationalization." Also, Fritz K. Ringer's *The Decline of the German Mandarins: The German Academic Community, 1890–1933* (Cambridge: Harvard University Press, 1969) documents the acute effects of these general conditions on academics. While their status in society did not change, inflation undermined their ability to live up to that status and thus gave academics "the air of a superseded ruling class, and it inevitably increased their dissatisfaction with their modern environment" (63).

6. See Geoffrey Perkins, *Contemporary Theory of Expressionism* (Frankfurt am Main: Herbert Lang, 1974), esp. chap. 1, "The Background to Theories of Expressionism." See also Ron Manheim, *"Im Kampf um die Kunst: Die Diskussion von 1911 über zeitgenössische Kunst in Deutschland* (Hamburg: Verlag der Buchhandlung Sautter–Lackmann, 1987).

7. See Nigel Hamilton, *The Brothers Mann: The Lives of Heinrich and Thomas Mann, 1871–1950 and 1875–1955* (New Haven: Yale University Press, 1979), and Stanley Corngold's essay "Mann as a Reader of Nietzsche" in his *The Fate of the Self: German Writers and French Theory* (New York: Columbia University Press, 1986), 129–59.

8. Later in his study, Worringer even rejects explicitly his earlier position: "It would be untrue to claim for the Egyptian, as the author himself has done on a former occasion, a feeling for 'the awe-inspiring nature of the cubic,' and to assume that he overcame it by giving a geometrical form to his planes. This would be to introduce into the Egyptian's feeling for life a dramatic element utterly at variance with our present sober conception" (70 [84]). He continues his explicit refutation of that earlier position with a long summary and dismissal (81–88 [97–106]) of "anti-space metaphysic . . . dramatized and glorified." Instead, he now asserts that "[t]he Egyptian therefore was not hostile, but neutral and indifferent to space" (88 [105]).

9. An exemplary instance of the male perception that the advancement of women subverts patriarchal Wilhelminian culture, and a histrionic display of male fears, can be found in the small, odd essay by Worringer that appeared untitled in *Zeit-Echo: Ein Kriegs-Tagebuch der Künstler* in 1914. There he announces that "[t]his war has become, beyond all question to the contrary about races [i.e., French or German] and nations, something much more terrible: a sort of battle between the two different sexes" (20). Worringer provides no explanation of context for his remarks and it is difficult to imagine what would bring him or anyone to such a conclusion. Worringer seems to equate the Allied opposition to Germany with what he perceives as female hysteria (*weibliche Hysterie,* 20). Interestingly, he uses the latter term in a very pejorative sense, entirely in contrast to his use of "sublime hysteria" *(erhabene Hysterie)* to describe the Germanic, Gothic sensibility in Gothic (and therefore Expressionist) art. He even subordinates the war and military victory to the certain inevitable loss to be endured vis-à-vis the opposite sex, which guarantees male impotency: "We will sit there, like the male characters of Strindberg, when the battle has been fought and they [the men] to all appearances control the field [of battle], we will sit there with a laugh distorted by secret disgust and a feeling of impotency that slowly sucks away all [the feeling of] triumph in victory" (20). The impotence is both political and sexual, as in the remarkable and grotesque last line. He then blames neutral Germanic countries for their treason of German manliness! This frightening little essay is followed on the last page by a woodcut of a firing squad firing at writhing, unarmed figures standing blindfolded before a wall.

I wish to thank Peter W. Guenther of the University of Houston for calling this article to my attention; Professor Guenther found the article at the Robert Gore Rifkind Center for German Expressionist Studies at the Los Angeles County Museum of Art. Hofstra University also has issues of *Zeit-Echo* in its Weingrow Collection of Avant-Garde Art and Literature.

10. Interesting work on the position of women in the shaping of Weimar culture has been done in film studies, beginning with Emilie Altenloh's dissertation, *Zur Soziologie des Kino: Die Kino-Unternehmung und die sozialen Schichten ihrer Besucher* (Jena: Eugen Diederichs, 1914). Recently, Patrice Petro's study *Joyless Streets: Women and Melodramatic Representation in Weimar Germany* (Princeton: Princeton University Press, 1989) has illuminated the contours of female identity in the forms and formation of mass culture in Weimar Germany:

> The high percentage of women in early film audiences was in fact perceived as an alarming social phenomenon, one which confirmed the breakdown of traditional values elsewhere evidenced by the declining birthrate, the rising marriage age, and the influx of women into the industrial labor force. The presence of a female audience, in other words, not only represented a threat to traditional divisions between public and private, cultural and domestic spheres; it represented a threat to the maintenance of social legitimacy, to the distinctions preserving traditionally defined male and female gender roles and responsibilities. (8)

See also the essay by Atina Grossmann, "The New Woman and the Rationalization of Sexuality in Weimar Germany," in *Powers of Desire: The Politics of Sexuality,* ed. Ann Snitow, Christine Stansell, Sharon Thompson (New York: Monthly Review Press, 1983); as well as the collection edited by Atina Grossman, Renate Bridenthal, and Marion Kaplan, *When Biology Became Destiny: Women in Weimar and Nazi Germany* (New York: Monthly Review Press, 1984). Also, Claudia Koonz, *Mothers in the Fatherland: Women, the Family and Nazi Politics* (New York: St. Martin's Press, 1987), chap. 2, "Weimar Emancipation"; and Ute Frevert, *Frauen-Geschichte zwischen Bürgerlicher Verbesserung und Neuer Weiblichkeit* (Frankfurt: Suhrkamp, 1986); English translation (New York: Berg, 1988), esp. part 3, chap. 14.

11. Jean Baudrillard, *Amérique* (Paris: Grasset, 1986); American edition, *America,* trans. Chris Turner (London: Verso, 1988). Page references to the original edition are given in brackets. Where necessary, I have made alterations to the translation.

12. Steven Conner, *Postmodernist Culture: An Introduction to Theories of the Contemporary* (Oxford: Oxford University Press, 1989).

13. In Andreas Huyssen's excellent essay on Baudrillard's rewriting of McLuhan, "In the Shadow of McLuhan: Jean Baudrillard's Theory of Simulation," *Assemblage: A Critical Journal of Architecture and Design Culture* 10 (1989), 7–17, he notes in McLuhan also "a large-scale historical periodization of cultural stages, . . . (that) . . . results in a kind of technological *Geistesgeschichte,* a pattern that will reappear in Baudrillard" (12). Huyssen finds in Baudrillard "a binary reversal of McLuhan, but McLuhan nevertheless" (15). Though it is uncertain that Baudrillard might know Worringer's work directly, he has done translations from German and is familiar with German traditions, and one can at least speculate on the migration of ideas from Worringer to Baudrillard through Wyndham Lewis and Marshall McLuhan. Lewis knew Worringer's work from his days in Munich and through T. E. Hulme. In his biography of Lewis, *Wyndham Lewis: A Portrait of the Artist as Enemy* (New Haven, Yale University Press, 1957), Geoffrey A. Wagner notes that "in his dislike of art and life Lewis is closer to the German aestheticians, and particularly Wilhelm Worringer" (110) and remarks that Worringer's "reduction of chaotic 'life' to the deathlike stillness of artistic (or real) life, is most important to Vorticism" (111). After the Second World War, Lewis stayed in Toronto (see his novel *Self-Condemned,* 1954), where McLuhan become his acolyte and advocate. In this context, see also Jost

Hermand, *Literaturwissenschaft und Kunstwissenschaft* (Stuttgart: Metzler, 1965), especially 28–29, "Seelischer Universalismus."

14. Franz Kafka, *Amerika* (Frankfurt am Main: Fischer, 1983). One is tempted to recall Kafka's Karl Roßmann's similar awe and the irony of his uncle's trenchant understatement, both confirming Karl's impression and deflating his naive sense of wonder:

> 'Das grenzt ja ans Wunderbare', sagte Karl.
> 'Alle Entwicklungen gehen hier so schnell vor sich', sagte der Onkel, das Gespräch abbrechend. (45)

15. Douglas Kellner, *Jean Baudrillard: From Marxism to Postmodernism and Beyond* (Stanford: Stanford University Press, 1989). His critique of Baudrillard issues in a critique of idealism of all sorts, and offers an important critical insight into Baudrillard's *Amérique* that inverts Baudrillard's use of Disneyland as metonymy of the United States and its culture:

> My analysis has suggested that metaphysics is a supremely projective imaginary, in which the metaphysician projects his or her imaginary on the world, interpreting the world in terms of its *subjective* categories, fantasies, hopes and fears. Baudrillard arguably does the same thing, projecting his subjectivity on the object itself, ascribing his own privileged subjective experiences to the being of the object world itself in a typical imaginary of idealism. On this reading, Baudrillard comes off as the Walt Disney of contemporary metaphysics, anthropomorphizing objects in imaginary (ideological) projection in the same way in which Disney anthropomorphized animals and things, thereby turning animals and the object into the simulacra of small-town America as envisaged in his conservative imaginary. Baudrillard's metaphysical world, however, is more malefic than Disneyland, for its objects seduce and revenge themselves on hapless objects. (179)

Though I would hesitate to make Baudrillard representative of all philosophical idealism, which elsewhere can attain at least a greater degree of intellectual rigor, Kellner's critique captures Baudrillard's own willingness to subordinate, even eliminate, history and careful perception of the world, to a private vision for popular consumption. I prefer Huyssen's characterization of that *Weltanschauung*, which Baudrillard adopted from McLuhan, as a "media theology" (12), though again of course, Baudrillard glorifies the demonic aspects of the media, unlike McLuhan.

16. Baudrillard, like Worringer, is much indebted to Hegel, though the influence of Hegel on Baudrillard passes over Georg Bataille and his understanding of Alexandre Kojève's Hegel. Baudrillard's thought retains the contours of Hegelian dialectic, but the hyperbolic excesses of his discourse, which annul the third term of that dialectic, attempt to enact Bataille's notion of *dépense* (derived in turn from Marcel Mauss) as symbolic expenditure and transgression. In a discussion of Jacques Derrida, "U-topian Hegel: Dialectic and Its Other in Poststructuralism," *German Quarterly* 60, no. 2 (1987), 237–61, John Smith gives an excellent account of how Hegel figures generally in post-Structuralist discourses; his comment that "the self-conscious post-Hegelian, when searching for a mode of writing other than the Hegelian dialectic, is caught in the uncomfortable position of always having to sink or swim with Hegel's rhetorical tide" (252) applies equally to Baudrillard. Yet the tradition of philosophical anthropology in France, not dealt with by Smith, provides, if not fully an escape from Hegelianism, at least an added dimension with a different genealogy. See also Julian Pefanis, *Heterology and the Postmodern: Bataille, Baudrillard, and*

Lyotard (Durham: Duke University Press, 1991), here 1–81, and Denis Hollier's study, *Against Architecture: The Writings of Georges Bataille* (Cambridge: MIT Press, 1989), originally *La Prise de la Concorde* (Paris: Editions Gallimard, 1974), which treats at length his relation to Hegel.

17. A welcome tonic to Baudrillard's overblown desert hallucinations is a work by Reyner Banham, who figures more prominently in this discussion in another context (see page 144). His *Scenes of America Deserta* (Cambridge: MIT Press, 1982) is a sensitive exploration of desert landscapes, casual and understated in tone, focusing on tangible details of terrain, human structures and the foibles of human perception, including his own. In stark contrast to Baudrillard, Banham is wary of the inevitable tendency to impose the values of one's own cultural training on the apparent semantic emptiness of the desert. Likewise, again in contrast to Baudrillard, he remains conscious of the limits of language to capture the enormity of desert impressions. His repeated use of the word "sheer" marks that limit, and consequently, through careful diction, his respectful and credible evocations of what he sees attain both a subtle lyricism and a real intensity of heartfelt appreciation—as opposed to the hype of rhetorical self-indulgence in Baudrillard. Banham's unpretentious account is rich in insights; especially instructive in this context are his discussions of Gaston Bachelard and Vincent Scully, but one example will have to suffice:

> My transcontinental co-driver, as the Interstate finally fell off the edge of the infinitely tedious Texas panhandle into the first huge vista of the promise of New Mexico, asked:
> "May I say something?"
> "Sure."
> "Wow!"
> "Is that it?"
> "Enough, innit?"
> Said with emotion it is indeed enough and it avoids the entangling rhetorics of more literary attempts to give articulate form to a response that seems to come from deep in the interior of one's being, and to come without warning. (66)

18. See also Stephen Greenblatt's discussion of American "National Parks" in his essay "Towards a Poetics of Culture," in *The New Historicism*, ed. H. Aram Veeser (New York: Routledge, 1989), 1–14, here 8–10.

19. Reyner Banham, *A Concrete Atlantis: U.S. Industrial Building and European Modern Architecture, 1900–1925* (Cambridge: MIT Press, 1986). I wish to thank my colleague at Hofstra University, Joseph Masheck, for pointing out this book and this author to me. His own discussion of Banham's book is in his *Modernities*, 55–61.

20. In contrast to the traditional view of him as simply a "fanatical purist" (98), Miriam Gusevich, in "Decoration and Decorum: Adolf Loos's Critique of Kitsch," *New German Critique* 43 (1988), 97–123, gives a more differentiated understanding of Loos's complexity.

21. Le Corbusier in his *Vers Une Architecture* (Paris: Editions Crés, 1923) also includes some of the images from Gropius's publication and as Banham notes "conspicuously ignores the achievements of the European concrete tradition" (216) of Auguste Perret, Hennebique, and Freyssinet (whom he does briefly mention) in preference for the now well-established myth of American industrial builders as noble American savages.

22. Here Worringer cuts a tangent with the work of Siegfried Kracauer. Worringer reads ancient Egyptian hieroglyphs as a metonym for the whole culture in all its forms; Kracauer reads the city of Berlin as a hieroglyph, as a metaphor for a decipherable text that will reveal the inner workings of its society. The different aspects of the city will, with difficulty,

reveal their significance about that society. Whereas Worringer cites actual Egyptian hieroglyphs, negates their mystery and forecloses further inquiry, offering them merely as proof of his tendentious comparison, Kracauer uses the hieroglyph as a metaphor for a *process of critical decipherment*: "Die Raumbilder sind die Träume der Gesellschaft. Wo immer die Hieroglyphe irgendeines Raumbildes entziffert ist, dort bietet sich der Grund der sozialen Wirklichkeit dar" (from *Über Arbeitsnachweise,* quoted in Inka Mülder's *Siegfried Kracauer—Grenzgänger zwischen Theorie und Literatur: Seine frühen Schriften, 1913–1933* [Stuttgart: Metzler, 1985], especially "Oberflächenanalyse," 86–95; the quotation is on 88).

23. For a catalogue of these traits, see Wolfdietrich Rasch, *Die literatische Décadence um 1900* (Munich: Beck, 1986), and my review in *Germanic Review* 63, no. 2 (1988), 111–12.

24. The word "Entartung" simultaneously refers back to Max Nordau's 1895 text of that name, which gave the term currency, and of course to National Socialist ideology and its exhibit of so-called degenerate art in 1937. Worringer remained in Germany during the Nazi period, but apparently did not publish. Heinrich Dilly makes no mention of him in his study, *Deutsche Kunsthistoriker, 1933–45* (Munich: Deutscher Kunstverlag, 1988). Although his use of this term, and the general tenor of his study of Egyptian art, would suggest a later allegiance to Nazism, I hesitate to draw that conclusion in this serious matter without knowing further details of his activities and attitudes during that period.

8

After Worringerian Virtual Reality: Videodromes and Cinema 3, MassCult and CyberWar*

Geoffrey C. W. Waite

> The little beginning of little academic conflicts is a great beginning, for after it—if not today then tomorrow, if not tomorrow then the day after—will follow big continuations.
>
> —Lenin[1]

> Therefore, we may never, while we are concerned with inquiries into actual things, draw any conclusion from abstractions; we shall be extremely careful not to confound that which is only in the understanding with that which is in the thing itself *(in re)*.
>
> —Spinoza[2]

> Hallucinations are also facts.
>
> —Althusser[3]

ON RELEVANCE: SOME METHODOLOGICAL PRECAUTIONS

Do "little academic conflicts"—such as about Worringer, yesterday and today—*really* promise "big continuations" in the near or distant

*I am grateful to Neil H. Donahue for causing me to rethink Worringer and particularly grateful to Nora M. Alter for her meticulous comments on this essay, which is dedicated to her.

future, as Lenin suggested in 1908, the same year Worringer published his most influential text?

From the perspective of Worringer, were he still alive, current technologies such as virtual reality and cyberspace, along with their technocultural and technosocial realizations, would likely confirm his sense of the periodic, historical priority of "abstraction" over "empathy," and might well appear to confirm, too, the way supposedly transhistorical forces of abstraction (such as Gothic or Egyptian "forms") mysteriously manage to insinuate themselves, realize themselves again and again in specific historical periods in specific regions, nations, national and aesthetic identities. Alternatively, from the perspective of virtual reality and cyberspace, as it were, Worringer's key terms would indeed appear relevant, even though he did not significantly or directly influence current techologies. But both these perspectives of "Worringerian virtual reality" (that of "Worringer on virtual reality" and that of "virtual reality on Worringer"), along with the underlying assumptions informing each, need to be looked at carefully and critically.

Of course, simply by asking whether something is relevant, automatically and surreptitiously makes it relevant, makes it influential. To this extent at least, questions of influence and relevance are self-fulfilling prophecies. Just by (re)posing the question of Worringer's relevance—by "predicting" in this way—one ensures (however modestly) that Worringer is still relevant and will be so tomorrow, perhaps more so than before. Such proleptic discursive acts are never innocent. "Anybody who makes a prediction," Antonio Gramsci wrote, "has in fact a 'programme' for whose victory he is working, and his prediction is precisely an element contributing to that victory."[4] The next big question is why and to what purpose any topic enters (no matter in how mediated or implicit a fashion) into the current mode of production and reproduction of a given social formation. In our case here—in this book and this essay—the topic is Wilhelm Worringer in the midst of global neo-capitalism, at its moment of swaggering self-proclaimed triumph over all alternative possibilities—a neo-capitalist world order characterized by a transitional-information-technology and by a postindustrial, post-Fordist, postunionized, anticommunism.[5] In comparison to the global social and historical scheme of things, Worringer is *irrelevant simply.* My essay here starts not inside the Worringerian corpus but on the outside, in that global scheme of things, not because this maneuver is sufficient to grasp Worringer but because it is necessary to grasp his current influence. (After all, what is worse: never having read Worringer or reading him too much?) "The problem of all philosophical (and political and military) problems," wrote Althusser in 1976, is "to know how to exit from a circle while remaining within it."[6]

Certainly the question of relevance not only conceals tacit epistemological and linguistic presuppositions, which to some extent are a matter of *philosophia perennis,* but it also has to do with history. Worringer's fortunes have changed dramatically over time, apparently, so it is well to be alert to the possibility of a more radical change in them recently—especially alert in this, the first collection on him ever in any language. In a moment we need to return to the likelihood that a major change in the reception of Worringer *has* taken place, and to what this might mean.

Like his rather complex legacy, Worringer's own historical position on any simple ideological spectrum arranged from "Left" to "Right" is—or ought to be—a matter of continuing debate, especially on occasions where his significance is simply assumed or unselfconsciously (re)produced. But it is equally important to insist that such debates (which, as a type of "difference-engine," typically turn out to conceal an unacknowledged consensus about other equally or even more important matters under the guise of pluralistic difference)[7] require continual contextualization and reinscription in larger theoretical, political, and economic narratives and matrices—many of which have almost nothing to do with academic discourse in the narrow sense, and which surpass any mode of discourse limited to written texts alone, and certainly to those by single authors. Most current individual and collective scholarship on Worringer remains locked in a dual-problematic of art history and historicism (meaning precisely that one does buy into the undertheorized and uncriticized desire to write about Worringer without asking if, how, and why it is relevant to do so). For this reason, it is especially important to insist that it is legitimate to reflect on Worringer in historical terms—indeed to study history itself—only on condition that such reflection and study leads us to *contest the present:* for example, by letting us see that if something comes to be, it can also pass away and return; and that significant alternatives exist—at least in the past—to business as usual, *Germanistik* as usual, art history as usual, politics as usual, history as usual.

Good history, like good art, good science, good criticism, and good theory, is about perspectives, possibilities, alternatives. Even art historians (at least Panofsky) have understood that, while "we understandably think of perspective as a device of only the two-dimensional arts," nonetheless "this new way of seeing—or, rather, of designing with reference to the very process of sight—was bound to change the other arts as well."[8] But not merely other arts. It is the totalizing aspect of virtual reality and cyberspace, including their explicitly tactical and strategic uses by the military-industrial complex, that may pose the greatest challenge to date to alternatives to neo-capitalist domination and hegemony. Be this as it may, if Worringer and debate about his work are going to be of any immediate relevance in the context of the current or impending "defeat" of "socialism" and "victory" of neo-capitalism (also known as the *pax americana*), then attention must be turned not merely to art criticism or even "interdisciplinary work" and "cultural studies" (all of which turned back on themselves are hopelessly anachronistic terms and pursuits)[9] but also toward what is—in effect, if not fact—a "Worringerian" theory and practice of that *virtual reality,* which is increasingly what is left of "art" and "art history" and "architectural" theory and practice. But this means also turning toward those military-industrial manifestations of virtual reality which inform mass culture and recent technologies of warfare: this is to say, culture and war directed not only *externally* against remaining (to some extent growing) pockets of global resistance to neo-capital but also *internally* in the struggle for still-resisting hearts and minds within the belly of the beast. *This* aspect of Worringer's "influence" and "relevance" involves a huge call to arms, obviously, and only a noncommunist would ever dream that it could be adequately formulated let alone answered by one person alone. In any case, the best *this* communist can do is to make a rather abstract start, I hope, along with some empathetic readers.[10]

The Worringer Industry, such as it is or has been up to now, has achieved a workable but, from my perspective, largely unquestioned consensus about what Worringer's texts mean and what their significance is in terms of art history and theory. Basically, this significance turns out to be remarkably homogenous and often rather boring in spite of its apparent vitality. Architecture and historians of architecture along with film and film theorists represent a somewhat exceptional case, as we shall be seeing shortly. But the problem is that the more contemporary questions of Worringer's "influence" and "relevancy" have little or nothing to do with art or art criticism as they are conventionally conceived, though they have a lot to do with them as they *might* be conceived, theorized, and even put to work for good or ill. This is not to deny that Worringer continues to influence certain painters, art historians, and literary critics (as he has long done) or that he does so in a way that remains at root (with a few notable exceptions) embarrassingly uncritical and affirmative. My point is only that what we have now in terms of Worringer's most interesting and profound "influence" and "relevance" no longer has much significant to do with literary criticism, painters, art historians and theorists, and so forth.

In the remainder of this essay, I argue that the real influence and relevance of "Worringer" today is bipartite; and it is this that we must get "after"—in the combative as well as temporal sense of the word. The first is an almost entirely indirect, implicit, unconscious "influence" on mass culture or what might be termed *MassCult*. The second is an equally ignored impact on theories of modern warfare, including what is now widely called *CyberWar*. By contrast with the first current sphere of "relevance," this second one is remarkably direct and explicit, especially in light of the multiple additional determinations of it and of what is at stake globally. The battle for the hearts and minds of at least some intellectuals in the recently enormously expanded domain of advanced capitalist society (in which New Social work has significantly supplemented though not yet entirely displaced systems of Fordist and even neo-Fordist production)[11] is taking place in part—symbolically and even actually—in the two Videodromes and in the interstices between them. At least in the West.[12] If Worringer really was—or can be seen as—a protocyberpunk warrior, what might this mean for his work, for its reception (including the volume and essay at hand), and for the unacknowledged consensus, the prison-house, the difference-engine that is contemporary critical discourse? What matters most in this essay, in any case, are the implications of Worringerian theories for postmodern conceptions of warfare. Nonetheless, MassCult—as it manifests itself as film and film theory *explicitly* with reference to Worringer—provides a convenient transition from the movie theater to the theater of war—precisely the two theaters articulated historically and theoretically by Virilio in *War and Cinema*.[13] (It is necessary from now on to understand Worringer's name always in scare quotes—as "Worringer"—in order to register the need to grasp the *implicit* as well as *explicit* nature of Worringerian virtual reality.)

Basically and generally, as I have intimated, the question of Worringer's relevance today is the question of virtual reality: that is, a type or facet of reality in which the very distinction between what is implicit to the point of irreality and explicit to the point of brute fact becomes exceedingly difficult to determine, may even be obviated sooner or later for all practical and theoretical purposes. Two points of more or less fluid articulation between implicit (MassCult) and explicit (CyberWar) relevance, and between the more real and the more virtual, are provided by architecture and architectural theory, film and film theory—as theories and practices of space and time grasped within primarily spatial and temporal problematics respectively. Henri Lefebvre's great dictum that *"The space of a (social) order is hidden in the order of space"*[14]—and into which "time" can be substituted mutatis mutandis for "space"—demands to be taken seriously: in this context, that is, in tandem with and against Worringer's own theories, say, of "abstract" versus "empathic" space and of "Gothic" or "Egyptian" form; and in tandem, too, with and against his not insubstantial influence on "our" understanding of time and space, of points, surfaces, planes—concepts that for all their apparent increasing abstraction still remain remarkably dependent on . . . empathy.

VIRTUAL REALITY (VR)

It is a vast thing, beyond knowledge, a sea of [abstract] information that only the body, in its strong blind way, could ever read [ever empathize with].

—Gibson[15]

It was a place shunned as a rule, and the country all round was so arid and desolate that there were no residents near it. As it was kept for State use, and might be serviceable in time of war, it was closed with massive iron doors, which were kept locked except upon certain occasions.

—Stoker[16]

Unexpectedly, this country is pleasant, yes, once inside it, quite pleasant after all. Even though there is a villain here, serious as death.

—Pynchon[17]

"Testing bounds of reality," as the mass media for the moment have it. "The capacity to redefine radically the relation between fiction and reality," or so we are being informed. Videoplace: a corner of the Connecticut Museum of Natural History, defined by its inventor-curator as a site (in the provinces) where "visitors can play 'Light up the Town,' shading in the night sky above New York with the wave of a hand." Artificial reality: "an experience in which the computer perceives the movement of your body, interprets it in terms of a graphic world and then displays it to your senses." Architects do walk-throughs of unbuilt buildings or, if the spirit moves them, unbuildable buildings. Or just go to the Matsushita storefront in Tokyo where the cutting edge of consumer capitalism is buying kitchen equipment wearing VPL datasuits and feeling as if in a model kitchen, but one that can be transformed by voice activation to suit your tastes and credit line—rearrange the appliances and lighting, even the walls, ceilings, and so on. Brain surgeons perform computer-simulated operations feeling the warmth of the pineal eye, the weight of the laser scalpel. Mattel Toy Corp.'s Power Glove: a prosthesis to translate hand movements into electronic signals that "control" Nintendo games. Eyephones, datagloves, datahelmets, datasuits. Have teledildonic sex (good sex, bad sex, any sex) with the Lacanian *objet petit a*" of your choice: "smart skin," "embracing technology," "cyberdermis fucksuits." And withal comparatively easy to clean.[18]

The cockpit of a stealth bomber or a high-tech Abrams tank. "VR is not a passive medium," Jaron Lanier of VPL Research in Redwood City, California, explains, "it's a world in which you do things, a tool you're using to accomplish something." What, for instance? To penetrate deep into countries beneath their radar-shield, then pull up before the very real aftershock catches up to you, snatches you back to incinerate you.

> With the supersonic vector (airplane, rocket, airwaves), penetration and destruction are one. The instantaneousness of action at a distance corresponds to the defeat of the unprepared adversary, but also, and especially, to the defeat of the world as field, as distance, as matter. Immediate penetration, or penetration that is approaching immediacy, becomes identified with the instantaneous destruction of environmental conditions, since after *space-distance,* we now lack *time-distance* in the increasing acceleration of vehicular performances (precision, distance, speed).[19]

Abstraction with the illusion of reality, its absolute simulacrum: all different, yet the same; all the same, yet different. Accident-free—in theory. "Jacked into a custom cyberspace deck that projects your disembodied consciousness into the consensual hallucination that was the matrix."[20] Consensual hallucination. . . . But, as Donna Haraway (author of *A Cyborg Manifesto*) is still able to note: "Politics rests on the possibility of a shared world. Flat out."[21] Dare one say any longer: "An *empathic* world. Flat out"?

With what the architect and theoretician of film and warfare Paul Virilio calls "the lost dimension," which encompasses a certain disappearance of both time and space, distance disappears also; and, as distance shrinks, the ability to compare anything (say, VR to an alternative reality) recedes into the past.[22] While this loss may not be *qualitatively* different from certain experiences of previous eras mutatis mutandis, there does appear today to be a *quantitative* increase in the sheer velocity with which space and time are compressed.[23] This apparent reduction of "empathic" distances themselves to "abstractions" (due in part to technological advances like fiberoptics and so on) is related to a shift in perception that the Japanese critic Takayuki Tatsumi (with reference to the cyberpunk novels of Gibson) has called "the postmodernist paradox" ("East" and "West" alike): namely, *the perceiver literally becomes the perceived.*"[24] In this regard, "abstraction" and "empathy" become functions of time as well as space, both of which are threatening to reach some sort of conceptual if not also material threshold. But, again, a basic question to pose is how "new" all these developments really are and whether we require novel periodizations to describe them.[25] For example, in the philosophical terms of Spinoza in the seventeenth century, as well as David Cronenberg's filmic ones in the late twentieth, the human body is also transformed by the very act of imaging an external body.[26] Indeed, in Spinozism, "The images of things are modifications of the human body."[27] Think now of the Videodromes and Interzones, mind-body interfaces, interchanges, viral communications, metamorphoses, mutations, omnisexuality, bio-psycho-hardwiring, psychoplasmic metaphysics, and implicit monism in those Cronenbergian films that are about nothing if they are not also about (whether the actual "influence" is direct, indirect, or even nonexistent) Worringerian "abstraction and empathy," "Gothic form," and so on. (It is also at this fundamental "phenomenological" point described by Takayuki Tatsumi that the distinction between "Eurocentric" and some "Other" kind of discourse seems to evaporate into the thinnest air of cyberspace.)

Now let us assume *ex hypothesi* that a comparatively obscure German art historian Wilhelm Worringer (1881–1965) was VR's uncanny "first" theorist and practitioner. This provisional thesis should come as small surprise for those who have already begun reading him not merely as the first German Expressionist but also, as will be seen presently, as the first theoretician of postmodern CyberWar. Said differently, Worringer would then be qua "uncanny 'first'"—among several major theorists and even (though in his case merely textual) practitioners of VR—simultaneously the most influential on us post-contemporaries and yet by us the most ignored. His written texts would be not merely examples of "Expressionist" rhetoric but also the proto-technocultural equivalent of VR; and his applications would be far beyond art, art history, criticism, and theory.

VIDEODROMES

It can be said that today, at the turn to the twenty-first century, there are two fundamental arenas—call them *Videodromes*—in which Worringer's theories such as "abstraction and empathy" and "Gothic form" have been having an especially interesting and relatively unprecedented impact. Again, one Videodrome is entirely implicit and unconscious, the other remarkably explicit and conscious. In comparison with the modernist, working-class "velodrome" of concrete and multiday bicycle races, "Videodrome" is the much more abstract, properly postmodern arena of combat with mind-body cyborg interfaces and metamorphoses, within and by means of which the struggle for total capitalist hegemony is sadomasochistically played out on—*and as*—public-access TV and other "aesthetic" practices.[28] Note that today "aesthetics" means not only a theory of beauty, or the intersection of the epistemological and the ethical, or any other (more or less post-Kantian) aspect of art or culture; it is also the sector of interface between organism and environment, the world either perceptible to the senses *(aisthetón)* or, by turns, anesthetically imperceptible to them. And thus aesthetics has come to refer to cyberpunk *prosthesis:* an extension of the material body and mind propelled onto death, a potential extension nonetheless of all senses and organs.[29] In the condition that Jean Baudrillard calls the "cybernetic peripeteia of the body," it is not so much that "passions have disappeared," it is rather that they "have materialized."[30] In Haraway's terms: "By the late twentieth century . . . we are all chimeras, theorized and fabricated hybrids of machine and organism; in short, we are cyborgs. The cyborg is our ontology; it gives us our politics."[31] Metaphysics and aesthetics are both becoming forms of *psychoplasmics* and vice versa. Psychoplasmics refers to a (theoretical if not actual) transferential psychoanalytical operation involving the self-replicating (including posthumous) body-free projections of subconscious and conscious fears, hatreds, and desires into an embodied, materialized corps of transsexually or asexually generated beings or "broods"—with certain salutary benefits for the projecting individual and with immediately disastrous consequences both for the latter's victims and potentially for society at large.[32] The Worringer industry helps manufacture Worringer's brood and (mass)cult. If so, we might wish to get after it in earnest.

At this point a brief speculation about Worringer's own ideologically determined attitudes toward technoculture seems to be in order. Strictly speaking, however, what is at issue in all current discussions of Worringer ought to be less his own theory or even rhetorical practice (say, of "abstraction and empathy") than the problem of the relationship between any one of his binary concepts and their current ideological functions, especially in what can be called the properly Worringerian problematic: namely, that one binary term tends to be more or less surreptitiously *valorized* at the expense of its adverse. Certainly all of Worringer's own work was informed by the inadequately theorized tendency, first, to favor "abstraction" (or, more precisely, the *ideological* baggage that comes with it, since the meaning of his term undergoes certain interesting changes from 1908 to the 1950s) and, second, to disparage "empathy," in spite of his occasional disclaimers to the contrary. This valorizing maneuver holds true even when Worringer eventually shifts his ground on what constitutes "abstraction," and whether he means by it something historical, ontological, epistemological, phenomenological, critical, or *something else besides.*[33]

Worringer's sporadic, contradictory, and always undertheorized attempts to assign either a necessarily reactionary or, alternatively, a necessarily progressive function to certain technological innovations ought to disturb more readers than have been disturbed.[34] While it is true that neither a theory nor a mass medium rarely, if ever, has only one ideological function or effect, they do tend to follow certain internally and externally imposed tendencies.[35] In any event, it is within this problematic of technoculture that the problem of the *Sublime* must be placed—not only the Sublime as understood by Worringer in his thoughts about "abstraction" or Gothic and Egyptian "form" but also the way that VR, too, is a videodromic variant of the Sublime. Worringer worked within an essentially neo-Kantian framework. And, in the Third Critique, Kant had written:

> We call that Sublime which is absolutely great, but to be great and to be a great something are quite different concepts (magnitudo and quantitas). In like manner *to say simply* (simpliciter) that anything is great is quite different from saying that it is *absolutely great* (absolute, non comparative magnum). The latter is what is great beyond all comparison. . . . The Sublime is that in comparison with which everything else is small. . . . *The Sublime is that, the mere ability to think which shows a faculty of the mind surpassing every standard of sense.*[36]

With regard to the problem of talking about the Kantian Sublime in the first place, Slavoj Zizek refers to a decisive "paradox": namely, "the conversion of the impossibility of presentation into the presentation of impossibility."[37] And clearly all of Worringer's key terms share this paradox but particularly "abstraction," and one really does suspect that there is something more than slightly mad about his writing and thinking. So it is interesting that Shoshana Felman once distinguished between *speaking* madness and speaking *of* madness as roughly equivalent to the difference between rhetoric and grammar— another consituent problem of Worringer's style.[38] Too, Jean-François Lyotard has recently summarized in quasi-Heideggerian fashion the enormous ambition behind the way that Kantianism needs to construct a feeling (or rather "enthusiasm") that would both respond to something vital in human nature and yet would not require verification by comparison with any known or unknown empirical fact. Lyotard is particularly interested in the philosophical implications of what he calls the *différend*, a labile linguistic and conceptual moment in which an assertion that for one reason *must* be phrased for some other reason *cannot* be, or cannot *yet* be.[39] And, again, Worringer's key terms are profoundly informed by such proleptic desires. Finally, Gilles Deleuze argues that a main point of the Kantian figuration of the Sublime was to force the imagination (in Kant's own phrase) to "recoil upon itself," and thereby to learn that (in Deleuze's words) "it is reason which pushes [imagination] to the limit of its power, forcing it to admit that all its power is nothing *in comparison to an Idea.*"[40] But it is also thus that the principle of comparability is recuperated by and for Idealism; in Deleuze's precise turn of phrase: "the Ideas of reason are speculatively indeterminate, practically determined" (52); and this recapitulation raises very serious questions about what the *practical* determinations are not only on the Sublime of Worringer and the Sublime of videodromic VR but also on the political consequences of each.

Be any Sublime as it may, however, Worringer's conceptual flabbiness and indecisiveness about the value to be assigned abstraction and technology, and their deeper relationship to Modernism, came to be invested by him, over the course of his career, with rather different affective and axiological charges. Nevertheless, his overall tendency to undertheorize his key terms never changed substantially. Why not? Certainly the basic structure of this problematic (as Neil H. Donahue is showing in this volume) remains intact in relatively late works such as *Egyptian Art* (1927).[41] In this text, in what is ostensibly an analysis of one of the most important "primitive" cultures, its art and architecture, Worringer *apparently* (as Donahue also notes, Worringer's slippery, protopostmodern "rhetorical Sublime" makes it particularly difficult to pin him down here) retracts his earlier positive judgment about things Egyptian (which continue to exert a powerful attraction in popular culture) as, in effect, the protoform of avant-garde Modernism, which is also to say of nonempathic abstraction. Initially for Worringer in the pre–World War I period, most notably in *Abstraction and Empathy* (1908), "abstraction" had been a salutary and quasi-dialectical cause/effect of an ostensibly profound need for "quiet points" *(Ruhepunkte)* in "our" anxious, aerophobic, paranoid confrontation with the sheer void of human existence, if not with Being Itself. On this onto-theological (not to say also quintessentially bourgeois) view—as Heidegger might depict it and as was depicted by Worringer himself in the next major stage of his work, *Form Problems in the Gothic* (1911)—"Gothic" architecture represented one of the most crucial phases (theoretically and rhetorically for him always more than historically) in the vast trajectory (or is it Nietzschean Eternal Recurrence?) of all human culture. According to Worringer's earlier, quasi-Existentialist position, recourse to "empathy" of any kind was ultimately inauthentic, unmanly, and so on. And, as such, it was for him in truth *un-* or even *anti*-artistic. As has been documented often, Worringer's early thinking about abstraction and empathy made a considerable impression on a European artistic and critical avant-garde that was quite eager, on the one hand, to buy into almost any return to non-Occidental, and supposedly "nontechnological" and "primitive," cultural formations in the name of Modernism, and equally willing, on the other, to avoid sorting out the technological and ideological implications of this paradoxical, more or less neo-aristocratic atavism. Were, then, for Worringer both Modernism and reaction to it imagined to be essentially technophobic or technophilic, and for which person or class exactly? A good part of what has been called the "displaced politics" of modernism's "aesthetic agency" can likely be traced to this aporia.[42] Thus, Worringer's own apparent reversal of judgment by the late 1920s about the abstract nature of primitive art can indeed be read (as Donahue does) as a thinly disguised—but decidedly *militant*—attack against "Americanism" and all that supposedly comes with it: for example, "democracy," "pacifism," "demasculinization," "feminism," and "technology," if not modernity *tout court*.[43]

In any case, the sixty-seven-year-old Worringer (writing in 1948, in the "year-zero" rubble of the Third Reich) did imply that at least one trend of his interventions into cultural politics (from at least 1921 to the present) had been "critical-skeptical, even defeatist."[44] But this was not at all to say that his had ever been a pacifistic mode of *writing*. Even this same 1948 essay—"The Problematic of Contemporary Art"—concludes with a ringing assertion that his own most basic theories were neither "refuted" nor "vanquished."[45]

What is crucial to grasp in Worringer, and his own (possible) sense of technoculture, is the exact nature of relative *continuities*—both internally, within his work, and externally, between it and the development of capitalism in his lifetime. But these continuities cannot be grasped adequately in arguments about whether Worringer's patented brand of idealism was relatively coherent or incoherent, or whether his rhetoric was internally consistent or not, crazy or not. One must always include in such discussions specific arguments about which *types* of idealism and rhetoric are generally most effective in attempting to manage the contradictions of the capitalist mode of production—contradictions that are ultimately insoluble without real communist social transformation and revolution. There is, for example, an obvious "neglect" in Worringer of the economic determinations, conditionings, and pressures on all cultural development (as pointed out by no one better or more obsessively than Georg Lukács). Such "neglect" exists not merely in Worringer's work, however, but also in most of its subsequent reception. It tends to reduce both Worringer's writing *and* that of his critics to the status of unreflected transitional objects. But what is particularly interesting is that such "neglect" is seldom—if ever—some mere aberration, mistake, lapse, or madness that might be made good, say, by more elaborate or rigorous *cultural* or *textual* criticism. Rather, it is, in its own terms, a quite *rational* facet of capitalist hegemony (in the Gramscian or Althusserian sense of "non-coercive coercion").[46]

The more basic point here, however, is that nowadays the first of the two most significant and influential variants of the Worringerian articulation of "abstraction" and "empathy" transpires not in scholarly discourse of *any* kind but rather in that mass culture about which he himself was at best ambivalent: namely, in technosocial VR, in all the military-cultural-industrial Videodromes that currently produce and reproduce the most significant false "alternatives" or "choices" between technophilia or technophobia.[47] Today, too, as was already the case with Worringer's own theory of "abstraction and empathy," the first term (technophilia, abstraction) tends to be covertly valued over the second (technophobia, empathy) in unstable ways that seem to betray deeper psychological anxieties and, especially, real social contradictions and oppositions. This labile valorization, cavorting rambunctiously as it does with the ideological continuities it conceals, lives on in the Videodrome of our own technoculture, where it continues to serve much the same indirect apology for neo-capitalism that, in the final analysis, was also Worringer's indirect apology for capitalism. And it does so with at least equal "genius."

MASSCULT

Thus, the first Videodrome for psychoplasmic operations à la Worringer (more conventionally put, his influence), the Videodrome that is almost entirely subconscious but also more extensive, is that of *MassCult*. Like its sometimes cognate "popular culture," the term "mass culture" is problematic for many reasons, not least because it is hardly produced by the masses (contrary to what many communists after 1917 hoped for) but sooner by an elite to manipulate the masses in more or less Fordist ways at the point of consumption as well as production. So it is that the term "mass culture" has, but also conceals, certain *cultic* dimensions. Further, since the study of mass culture itself functions as a kind of cult within academic-scholarly circles, it is appropriate to refer to mass culture as MassCult. The latter term also contains, at least for communists, an ironic and bitter allusion to original, properly Soviet hopes for what was called "masscult." Finally, MassCult is preferable to "the culture industry" in so far as it designates the object against which culture is directed: namely, those "masses" whose possibility of ever attaining something like the empathic moment once known as "class consciousness" is precisely what is proleptically eliminated in advance of its potential formation by the commodifying and abstracting mechanisms of both "high" and "low" culture equally.

MassCult includes especially Science Fiction (SF) and cyberpunk writing (most notably perhaps Philip K. Dick and William Gibson) and the films of the SF, New Bad Future, and SFSlash genres (for example, referring only to relatively mainstream filmic production: *Blade Runner, Alien, Shocker, Brazil, Terminator I* and *II, Total Recall, Lawn Mower Man*, and nearly the entire filmic oeuvre of Cronenberg). To my knowledge, Worringer has had no substantial direct influence on MassCult, but his direct influence can be felt everywhere when one reads/views back and forth between the two, channel surfing though the matrix.

Consider a passage from Dick's *Do Androids Dream of Electric Sheep?* (1968), the novel that inspired Ridley Scott's seminal film *Blade Runner* (1982). In both artifacts, a private detective dick, Rick Deckard (in the film, H. Ford), is supposed to kill or "retire" the "more-human-than-human," slave-class androids who have returned to Earth from outworld labor colonies in revolt against their programmer-producers. Deckard (who, particularly in the novel and in one dream sequence in the director's cut of the film, must increasingly confront the possibility that he himself is, in effect or fact, less than human) has to administer an examination to those suspected of being (more human than human) android Spartacists (so to speak) led by Roy Batty (R. Hauer)—whose capacity, "even" (or rather *especially*) as an abstractly constructed and programmed being, precisely to empathize not only with his cell members but with Life provides the major narrative impulse of the film. The "life or death" exam is called "the empathy test"; originally developed by the Pavlov Institute in the Soviet Union, it has been updated in the West and rechristened "Voigt-Kampff." Interpolate Worringer while reading this passage.

> The nexus-6 android types, Rick reflected, surpassed several classes of human specials in terms of intelligence. In other words, androids equipped with the new Nexus-6 brain unit had from a sort of rough, pragmatic, no-nonsense standpoint evolved beyond a major—but inferior—segment of mankind. For better or worse. The servant had in some cases become more adroit than its master. But new scales of achievement, for example the Voigt-Kampff Empathy Test, had emerged as criteria by which to judge. An android, no matter how gifted as to pure [read: abstract] intellectual capacity, could make no

> sense out of the fusion which took place routinely among the followers of Mercerism [one of the popular religions based on empathic identification with others]. . . .
>
> Empathy, evidently, existed only within the human community, whereas abstract intelligence to some degree could be found throughout every phylum and order including the arachnida. . . . Evidently the human robot constituted a solitary predator.[48]

In short, in this (Dickian) world, empathy is the *only* feature that distinguishes—or, more precisely, may *possibly* distinguish—the human from the nonhuman or the android and, hence, from the pure abstraction of paranoia. The latter condition most radically excludes empathy (even self-empathy) and, as such, it becomes a particularly effective means of waging the kind of warfare to which we will return.[49]

Due in part to its peculiar binary function, empathy cannot be ultimately destroyed (yet), and (for now) it tends to merge in Mass-Cult with the abstract, bio-mechanical world in strange and mysterious ways. The final scene of Scott's *Blade Runner* has generated some controversy because it (unlike the recently released director's cut and unlike Dick's novel) seems to fold the neo-*noir* Rick and his android lover Rachel (S. Young) back into an unapologetically "humanist" discourse.[50] So it is, too, that at the end of this particular movie, the retired killer Rick and his former potential quarry Rachel (who in the meantime, however, has saved his life) escape the postmodern, nuclear winter, multinational squalor of L.A. (The City of Quartz, *the* city of the future) in a rocket cab—riding off into a previously unseen, indeed impossibly still intact, Nature. Empathy (not to say bathos) would thus seem to triumph at the end of the day over abstraction—and even Dick's original story had ended on a note of bourgeois domesticity (though rather more understated, neurotic, everyday, and ironic than in the film).

But it is possible to view the closure of Scott's film very differently.[51] The very last shots of the originally released *Blade Runner*, viewed through the windscreen of Rick and Rachel's rocket car, are from the perspective—simultaneously—of one human and one android. What this means is that, both diegetically (in the imaginary space of the film's plot) and nondiegetically (outside this plot, both in its story and in our actual viewing space), we viewing subjects have been momentarily "interpellated" (in the Althusserian sense of constructing them ideologically by "hailing" them)[52] as a construction that is *literally* part human/android, part abstract/empathic. Thus, in Worringerian terms, the videodromic radicality of the original *Blade Runner* turns out to be "abstract" precisely where the "empathy" seems greatest and vice versa: the lens of the camera and the lens of the human eye/I are for a few seconds indistinguishable—as are virtually all the traditional biological and moral issues raised by assuming that there is any difference between the human and the machine, and that such difference really matters. (In other terms of the film, the distinction between the nondiegetic and the diegetic collapses as well since, to repeat, we have been given no prior indication that the Nature into which Rick and Rachel escape from the postcivilization of L.A. still exists or will ever exist again, including *these* ozone-depleted spaces in which we view and review the film *hic et nunc*.)

Almost exactly as in all of Worringer's writing, it is appropriately unclear from the point of view of (patriarchal, heterosexist, bourgeois) ideology whether the techno-somatic undecidability of the end of *Blade Runner* is intended by Scott. And, if it is intentional, whose specific ends does it serve in any of our available "architectural" or "filmic" spaces? Indeed it appears that such spaces are constructed by MassCult films so that all questions of the difference between intentionality or nonintentionality, between technology and the human, between abstraction and empathy are *apparently* elided a priori. But this is not to say that such differences are *really* elided beneath the surface of the audiovisual appearance and its apparatus. Nor is it to say simply that technology = abstraction, whereas human = empathy, either in MassCult *or* in Worringer. My point is rather that, even as such distinctions are obviated, real space and time are (still) only *virtually* obviated—leaving the space and time of political economies, notably neo-capitalism, remarkably intact and fortified. In *Blade Runner,* for instance, such political economy is comparatively visible and explicit in the explanatory scroll at the beginning of film, where the androids are explicitly linked to slave labor, but comparatively invisible and implicit at the end in the labor power that went into building the escaping rocket cab—not only the "imaginary" one in the plot and story of the film but also the "real" one that is the prop. The question of where political economy exists in Worringerian virtual reality, if indeed any is visible, must be approached slowly.

In the context of Worringer and his influence, it is significant that by far the greatest influence of the Dickian–Scotian *Blade Runner,* besides on films and film theory, has been on practicing architects and city planners. Indeed, no single movie has ever had a greater or more immediate, positive impact on their practices.[53] Of course, one *could* plausibly link this impact to Worringer's work on "abstraction and empathy" and on "Gothic architecture" with little difficulty, whether the architects and city planners in question know Worringer or not (though at least some of them undoubtedly do). But, in light of the overdetermined nature of MassCult, little would be served by the merely amusing juxtaposition of Worringer to current debates about urban planning and living—or to other matters that concern, much more literally, life and death.[54]

CINEMA 3

In *Cinema 2* (1985), Deleuze analyzes the post–World War II cinema as a Videodrome, so to speak, or rather as what he himself calls the "cinema of time."[55] Cinema 2 is composed of the "time-image" and the "action-image," as opposed to Cinema 1, the previous Videodrome or "cinema of movement," composed of the "movement-image" and the "mental-image."[56] Deleuze also seems to suggest in *Cinema 2* that Worringer is the link between his own cultural (film) theory and the properly Worringerian theory of warfare that he had analyzed already a half-decade earlier with the late Félix Guattari in *A Thousand Plateaus,* the second volume of their *Capitalism and Schizophrenia* (1972 and 1980). Deleuze himself only implies this articulating use of Worringer; nonetheless, it represents one of the most intriguing and pivotal moments in the entire history of the latter's reception.

A basic contention of *Cinema 2* is that there are two fundamental types of cinematographic optical signs (opsigns): *reports* or *constats* and *instats.* Deleuze proposes that *constats* provide "a vision with depth, at a distance, tending towards abstraction, the other [*instats*] a close, flat-on vision inducing involvement." He immediately adds: "This opposition corresponds in some respects to the alternative as defined by Worringer: abstraction or *Einfühlung*" (6).

For the sake of illustration, the filmic practice of *constats* is associated by Deleuze with Michelangelo Antonioni, that of *instats* with Federico Fellini. Deleuze argues: "Antonioni's aesthetic visions are inseparable from an objective critique . . . , whilst Fellini's visions are inseparable from an 'empathy,' a subjective sympathy" (6). But Deleuze does not develop this cinematographic analogy or isomorphism with reference to Worringer, preferring instead to warn that

[t]he distinctions, on the one hand between the banal and the extreme, and on the other between the subjective and the objective, have some value, but only relatively. They are valid for an image or a sequence, but not for the whole. They are still valid in relation to the action-image, which they bring into question, but already they are no longer wholly valid in relation to the new image that is coming into being. They mark poles between which there is continual passage. . . . As for the distinction between subjective and objective, it also tends to lose its importance, to the extent that the optical situation or visual description replaces the motor action. We run in fact into a principle of indeterminability, or indiscernibility: we no longer know what is imaginary or real, physical or mental, in the situation, not because we are confused, but because we do not have to know and there is no longer even a place from which to ask. (6–7)

Now, what Deleuze—rather nihilistically and (an)aesthetically—describes here *figuratively* for the contemporary cinema of abstraction is true, I argue, a fortiori and *literally* for VR—not merely the VR depicted or represented in films such as *Videodrome* or *Total Recall* (representing a genre of cinema oddly neglected by Deleuze) but VR as an *actual prosthesis* ("organ" or "tumor") and as an *actual war machine*. The latter practice is, or may be, most significantly, the Worrringerian Cinema 3. So once again we are compelled to exit, to sortie from cultural politics, in order to consider even more violent and lethal theaters of combat.

CYBERWAR

Our second contemporary Videodrome after MassCult—this one comparatively limited but also much more conscious, explicit, and intensive—is that of postmodern political theory and a more or less coeval postmodern theory of warfare, particularly as it is advanced by Deleuze and Guattari in and between the lines of the second volume of *Capitalism and Schizophrenia*. This theory builds on Virilio's various analyses of technology and warfare; but, unlike Virilio, who does not mention Worringer by name, the section in *A Thousand Plateaus* entitled "Treatise on Nomadology—The War Machine," in particular, appeals directly and decisively to Worringer.

Today, as Virilio suggested already in 1977, "[w]ar has . . . moved from the action stage to the conception stage that, as we know, characterizes *automation*."[57] And with this shift comes an obvious increase in abstraction, decrease in empathy. An example comes to mind. During the most recent global interventions by the United States and Allied multinational capitalist military into the affairs of their former bosom buddies in Iraq (on the principle that there's nothing like the wrath directed at a lover scorned) the dual tactico-moral—and in that sense *emphatic*—problem arose that (1) so-called smart bombs were hardly as clever as U.S. propaganda understandably insisted, and (2) that soldiers who are first trained and then fight in identical—*abstractly*—constructed cyberspaces or war simulators sometimes are unable to distinguish enemy from friendly "soft targets" (military jargon for human beings as opposed to "hard targets" such as buildings, incoming missiles, tanks). In other words, U.S. technosoldiers are incapable not merely of empathizing with the enemy (which is obviously counterproductive, even suicidal in training and especially when actual combat has begun) but also, sometimes, of distinguishing the enemy from compatriots in the first place. The result during the Gulf War was that some of the latter were occasionally "offed" by "friendly fire." "THIS BUD'S FOR YOU!" screamed one befuddled, dust-blinded tank gunner in Kuwait as he reluctantly obeyed the techno-order to fire off an optically guided projectile at a soft target that turned out, as he had feared, to be his own comrades. Confronted by his superiors (intent to scapegoat him), the young gunner retorted: "Nobody knows the fuck how fucking *abstract* it is out there"[58]— meaning by "out there" not only in the swirling sands of Desert Storm but also "in there" deep in the matrix, in the cyborg brain of Worringerian CyberWar.

Such incidents would indeed seem to exemplify instances when "the soldier's obscene gaze [but also—perfectly *audible* in the gunner's reference to the King of Beers—quite literally *commodified, reified, cyborgified*], on his surroundings and on the world, his art of hiding from sight in order to see, is not just an ominous voyeurism but from the first imposes a long-term patterning on the chaos of vision, one which prefigures the synoptic machinations of architecture and the cinema screen" (Virilio, *War and Cinema*, 49). Through a camera eye installed in its tip, the gunner in Desert Storm watched transfixed as his guided projectile approached his friends, until it (hard) and they (soft) exploded into abstraction.

But in order to spotlight one of my main contentions here, martial mechanization and automatization are (never) *quite* total, they are (still) *virtual,* still involve empathy. First World, Second World, Third World, Fourth World. . . . War of position, war of maneuver. . . . It does make a difference, at least for the time being. (A moral difference, as well as military and epistemological ones.) "Smart weapons" are (for now) more hype, more virtual than real. They are hallucinatory facts, propaganda aimed to coerce oppressed, potentially hostile people to be passive. So it was, for example, that the kill rate inflicted by Patriot missiles during the Gulf War was incessantly reported at the time to be 100%; but it turns out now, remarkably, to have been 0%. (The Iraqis had modified the Soviet-made Scud missiles beyond their stress thresholds, and they exploded as they began their downward descent on their targets; the Israeli and American Patriots aimlessly attacked the fragments, wholly unable to differentiate the warheads from the debris.) Today, therefore, many apparently discarded theaters of "architecture" and "cinema," and hence of warfare, remain present, even future necessities. The neo-capitalist state remains an "outer ditch, behind which there [stands] a powerful system of fortresses and earthworks: more or less numerous from one State to the next, it goes without saying—but this precisely [necessitates] an accurate reconnaissance of each individual country."[59] This Gramscian (and Leninist) perspective embraces the abstract, anti-empathic "country" represented by (post)-Fordist, transnational capital and by the (prematurely celebrated) VR that is the *pax americana.* In *Guerrilla Warfare,* Che Guevara noted: "In order to carry on warfare in country that is not very hilly, lacks forests, and has many roads, all the fundamental requisites of guerrilla warfare must be observed; only the forms altered. The quantity, not the quality, of guerrilla warfare will change."[60] Che could—must—have also been describing cyberspace, CyberWar.

In *The Production of Space* (an important text for Virilio and other theoreticians of CyberWar), Lefebvre wrote:

> We already know several things about abstract space. As a product of violence and war, it is political; instituted by the state, it is institutional. On first inspection it appears homogeneous; and indeed it serves those forces which make it a *tabula rasa* of whatever stands in their way, of whatever threatens them—in short of differences. These forces seem to grind down and crush everything before them, with space performing the function of a plane, a bulldozer or a tank. The notion of the instrumental homogeneity of space, however, is illusory—though empirical descriptions of space reinforce the

> illusion—because it uncritically takes the instrumental as a given. . . . For all that architectural projects have a seeming objectivity, for all that the products of space may occasionally have the best intentions in the world, the fact is that volumes are invariably dealt with in a way that refers the space in question back to the land, to a land that is still privately (and privatively) owned; built-up space is thus emancipated from the land *in appearance only*. At the same time, it is treated as an empty abstraction, at once geometric and visual in character. (*The Production of Space*, 285 and 338)

So already by the 1970s, at the latest, insight was possible into something like a political economy not only of space in the abstract but of virtually real space.

It is also interesting, I think, that the theory of Worringerian warfare is at least implicitly traced by Deleuze and Guattari to Worringer himself via Virilio via Lenin. Remarkable to say, the most extensive and explicit *political* use to which Worringer has ever been put is in the 1980 hymn to the postmodern, neo-barbarian, "nomadological war machine" entitled *A Thousand Plateaus: Capitalism and Schizophrenia*.[61] For it is to *Wilhelm Worringer* (alongside Heinrich von Kleist, who for Deleuze and Guattari is the crucial historical and conceptual pivot from the "schizoid" Hölderlin to the "schizoid" Nietzsche) that Deleuze and Guattari attribute the *"prodigious idea of nonorganic life—the very same idea Worringer considered the barbarian idea par excellence"* (411). And so it is that we arrive at an explicitly *Worringerian* politico-military theory and practice.

In order to legitimate their appropriation of Worringer's abstraction, Deleuze and Guattari point to Virilio's *Speed and Politics*, and especially to his theory of submarine and marine warfare, the theory of the nuclear fleet. This is the technological muscle, the coercion, that backs up the sophisticated noncoercive coercion that is the "culture" of the current capitalist "country" or State. Here we enter into an intertextual *mise-en-abîme* representing the most lethal VR: with Deleuze and Guattari citing Virilio citing Lenin on the strategic and tactical military implications and applications of the theory of abstract *points*. A key passage in *A Thousand Plateaus* consists of embedded quotations from Virilio and Lenin.[62] The pastiche reads:

> The strategic submarine has no need to go anywhere in particular; it is content, while controlling the sea, to remain invisible . . . the realization of the [abstract,] absolute, unin-

terrupted, circular voyage, since it involves neither departure nor arrival. . . . If, as Lenin claimed, "strategy means choosing which *points* we apply force to," we must admit that these "*points,*" today, are no longer geostrategic *strongpoints*, since from any given spot we can now reach any other, no matter where it might be . . . *geographic localization* seems to have definitively lost its strategic value, and, inversely, that this same value is attributed to the *delocalization of the vector*, of a vector in permanent movement. (*Plateaus*, 559 n. 65)

Points on a plane—one plateau or a thousand—that can be patrolled. But these are no longer points in a space beyond VR to which revolutionary pressure might be effectively applied in any recognizable Leninist sense; or so it seems to Virilio and Deleuze (Guattari, in some of his other writings, remained more Leninist). Following Cinema 3, then, we have World War Cyberspace: not only a Third World War *in* cyberspace but war *by means of* it. "Theater" in all senses of the word.

Thus, all this may start to sound like Worringer after all; at least it does to Deleuze and Guattari citing Virilio citing Lenin—Lenin against whom *all* virtual realities seem to be opposed. But with this thought, finally, we may have a really *inter-esting* thought—in the root sense of "between being"—and one to hold on to, if it is not too late. Lenin is figured here in and by Worringerian virtual reality as its—only—radical Other; its—only—alternative possibility. As *Worringerian* virtual reality, postmodern politics becomes not only just another nomadic politics or *abstract* politics and theory of warfare, but a specifically post-Leninist politics a priori.

In any event, it will undoubtedly surprise even his most enthusiastic and uncritical fans to learn that Worringer's greatest single insight, according to *A Thousand Plateaus*, was into *metal* and *metallurgy*. For Deleuze and Guattari, Worringer's theory is nothing less than "the nomadic war machine art par excellence"; and of course metal and metallurgy, as the material foundation of all known forms of warfare, are what bring "to light a life proper to matter, a vital state of matter as such, a material vitalism that doubtless exists everywhere but is ordinarily hidden or covered, rendered unrecognizable, dissociated by the hylomorphic model." If there is no metal and no *malleable matter* ("matter" in Greek is *hyle*, whence hylomorphic), then there is also no abstraction, no cyberspace, no VR. No mines, no computers, no nothing. If there is any lingering doubt about this, and since for Deleuze and Guattari the other last court of appeal besides Worringer is Kleist, the reader might wish at this point to jack into the famous dying words of the latter's Amazon queen, Penthesilea, as she forges the knife to kill herself out of words from the mine shaft of her soul.

> For now I will step down into my breast
> As into a mine and there will dig a lump
> Of cold ore I temper in the fires of woe
> To hardest steel; then steep it through and through
> In the hot, biting venom of remorse;
> Carry it then to Hope's eternal anvil
> And sharpen it and point it to a dagger;
> Now to this dagger do I give my breast:
> So! So! So! So! Once more! Now, it is good.
>   *(She falls and dies.)*[63]

The specific problem with VR, however, is that everything here must also *appear* "empathic-organic-natural" and not just "abstract-crystalline." Indeed, this *appearance* is the whole point.

In the notorious "last instance," however, VR is made out of nothing if not very real plastic and metal chips and generally the congealed labor power that produces them for surplus profit. Human miners still mine metals around the world; they cannot *just* be coerced to go into the shafts; they also have to go willingly. Workers still produce plastic or the machines to produce plastics; and they too must do so willingly, at least sometimes. And all these human beings can all still go out on strike, including general strikes that could help bring *any* government to its knees as fast as could any esoterrorist hardwire cyberpunk hacker. Ideally, these two groups would work and revolt together as a historical bloc.[64] But Deleuze and Guattari's explicitly Worringerian point about metal seems rather different, and less materialistic than, say, that of Kleist's Penthesilea—or that of Lenin. But it is not wholly unrelated. For Lenin, in one of the greatest works of Marxist history and historiography, the mining industry is especially significant in two respects: as an exceptionally clear index of the dynamic socioeconomic relations in all spheres of a national economy; and as an exemplary illustration of "the theoretical proposition that in a developing capitalist society there is a particularly rapid growth of those branches of industry which produce *means of production*, i.e., articles not of personal, but of productive, consumption."[65] In short, such intellectuals think they are out of the mine but actually remain down in it all along—whether the mine is real or virtual.[66]

According to the point of view of *A Thousand Plateaus* (in contrast to Lenin's):

> Metallurgy is the consciousness or thought of the matter-flow, and metal the correlate of this consciousness—the prodigious idea of nonorganic life—the very same Worringer considered the barbarian idea par excellence, was the invention, the intuition of metallurgy. Metal is neither a thing nor an organism, but a body without organs. The "Northern, or Gothic, line" is above all a mining or metallic line delimiting this body. (*Plateaus*, 411)

By this same neo-Worringerian logic, then, the "nomad war machine is the form of expression, of which itinerant metallurgy is the correlative form of content" (*Plateaus*, 415). But what, then, is the function and use of metal and metallurgy for neo-nomadic, Worringerian warfare "in the final analysis," *in letzter Linie*? It seems that Worringer's point was not quite the same as Deleuze and Guattari make it out to be—let alone what Lenin might say.

As for Worringer himself, the bottom line for every discussion of art, art theory, and cultural politics does indeed appear to hinge on what he regarded as the simple *fact* that the capacity to recognize true art is, as he put it in his *Problematic of Contemporary Art* (1948), an *organ*. One may, according to Worringer, learn to *develop* this organ (or, one might now say, psychoplasmic tumor or cyberpunk prosthesis) but basically either one is *born* with it or one is *not*. The presence or the absence of *this* organ was for Worringer, at least in 1948, *the* determining factor in human history, and its import explicitly supersedes the "fake" issue of class struggle.[67] It should come as small surprise that what Worringer was pleased to call his "pure logic" (wholly unencumbered, supposedly, by any particularly ideology)[68] never resolved a problem that it was not in his class-interest *to* resolve. That is, he was unwilling to grant to the social forces he most mistrusted—"the public," "the people," "the masses," "class," and "empathy"—anything like the flexibility and mobility that he gave freely and explicitly to forces he favored: such as "art," "art for artists," "artistic will," "organic culture," "abstraction," the more or less innate and natural "organ" that is genuine art appreciation (but, strangely, not empathy). In other words, Worringer never could have penetrated so deeply into mines or mining (or caves) as Deleuze and Guattari simply assume.

WORRINGERIAN VIRTUAL REALITY: SOME FINAL LINES, PLANES, POINTS

In the Videodrome called North America, Worringerian virtual reality of course "has a philosophy . . . that's what makes it dangerous."[69] The most *real* questions remain Lenin's: *which* philosophy are we then talking about, *whom* does it serve, *how* does it work, and is it a question of empathy or abstraction or both at once?[70] Abstraction and empathy always work in dialectical interchange, though not necessarily with any synthesis. To reformulate Kant, abstraction without (any) empathy is blind; empathy without (some) abstraction is empty.

A remark in *Abstraction and Empathy*, though uttered rather *en passant*, opens up a series of much more profound problems, both for this seminal text, for Worringer's work as a whole, and for whatever influence and relevance he may continue to have in the near future. "In so far," Worringer wrote, "as a sensuous object is still dependent upon space, it is unable to appear to us in its closed material individuality." He continued: "All endeavor was therefore directed toward the single form set free from space"—apparently finding its highest and most authentic degree of realization in the single *"point."*[71] But what *is* a (mathematical) point, and what exactly is *Worringer's* (philosophical or political and military) point? Can an object really ever be "independent" or "free" from space?[72]

If space does not allow itself to be individualized, or empathized with (and Worringer sometimes insisted quite vehemently that space and its imagined terror do *not* allow this), then what about *points*? (Yes, the leap from mathematical or geometrical to rhetorical or other more lethal points is a big one—but there seems to be no choice but to make it when reading Worringer and Worringerism.) The logician and mathematician Frege, writing in 1884, thought there might be apodictic proof that points are relational terms, not essential ones. In the *Foundations of Arithmetic*, he wrote: "One geometrical point, considered by itself, cannot be distinguished in any way from any other; the same applies to lines and planes. Only when several points, or lines or planes, are included together in a single intuition, do we distinguish them."[73] And, without Frege, (post)modern logic, semiotics, and mathematics might have taken a somewhat different turn, as might have VR eventually.

In not wholly dissimilar fashion, Kandinsky (an artist working somewhat under Worringer's influence and who by 1909 in *Point and Line to Plane* was arguably "the first abstract painter") also understood that points are in no meaningful sense "free" or "independent" of space.[74] Rather, they are shifting, mobile articulations between insides and outsides, windows and doors, art and nature—indeed, between any surfaces from two sides at once. It is certainly true that points are, in a sense, "abstract" but, Kandinsky added, there is simultaneously something irreducibly and uncannily *human* about them. "The geometric point is an invisible being" (21), Kandinsky noted in *Point and Line to Plane*—writing as much against Worringer as with him. "It must thus be defined as an immaterial being. Materially considered, the point equals a zero. But also a cipher, a sign. For in this zero, this nullity, different characteristics are concealed that are 'human'" (21).[75] He continued:

> In our conception, this nullity—the geometric point—is bound to the highest exactitude and brevity, that is with the greatest reserve—but one that speaks. Thus, the geometric point in our imagination is the highest and the most singular articulation of silence and speaking. Thus, the geometric form has found its material form in the first instance [*in erster Linie*] in writing—it belongs to speech and means silence. (21)

On the one hand, then, "the geometric line is an invisible being. It is the trace of a mobile point, a point moving itself, thus its product" (57). But, on the other, there is more here than meets the eye. "The point," still following Kandinsky, "is a small world or cosmos—separated more or less equally from all sides and *virtually* ripped out of its environment" (30).[76] But is this virtually violent act collapsible with the obscenely euphemized ocular *enucleation* (Bataille's gentle term for the self-inflicted peeling out of the human eye from its socket, its disembodiment)[77] that was hinted at by drugstore-cowboy cyberpunks like Worringer, in their conpensatory urge to "free" themselves from the real horrors of history, to stop thinking about anything but their own space, their own class—even while denying that it *was* a space, that it *was* a class perspective?

So with which eye, exactly, did Worringer ever see? A surrogate for the all-seeing eye of the deceased, Nietzschean God? The proto-cyborg, techno-human lens of a *Man with the Movie Camera* (Dziga

Vertov's film appeared in 1929, two years after Worringer's *Egyptian Art*)? The slightly earlier sliced eye of Salvador Dali and Luis Buñuel's *Un chien andalou* (1928)? The eye of the much later Foucauldian panopticon? The eye of Fichte's much earlier depiction of absolute self-consciousness as the "power into which an eye is implanted," "the implanted eye," "the in-oculated eye/I"?[78] As we can see from *Blade Runner* and MassCult generally, *all* lenses are in-oculated (and occulted) points, embodied-disembodied agencies, (proto)cyberpunk implants in matrices of (class) *power*. And, therefore, of (class) *struggle*.

Walter Benjamin (writing at the same time as Kandinsky, also vaguely under Worringer's influence) insisted that everything would come down to one point, on the assumption that "in every true work of art, there is the point at which anyone who puts himself into it will feel it blowing toward him like the cool wind of the coming dawn."[79] If all Worringerian *Einzelformen* (points, lines, planes, etc.) are not—cannot be—totally abstract *spaces* (i.e., are *only virtual* spaces) and vice versa, there can *be* no Worringerian theory of warfare *sensu stricto*—neither in Deleuze and Guattari nor anywhere else. Would Worringer then be totally irrelevant today?

As noted earlier, Worringer himself seems to have thought of space in quasi-*military* terms. So, for example, he wrote already in *Abstraction and Empathy*:

> Space is . . . the major enemy of all striving after abstraction, and hence is the first thing to be suppressed in the representation. [So ist der Raum also der größte Feind alles abstrahierenden Bemühens und er mußte. . . . IN ERSTER LINIE in der Darstellung unterdrückt werden.] (38 [75]; my emphasis)

But if space must be repressed and suppressed in Worringer's VR and theory of abstraction—as it must also be in Virilio's vision of CyberWar—then where does this occur? Exclusively in and by Worringer's own (or any other) *discourse*? In or by the origins of what he was so pleased to call *"art itself"*? Or just in and by *"abstract* art"? And when, how, and why does this repression or suppression of space occur? Already at art's most distant prehistoric "origins" and forever after? And, if so, in which millennium or social formation does it manifest itself in particular? Or is it (only) after 1908, 1909, 1910, and so on—one year at a time, year after year after year? And if this repression and suppression of space must indeed occur, to what ends might it be mobilized today? According to Worringer's own theory, spatial repression and suppression apparently happens always already in the first instance, *in erster Linie.* But that means, literally, that it is already IN THE FIRST LINE—the first "line of march," as it were. And therefore it would have always already been in the first *point* that space was to be repressed, suppressed. So, *pace* Worringer, not only space but also, therefore, in his terms, the possibility of *empathy,* is always already *there* after all—*within* abstraction. The enemy Other, according to this paranoid point of view, is inextricably within. So, have postmoderns like Deleuze and Guattari simply misread their modern masters in their burning desire to be schizoid, never paranoid?

What is relatively certain is that (according to Worringer) what used to be called "art history" or "the history of architecture" (not to say *all* prior history as it existed prior to *Abstraction and Empathy*) has been hysterically fixated (Worringer strongly implies) on what is thought of as "natural," "organic," and "bourgeois." Thus, Worringer will say things in *Abstraction and Empathy* such as: "The Renaissance, the great period of bourgeois naturalness [die große Natürlichkeit, die große Bürgerlichkeit] commences—and all artistic creation determined by the urge to abstraction goes under" (120 [164]). Richard Hamann, reviewing *Abstraction and Empathy* in 1910, intuited that something was left out of this Worringerian virtual reality, something at its base, something Real. (We have been recently reminded of Hamann's semi-Marxist critique—radicalized and turned into historical materialism by Jost Hermand—by the less Marxist West German historian of architecture Michael Müller.)[80] And what was omitted here has something to do with a relatively continuous, if often apparently "abstract," development of the political economy from the late nineteenth to the twentieth century. First, at a more initial stage of capitalist coercion, arose the attempt to "humanize" the sobriety of the nascent commodity world by the application of vital-organic sensuality and by arresting it with affective values. At this point, empathy was useful. But after a while hegemony was not working so well. At this somewhat later (but by no means "final" or even "late") stage of capitalist hegemony, abstraction replaced the function of empathy, and so was instaurated the denial of organic sensuousness, "the poeticization of the unpoetical." Abstraction (still roughly following the arguments of Hamann and Müller) is thus part and parcel of a modern need to justify the *"abstraction" of capital* by means of inarticulate, self-legitimating urges and desires, just as, at a time nearer the inception of capitalist modernity, empathy had striven to "poeticize" and "sentimentalize" abstractions, including geometrical images.

In short, according to this line of reasoning (which seems to me essentially correct, though sorely in need of neo-capitalist update), Worringer's original theories were just one of many attempts circa 1908 (but, judging from our continuing interest in him, it remains even today a relatively effective one) to legitimate "abstract" commodity production: that is to say, most uncannily mysterious—both perceptible and imperceptible to the senses *(sinnlich-übersinnlich)*—and, proleptically, the production of that which is the most socially devastating nonsensible-hypersensible, phantasmagoric VR of them all. For global neo-capitalism is arguably the ultimate VR, or would be if both become global "world-historically"; as Marx seems already in the nineteenth century to have "predicted."[81] By the late 1960s, Debord was arguing in *La société du spectacle* that under neo-capital "the *real* consumer" has been transformed into the "consumer of *illusions,*" since the commodity is already, "in fact and in effect, this real illusion" [*cette illusion effectivement réelle*]—with the society of the "spectacle" being its "general manifestation." In short, the overriding tendency of consumer capital is to shift attention from the "real" to its specular-spectacular "representation."[82] And, finally (less with a writer like Baudrillard—if there is anyone "like" anybody else—than with his acolytes), we end up with the aporia of the "hyperreal"—at which point we are really stuck in an aporia and can go no further, and certainly not back to Marx. Or can we? Was Marx, too, into *virtual* reality *only?*

According to Worringer's self-described "agnosticism" with regard to the epistemological and ontological status, the empirical facticity of "abstraction" and "empathy," one more or less "postmodern" answer to all such questions seems to be: "Relax, *everything* is virtually real, hyperreal." Such is the beauty—the aesthetics, the ethereal and rhetorical sublimity—less of all postmodernism, however, than of *liberal pluralism.* In VR, everything, every alterity, ultimately has only virtual form but gives off the appearance of maximum difference. Nonetheless, I have suggested, what remains is the material base of the haptic-optical field of VR, the hylomorphic *stuff* out of which VR is constructed. But precisely *this* material base is what is made imperceptible by VR and by Worringer and Worringerian virtual reality. It is here, to repeat, that Worringer is irrelevant simply. One can speak, therefore, of the *euphemized violence* both in Worringer and in his influence generally. "Euphemized violence" is defined for quasi-nomadic societies by Pierre Bourdieu as "overt (physical or economic) violence—*censored, euphemized,* i.e., unrecognizable [but nonetheless] socially recognized violence."[83] Euphemized violence is precisely the dominant mode of Worringer's writings and of Worringerian virtual reality. *And* of capital yesterday and today—but not necessarily tomorrow.

Make no mistake: to read not only all of Worringer (that is, to take his historico-theoretical model, his VR, seriously) but also the growing literature on his influence one is almost required to "forget" about political economy, about economic history. At least Worringer himself does, even when his interventions are most explicitly "political."[84] Forget slave labor, wage labor. Worringer does. Forget *socio-economic* prehistory, current history, all history. Nothing but dreams. It's all protopostmodern nostalgia not for lived social history but for the moment when one first decided to jack into the media matrix, to be a player on its market. Nostalgia follows fast in the wake of the initial hallucinogenic rush of the decision to leave forever a state one can already no longer remember. For *this* is the effect of Worringer's prose, if not also of the neo-Worringerian, postmodern sense of time and space, of temporality, of history, of historicity, and of warfare. Fredric Jameson has developed a conceptual thread in Deleuze and Guattari's *Capitalism and Schizophrenia* to suggest that this type of infatuation with the "perpetual present" is "a terrible indictment of consumer capitalism itself," and "at the very least, an alarming and pathological symptom of a society that has become incapable of dealing with time and history."[85] Jameson worries about "[t]he *insensible* colonization of the present by the nostalgia mode."[86] But what is precisely the problem is that the "colonization" in question *is* "sensible." Inside Worringerian virtual reality, one might add. The real problem, however, is *to whom* and *on whose behalf* such "colonization" is sensible or insensible, and to and for whom it makes *very* good sense, indeed.

If such questions must be asked, *if* they can be answered, and *if* they are really important, really real, *then* I suggest they *cannot* be asked or answered in the incomparably sublime consensual hallucination that is Worringer or Worringerian virtual reality, at least not as he and it are represented by Deleuze and Guattari and their simulacra. (Let alone as they are represented by art historians.) But how about by "*us*"—writing and reading here and now in the spatiotemporal matrix, the VR, the miniaturized, textualized "Research Institute" that is *this* essay and *this* anthology, among so many others? But "my" point here is that when we are *alone* "we" are *all* incapable. *Collective, communal* action—alongside individual, singular action—

is needed to combat what is already the deformed collectivity of VR, the consensual hallucination of cyberspace. And if there are really *no* (communist) alternatives here, then this does not mean that they cannot materialize in some other space, at some other point in time. Virtual realities, it turns out, are never quite so stable as they seem. No points or spaces are. Even bio-mechanically induced and constructed brain tumors (such as those clearly visible in Cronenberg's *Videodrome* or Paul Verhoeven's *Total Recall,* or the ones barely visible between the lines of *all* Worringer's writings) occasionally, or even perhaps inevitably, malfunction. Accidents do happen (still); empathic consolation is possible (still)—even politically necessary (always).

EPILOGUE: ACCIDENTS DO HAPPEN

Heading toward closure (here), jack into two passages more or less at random, three trial runs in Worringerian virtual reality.

First Run

> The line escapes geometry by a fugitive mobility at the same time as life tears itself free from the organic by a permutating, stationary whirlwind. This vital force specific to the Abstraction is what draws smooth space. The abstract line is the affect of smooth space, just as organic representation was the feeling presiding over striated space. The haptic-optical, near-distant distinctions must be subordinated to the distinction between the abstract line and the organic line; they must find their principle in a general confrontation of spaces. The abstract line cannot be defined as geometrical and rectilinear.

—This just happens to be produced by Deleuze and Guattari (*Plateaus,* 499).

Second Run

> Gothic man is insensible to the latent demands of atmospheric space, for beneficent, rhythmic limitation. Indeed, for the sake

of his morbidly strained need for expression, he violates atmospheric life. Where classical man only listened to it and served it with understanding, he faces it aggressively. He imprisons it, places obstacle after obstacle in its path, violently wrestling from it a quite definite rhythm of movement, intensified to the utmost, the aim of which is infinite height. Repelled on every side, shattered against a thousand oppositions, atmospheric life leads a tormented, agitated, restless existence within the limits of the interior, until finally, as if with an audible roar, it breaks against the vaulted roof. There a whirlwind, as it were, is formed which rises irresistibly upwards; any one at all sensitive to the impressions of space can never enter the great Gothic cathedrals without experiencing a dizziness caused by space. It is the same dizzy feeling set up by the chaotic intricacy of line in early Northern ornament. "Plus ça change, plus ça reste la même chose."

—And this just happens to be produced by Worringer.[87]

But also, to get after and out of this totalizing and vertiginous Worringerian matrix, consult finally Kleist (according to Deleuze and Guattari, the second greatest protopostmodern theorist after Worringer himself). *Third Run.* (A possible alternative Cinema 3.) Ask Kleist what transpired once in 1800 in a *visible* fortress, but *invisible* cathedral and prison. On the day he described to his lover as "the most important of my life," Kleist found himself in the vaulted space of a city fortress gate. (No doubt about it—in terms of Worringerian virtual reality—it was a *Gothic* space, a *cyber*space, an *electroplasmagothic* space).

Kleist (the "aristocrat" who, as such and otherwise, built nothing with his hands save his texts) dared to ask himself (in a space created by Roy Batty and other slaves, workers, and androids among us): "Why does the entire ceiling not collapse, since it has *no* support?" "It stands," Kleist answered:

> *because all the stones want to collapse at once*—and I drew out of this thought an indescribably refreshing consolation that stands at my side, right up to the decisive moment, with its hope that even I would hold myself up when everything lets me fall.[88]

So accidents *do* happen, and there is at least *one* consolation coming from somewhere deep inside VR. In fact, this consolation—this empathic alternative to abstraction—is so deep in Kleist's case (but never *really* in Worringer's), that it is virtually coterminous with its own potential collapse, its own crash. But where the potential for—cyberspatial *and* economic—collapse and crash exists, it's no longer just *business* as usual, Worringer industry as usual, Worringerian virtual reality as usual. Sure, this is a negative (not to say also nihilistic) conclusion to this first attempt to get *after* Worringerian virtual reality. But precisely such endings may be, for the time being, the absolute horizon and limit of Worringer's relevance and influence, at least they are right *now*, in *this* text, *this* virtual reality—as we all await, but also some of us begin to combat and produce, possible, alternative, nontextual realities to come, including perhaps even those "big continuations" spoken of by Lenin back in the prerevolutionary year 1908 (known in some quarters only as the date of the publication of the first book of one Wilhelm Worringer).

NOTES

1. V. I. Lenin, "The Student Movement and the Present Political Situation" [1908], in his *Collected Works*, various translators (Moscow: Progress Publishers, 1963), 15:213–19; here 219. "The proletariat will not be behindhand. It often yields the palm to the bourgeois democrats in speeches at banquets, in legal unions, within the walls of universities, from the rostrum of representative institutions. It never yields the palm, and will not do so, in the serious and great revolutionary struggle of the masses. All the conditions for bringing this struggle to a head are not ripening as quickly and easily as some of us would hope—but those conditions are ripening and gathering head unswervingly. And the little beginning of little academic conflicts is a great beginning, for after it—if not today then tomorrow, if not tomorrow then the day after—will follow big continuations."

2. Benedict de Spinoza, *On the Improvement of the Understanding* [1661, unfinished], in his *On the Improvement of the Understanding, The Ethics, Correspondence*, trans. with an introduction by R. H. M. Elwes (New York: Dover, 1955; reprint of the 1883 ed.), 1–41; here 34.

3. Louis Althusser, *L'avenir dure longtemps [suivi de] Les faits: Autobiographies* (Paris: Stock/IMEC, 1992), 74 *(L'avenir)*. These two, very different and both unfinished, attempts at an autobiography were written in 1985 and 1976, respectively.

4. *Selections from the Prison Notebooks of Antonio Gramsci*, ed. and trans. Quintin Hoare and Geoffrey Nowell Smith (New York: International Publications, 1971), 170–71.

5. For a useful survey of the literature linking postmodernism to postindustrialism, see Margaret Rose, *The Post-Modern and the Post-Industrial: A Critical Analysis* (Cambridge: Cambridge University Press, 1991). See further David Harvey, *The Condition of Postmodernity: An Enquiry into the Origins of Cultural Change* (Oxford: Basil Blackwell, 1989).

6. Althusser, *L'avenir dure longtemps [suivi de] Les faits: Autobiographies*, 313 *(Les faits)*.

7. On difference-engines, see Marvin Minsky, *The Society of Mind* [1985], illustrations by Juliana Lee (New York: Simon and Schuster/Touchstone, 1988), 78. For an imaginative

account of the "first" such engine, see William Gibson and Bruce Sterling, *The Difference Engine* (New York: Bantam Books, 1991).

8. Erwin Panofsky, *Gothic Architecture and Scholasticism* [1951] (New York: New American Library, 1976), 17. For more current discussions of perspective and related matters, see *Vision and Visuality*, ed. Hal Foster (Seattle: Bay Press, 1988) and *Incorporations*, ed. Jonathan Crary and Sanford Kwinter (New York: Zone, 1992).

9. For a pellucid and timely criticism of "interdisciplinary" work along these lines, see Althusser, "Philosophy and the Spontaneous Philosophy of the Scientists" [1967], in his *Philosophy and the Spontaneous Philosophy of the Scientists and Other Essays*, ed. and with an introduction by Gregory Elliott, trans. Ben Brewster et al. (London: Verso, 1990), 69–165; esp. 92–100. For attempts to apply a communist theory of unacknowledged consensus to specific cultural and philosophical artifacts, see Geoff Waite, "Lenin in Las Meninas: An Essay in Historical-Materialist Vision," *History and Theory* 25, no. 3 (1986), 248–85; "Truckin' under a Pink Sky, Seeing Red" [essay on Lyonel Feininger], in *Human Rights/ Human Wrongs: Art and Social Change*, ed. Robert Hobbs and Fredrick Woodard, afterword by Robert Hughes (Iowa City: University of Iowa Museum of Art Press, 1986), 71–105; and the forthcoming *Nietzsche's Corps(e): Aesthetics, Politics, Prophecy, or, the Spectacular Technoculture of Everyday Life*.

10. For a preliminary (and I think flawed) attempt to articulate the reception of Worringer's *Abstraction and Empathy* and its reception in terms of their respective "rhetorics" and by means of a more internal reading, see Chapter 1.

11. On New Social or Socialized Work, see Félix Guattari and Toni Negri, *Communists Like Us: New Spaces of Liberty, New Lines of Alliance* [1985], with a "Postscript, 1990" by Toni Negri, trans. Michael Ryan (New York: Semiotext[e] Foreign Agents Series, 1990); and another key document of twenty-first-century thought, *Autonomia: Post-Political Politics*, ed. Sylvère Lotringer and Christian Marazzi, special issue of *Semiotext(e)* 3, no. 3 (1980).

12. I don't know what it means that Worringer's first book has just been translated into Chinese in the People's Republic of China, based on an East German edition, or that his work has long been influential in Japan. In 1987, a Chinese edition of *Abstraction and Empathy* appeared as *Cho xiang Yu Yiq ing*, translated from a recent East German edition *Abstraktion und Einfühlung* (Leipzig: Gustav Kiepenheuer, 1981). According to Worringer's bibliographer, his work has appeared in translation "among other places in England, France, the Netherlands, Spain and the Spanish-speaking States of Latin America, in the USSR and the USA." Wulf Schadendorf, "Bibliographie," in Worringer, *Fragen und Gegenfragen*, 189–92; here 189.

13. See Virilio, *War and Cinema: The Logistics of Perception* [1984], trans. Patrick Camiller (London: Verso, 1989).

14. Henri Lefebvre, *The Production of Space* [1974], trans. Donald Nicholson-Smith (Oxford: Basil Blackwell, 1991), 289.

15. William Gibson, *Neuromancer* (New York: Ace Books, 1984), 239.

16. Bram Stoker, *The Lady of the Shroud* [1909] (London: Jarrolds, 1966), 178.

17. Thomas Pynchon, *Gravity's Rainbow* (New York: Viking, 1973), 674.

18. On teledildonics, see Howard Rheingold, *Virtual Reality* (New York: Simon and Schuster/Summit Books, 1991), 345–53. But, for a more theoretically informed discussion of the erotic and virtual reality, see David Tomas, "Old Rituals for New Space: *Rites de Passage* and William Gibson's Cultural Model of Cyberspace," and Michael Heim, "The Erotic Ontology of Cyberspace," both in *Cyberspace: First Steps*, ed. Michael Benedikt (Cambridge: MIT Press, 1991), 31–47, and 59–80, respectively.

19. Paul Virilio, *Speed and Politics: An Essay on Dromology* [1977], trans. Mark Polizzotti (New York: Semiotext[e], 1986), 133–34.

20. Gibson, *Neuromancer*, 5. Also see his *Count Zero* (New York: Ace Books, 1987).

21. "Cyborgs at Large: Interview with Donna Haraway," in *Technoculture*, ed. Constance Penley and Andrew Ross (Minneapolis: University of Minnesota Press, 1991), 1–20; here 4. See further Donna J. Haraway, "A Cyborg Manifesto: Science, Technology, and Socialist-Feminism in the Late Twentieth Century" [1985], in her *Simians, Cyborgs, and Women: The Reinvention of Nature* (New York: Routledge, 1991), 149–81.

22. See Virilio, *The Lost Dimension* [1984], trans. Daniel Moshenberg (New York: Semiotext[e], 1991).

23. In terms of their theoretical and practical implications, there may not be much that is radically *new* or even all that *different* about cyberspace, cyborgs, VR, and other computer-generated, bio-mechanical, and supposedly "interactive" technologies or hyperrealities. Certainly (for the time being) they can be compared to other, older things; and this very ability to compare means that the type of reality entailed is precisely still virtual rather than totally actual. Novelty for its own sake is rarely interesting, nor is the nostalgic desire for origins that tags along with it. What matters rather more is why such comparisons occur to us *even* in VR, and what we can make out of them—their politics, as it were.

Numerous, very diverse technosocial forerunners of VR have been suggested; for example, the Lascaux caves. See Rheingold's popularizing account, *Virtual Reality* (with the rather expansive jacket blurb: "The Revolutionary Technology of Computer-Generated Artificial Worlds—and How It Promises and Threatens to Transform Business and Society"), 379–82. For more precise discussions of the question of how "new" cyberspace really is—at least in its current manifestations—see Tomas, "Old Rituals for New Space," and Heim, "The Erotic Ontology of Cyberspace." See further Michael Herr, *Dispatches* (New York: Avon Books, 1978), where the Vietnam War takes on an uncanny resemblance to cyberspace before the fact.

For some (necessarily very preliminary) accounts either of virtual reality itself or of relevance to it, see the following books and anthologies: Rheingold, *Virtual Reality; Cyberspace: Ausflüge in virtuelle Wirklichkeiten*, ed. Manfred Waffender (Reinbek bei Hamburg: Rowohlt, 1991); *Mirrorshades: The Cyberpunk Anthology* [1986], ed. Bruce Sterling (New York: Ace Books, 1988); Benjamin Woolley, *Virtual Worlds: A Journey in Hype and Hyperreality* (Oxford: Basil Blackwell, 1992), and, especially for the time being, *Cyberspace: First Steps*. Finally, on reification, see Georg Lukács, *History and Class Consciousness: Studies in Marxist Dialectics* [1922; 1968], trans. Rodney Livingstone (Cambridge: MIT Press, 1971).

24. Example: "Gibson's Chiba City may have sprung from his misperception of Japan, but it was this misperception that encouraged Japanese readers to correctly perceive the nature of postmodernist Japan. In short, the moment we perceive cyberpunk stories which misperceive Japan, we are already perceived correctly by cyberpunk." Takayuki Tatsumi, "The Japanese Reflection of Mirrorshades," in *Storming the Reality Studio: A Casebook of Cyberpunk and Postmodern Science Fiction*, ed. Larry McCaffery (Durham: Duke University Press, 1991), 366–73; here 372.

25. Too often, for example, the term "postmodern" is prematurely employed to designate an absolute epistemological, aesthetic, or even global economic break with Fordist modernity; for the moment it is usually better to reserve the term for the still manifest global *overlap* between Modernism and emerging but still deeply related modes of production.

26. See David Cronenberg's *Stereo* and *Crimes of the Future* (both late 1960s), *Shivers/ They Came from Within* (1975), *The Brood* (1979), *Scanners* (1981), *The Dead Zone* (1983),

Videodrome (1983), *The Fly* (remake, 1986), *Dead Ringers* (1988), *Naked Lunch* (1991),
etc. Much of the literature to date on Cronenberg is lacking in incisiveness or even interest.
The notable exception is Fredric Jameson's extended analysis of *Videodrome* in terms of
the postmodern conspiracy theory in his *Geopolitical Aesthetic: Cinema and Space in the
World System* (Bloomington: Indiana University Press, and London: BFI, 1992), 11–35.
For a briefer discussion of another of Cronenberg's films *(Dead Ringers)* in terms of the
logic of the simulacrum, see Arthur W. Frank, "Twin Nightmares of the Medical Simulacrum," in *Jean Baudrillard: The Disappearance of Art and Politics,* ed. William Stearns
and William Chaloupka (New York: St. Martin's Press, 1992), 82–97.

27. Spinoza, *The Ethics* [completed 1675; published 1678], in his *On the Improvement
of the Understanding, The Ethics, Correspondence,* 42–271; here 148 [part III, prop.
XXVII, proof].

28. See *Videodrome* (Cronenberg, Canada, 1983).

29. For the now-classic ecstatic view of the mass media as human prosthesis, see Marshall
McLuhan, *Understanding Media: The Extensions of Man* (New York: McGraw-Hill, 1964);
for the equally classic counterview a few years later of the mass media as a hyperreification
of commodity capitalism, see Guy Debord, *La société du spectacle* [1967] (Paris: Champ
Libre, 1971). On these two takes on modernity, finding a common (though, I think, to
some extent itself contradictory) source in the work of Walter Benjamin, see Hal Foster,
"Postmodernism in Parallax," *October* 63 (Winter 1993), 3–20, esp. 16–19.

30. Jean Baudrillard, *Forget Foucault* [1977], in *Forget Foucault and Forget Baudrillard,*
trans. Nicole Dufresne, Phil Beitchman, Lee Hildreth, and Mark Polizzotti (New York:
Semiotext[e] Foreign Agents Series, 1987), 7–64; here 53.

31. Haraway, "A Cyborg Manifesto," in *Simians, Cyborgs, and Women,* 150. But in
several important respects Haraway's vision of cyborgs is premature, as other students of
the future are suggesting. For example, William Gibson (self-described "computer illiter-
ate" and coiner of the term "cyberspace") has significantly inspired NASA scientists, plastic
surgeons, and inventors generally, as well as cyberpunks and other cyborgs; at the same
time, however, in interviews he emphasizes that humans continue to exist around most of
the globe—often, indeed most typically, in extreme and dehumanizing illiteracy, disease,
and poverty. For the time being, cyborg posthumanity is still reserved for the capitalist:
for example, the man safe in Beverly Hills above the rubble of The City of Quartz, say,
who can afford a new kidney, heart, hip, leg, hand, eye, etc. (though not, just yet, brain
or spinal column), when the old ones go the way of all flesh; he can even have himself frozen
when he dies—perhaps to be reborn again, to Return Eternally, as the poor person cannot.

32. See *The Brood* (Cronenberg, Canada, 1979). Note also that an elaborate political
discourse circulating around "the brood" (German *Brut,* French *couvée,* Spanish *cría,* Italian *covata*) was ubiquitous in Northern and Southern Europe throughout the 1970s—used
not only negatively by the state and mass media to stigmatize "terrorist" groups such as
the Red Army faction, but also as positive self-descriptions by the groups themselves. Of
course the theme of psychoplasmics runs throughout the history of SF. *Forbidden Planet*
(1956) is arguably the classic cold war, "rightwing Freudian" version of this problematic.

33. Such fluidity between categories is symptomatic of all his writing; this is one reason
not only for the logical vertigo one often experiences reading him but also for his fairly
variegated influence. One suspects (in quasi-psychoanalytic terms) that Worringer never
"worked through" the deep ambivalence (inhabiting already his earliest and most influential
work of 1908) with regard to the relationship between such categories as "primitivism,"
"modernism," "technologism," and "Americanism"; we are (too obsessively) reminded by
Freudians that one must perpetually and more or less blindly "act out" in practice that

which is inadequately "worked through" in theory. *Where denegation proposes, repression disposes.*

34. But, then, writers of the much greater conceptual sophistication of Walter Benjamin on the Left or Martin Heidegger on the Right hardly solved the problem of what might be called the political ontology of technology, either.

35. Thus, for example, film *(parole)* may be seen, with the communist filmmaker and theorist Pier Paolo Pasolini, to begin where cinema *(langage)* ends, ends where cinema begins; and cinema and film begin where reality ends, end where reality begins. Such is one play of the "proximate" or "differend"—the dialectic-often-without-synthesis within cultural politics between culture and politics. Pasolini noted in this regard that the "porter of cinema is the same porter of reality . . . and because cinema is an audiovisual technique, the porter of cinema appears and speaks as in reality." Pier Paolo Pasolini, "The Fear of Naturalism" [1967], in his *Heretical Empiricism* [1972], ed. Louise K. Barnett, trans. Ben Lawton and Louise K. Barnett (Bloomington: Indiana University Press, 1988), 244–46; here 245. Recall, too, Althusser's binding remark that in really revolutionary theater "the play is really the production of a new spectator, an actor who starts where the performance ends, who only starts so as to complete it, but in life." Althusser, "The 'Piccolo Teatro': Bertolazzi and Brecht (Notes on a Materialist Theatre)" [1962], in his *For Marx* [1965], trans. Ben Brewster (New York: Vintage, 1969), 129–51; here 151.

The point here, however, is only that if VR is going to turn out to be only the most advanced, avant-garde form of tele-trans-portation, then it may well not serve the "porters" of history: the peasants and workers. But then no technology, no art, no concept in criticism or philosophy has served them very long, even if technology per se is not wholly reducible to the ideology it *has* tended to serve.

36. Immanuel Kant, *Kritik der Urteilskraft* [1790], ed. Wilhelm Weischedel (Frankfurt am Main: Suhrkamp, 1974), 169–72; *Critique of Judgement*, trans. J. H. Bernard (New York: Hafner, 1974), 86–89.

37. Slavoj Zizek, *For They Know Not What They Do: Enjoyment as a Political Factor* (London: Verso, 1991), 144.

38. Shoshana Felman, *Writing and Madness* [*La folie et la chose littéraire*, 1978], trans. Martha Noel Evans and Shoshana Felman (Ithaca: Cornell University Press, 1985), 12–13.

39. See Jean-François Lyotard, *The Differend: Phrases in Dispute* [1983], trans. Georges Van Den Abbelle (Minneapolis: University of Minnesota Press, 1988), 12–13. On the related Heideggerian notion of the "proximate," see Emil Kettering, *Nähe: Das Denken Martin Heideggers* (Pfüllingen: Neske, 1987).

40. Gilles Deleuze, *Kant's Critical Philosophy: The Doctrine of the Faculties* [1963], trans. Hugh Tomlinson and Barbara Habberjam (Minneapolis: University of Minnesota Press, 1990), 50–52 (my emphasis).

41. See, in this volume, Neil H. Donahue, "From Worringer to Baudrillard and Back: Ancient Americans and (Post)Modern Culture in Weimar Germany." See further Wilhelm Worringer, *Egyptian Art* [*Ägyptische Kunst: Probleme ihrer Wertung* (Munich: Piper, 1927), authorized trans. Bernard Rackham (London: Putnam, 1928)], and several of the essays written soon after World War I that are now contained in his *Fragen und Gegenfragen: Schriften zum Kunstproblem* (Munich: Piper, 1956), including: "Kritische Gedanken zur neuen Kunst" (1919) and "Künstlerische Zeitfragen" (1920/21), 86–105 and 106–29, respectively. Also see Worringer's earlier (bizarre, wildly misogynist, and never reprinted or translated) essay "Geschlechterkampf" ("Battle of the Sexes"—though this may not be his own title), in *Zeit-Echo: Ein Kriegs-Tagebuch der Künstler* 2 (1914), 20–22.

42. See Neil Larsen, *Modernism and Hegemony: A Materialist Critique of Aesthetic Agencies,* foreword by Jaime Concha (Minneapolis: University of Minnesota Press, 1990).

43. And we must be continually reminded these days that not all attacks on modernity lay the groundwork for a progressive postmodernity; many are very reactionary—perhaps Worringer's among them, although the jury is still out.

44. See Worringer's important monograph *Problematik der Gegenwartskunst* (Munich: Piper, 1948), 5–10; reprinted in *Fragen und Gegenfragen*.

45. Worringer, *Problematik der Gegenwartskunst*, 18–28.

46. There are many relevant introductions to the concept hegemony. See, for example, *Gramsci and Marxist Theory*, ed. Chantal Mouffe (London: Routledge and Kegan Paul, 1979); Joseph V. Femia, *Gramsci's Political Thought: Hegemony, Consciousness, and the Revolutionary Process* (Oxford: Clarendon, 1981); and John Hoffman, *The Gramscian Challenge: Coercion and Consent in Marxist Political Theory* (New York: Basil Blackwell, 1984).

Too, the Worringer industry seems not to have recognized sufficiently yet that Worringer's oscillating attitude toward modernity—economic as well as technological—was also specifically "Heideggerian" in important respects, in addition to being an effect of the ubiquitous "mandarin" discourse circulating in and around Weimar Germany. For discussions of this problematic that bear at least indirectly on the Worringer case, see Michael E. Zimmerman, *Heidegger's Confrontation with Modernity: Technology, Politics, Art* (Bloomington: Indiana University Press, 1990); and Fritz K. Ringer, *The Decline of the German Mandarins: The German Academic Community, 1890–1933* (Cambridge: Harvard University Press, 1969), along with Jürgen Habermas's review article "Die deutschen Mandarine" [1971], now in the new version of his *Philosophisch-politische Profile*, 2d expanded ed. (Frankfurt am Main: Suhrkamp, 1987), 458–68. On at least two recent occasions, Ringer's theory of the German mandarins has been applied to Heidegger (but not Worringer): in passing by Habermas, and more systematically by Bourdieu. See Habermas, "Heidegger-Werk und Weltanschauung," in Victor Farías, *Heidegger und der Nationalsozialismus,* 2d expanded ed., trans. Klaus Laermann, with an introduction by Jürgen Habermas (Frankfurt am Main: S. Fischer, 1989), 11–37; esp. 16–17. Also see Pierre Bourdieu, *L'ontologie politique de Martin Heidegger,* 2d ed. (Paris: Editions de minuit, 1988), 15–65.

47. For analyses of the false dialectic between technophobia and technophilia, and its effects, see Michael Ryan and Douglas Kellner, *Cinema Politica: Politics and Ideology of the Contemporary Hollywood Film* (Bloomington: Indiana University Press, 1988); James H. Kavanagh, "Feminism, Humanism and Science Fiction in *Alien*" [1980], in *Alien Zone: Cultural Theory and Contemporary Science Fiction Cinema,* ed. Annette Kuhn (London: Verso, 1990), 73–81; and Michael Parenti, *Make-Believe Media: The Politics of Entertainment* (New York: St. Martin's Press, 1992).

48. Philip K. Dick, *Do Androids Dream of Electric Sheep?* [1968] (New York: Ballantine Books, 1984), 25–27. There is today an extensive literature on *Blade Runner*: for the first major study, see Giuliana Bruno, "Ramble City: Postmodernism and *Blade Runner*" [1987], in *Alien Zone,* 183–95; for more recent criticism, see *Retrofitting "Blade Runner": Issues in Ridley Scott's "Blade Runner" and Philip K. Dick's "Do Androids Dream of Electric Sheep?"* ed. Judith B. Kernan (Bowling Green: Bowling Green State University Press, 1991).

49. One of the things that links the conceptual world of Worringer to contemporary technoculture is his *paranoia*—in a metaphorical, if not also literal, sense of the word. This is clearly exhibited in the prefaces he wrote (in 1948 and again 1959) to *Abstraction and Empathy,* especially in his concern to defend his theories from all future objections. According to Dick, in a 1974 interview: "Paranoia, in some respects, I think, is a modern-day development of an ancient, archaic sense that animals still have—quarry-type animals—that they're being watched. . . . I say paranoia is an atavistic sense. It's a lingering

sense, that we had long ago, when we were—our ancestors were—very vulnerable to predators, and this sense tells them they're being watched. And they're being watched probably by something that's going to get them. . . . And often my characters have this feeling. But what really I've done is, I have atavised their society. That although it's set in the future, in many ways they're living—there is a retrogressive quality in their lives, you know? They're living like our ancestors did. I mean, the hardware is in the future, the scenery's in the future, but the situations are really from the past." Cited as the motto of *The Collected Stories of Philip K. Dick,* introduction by Norman Spinrad (New York: Citadel Twilight, 1990), vol. 2. But Dick's most extraordinary depiction of paranoia as *social* and *military* mode of organization and combat occurs in his *Clans of the Alphane Moon* [1964] (New York: Carroll and Graf, 1988), esp. 92–99.

As Leo Bersani has also implied, paranoia bears directly on theories of *warfare:* "the paranoid imagination operates on precisely that assumption which its enemies—*if they existed*—would wish it to operate on: the assumption that simulations belong to the other side, that doubles have no reason to appear or to exist except to prevent us from seeing the original. The self-protective suspicions of paranoia are, therefore, already a defeat. The paranoid We *must* lose out to the enemy They, and this by virtue of the fact that it authorizes, or creates, the condition of possibility of They-ness by a primary, founding faith in the unicity of the Real. . . . In paranoia, the primary function of the enemy is to provide a definition of the real that makes paranoia necessary. We must therefore begin to suspect the paranoid structure itself as a device by which consciousness maintains the polarity of self and nonself, thus preserving the concept of identity. In paranoia, two Real Texts confront one another: subjective being and a world of monolithic otherness." Leo Bersani, "Pynchon, Paranoia, and Literature," *Representations* 25 (Winter 1989), 99–118; here 108–9.

For the classic (very disputable, generally speaking, but in the case of Worringer's famous depictions of his encounter with Georg Simmel in Paris, perhaps also relevant) notion that paranoia represents a defense mechanism against a subconsciously desired homosexual attack, see Sigmund Freud, "Psycho-Analytical Notes on an Autobiographical Account of a Case of Paranoia (Dementia Paranoides)" [1911], in his *Three Case Histories,* ed. Philip Rieff (New York: Collier Books, 1972), 103–86. (Whether Worringer himself "was gay" or not is a matter of some debate, but of no concern here.)

Particularly symptomatic with regard to his at least rhetorical paranoia, is Worringer's preoccupation with regard to the point of obsession with what went on in Paleolithic *caves* (the deep lime pits of Lascaux having been discovered on 12 September 1940) since whatever it was is imagined by him to have been originary—determining subsequent history. Even though he sometimes says that the evidence of caves is "merely a last, sequel-less final terminus of *their* development," not *"ours,"* this remark hardly captures the importance of caves for him as a determination on the subsequent development of cultural history. See Worringer, "Schlußwort nach fünfzig Jahren—Zur Neuausgabe 1959," in *Abstraktion und Einfühlung: Ein Beitrag zur Stilpsychologie* [1908] (Munich: Piper, 1959), 15–33; here 30. For the standard (but not entirely satisfactory) English translation, see *Abstraction and Empathy: A Contribution to the Psychology of Style,* trans. Michael Bullock (New York: International Universities Press, 1953). This preface (and self-described "final word") was written after the English translation was published.

Caves are important to understand Worringerian virtual reality because, as noted earlier, what went on in them arguably represented the first VR technology—perhaps as a way of manipulating initiation rituals by dominant elites. Using terms borrowed from Octave Mannoni, I would suggest also that caves are the "keys to the imaginary" of Worringerian virtual reality, in that they are its most basic "other scene," its "I know [it isn't really true] but [I believe it nonetheless]." Mannoni spoke of the deep psychoanalytic, anthropological, and societal need to posit "another scene" of absolute, untroubled faith. Such need may be variously projected: for instance, onto another culture, onto the past of one's own epoch or society, onto a stage of an initiation ritual, or onto an individual's childhood. Most important, this need generates a type of myth or "other scene" that persists even—indeed *especially*—when it has been exposed as *empirically untrue*. In part, this is a defense mechanism: the possibility of legitimation crises to one's theory is interdicted, for example. Thus is produced what Mannoni called the *"je-sais-bien-mais-quand-même"* structure, in which the belief in an illusion is grounded on some element of the illusion and *vice versa:* an intricate (im)balance of faith and disavowal, such as the "caves" in Worringer's theory of abstraction and empathy, but also, I am suggesting, the general problematic of his "reception": that is, the reality-effect of (Worringerian) virtual reality. See Octave Mannoni, *Clefs pour l'imaginaire ou l'autre scène* (Paris: Editions du Seuil, 1969), esp. 163–64.

For a discussion of caves both relevant to and extending beyond Worringer's concerns, see Georges Bataille, *Lascaux or the Birth of Art* [1955], trans. Austryn Wainhouse (Geneva: Skira, 1955), even though Mario Ruspoli finds Bataille's work on cave painting to be "of debatable interest in the eyes of the prehistorian." See Ruspoli, *The Cave of Lascaux: The Final Photographs,* trans. Sebastien Wormell (New York: Abrams, 1987), 205, and Steven Ungar, "Phantom Lascaux: Origin of the Work of Art," in *On Bataille,* ed. Allan Stoekl, Yale French Studies 78 (New Haven: Yale University Press, 1990), 246–62. On some of the problems of ever knowing for sure what went on in prehistoric caves and whether it matters very much, see Donald Preziosi, *Rethinking Art History: Meditations on a Coy Science* (New Haven: Yale University Press, 1989), 122–55. Finally, for a particularly brilliant essay on the caves, but not Bataille nor Worringer, see the great Marxist art critic Max Raphael's *Prehistoric Cave Paintings,* trans. Norbert Gutermann (New York: Pantheon Books, 1945).

50. Borrowing and conflating key phrases from Alfred Hitchcock, François Truffaut, Robert Ray, Raymond Bellour, and Zizek, it is important to add that the "certain tendency of the Hollywood cinema," virtually in its entirety, is to become "a *machine* for the production of the [heterosexual] couple"—no matter what the historical or social frameworks are in which people happen to find themselves. See François Truffaut, "A Certain Tendency of the French Cinema" [1954], in *Movies and Methods,* ed. Ben Nichols (Berkeley and Los Angeles: University of California Press, 1976), 224–37; Robert Ray, *A Certain Tendency of the Hollywood Cinema, 1930–1980* (Princeton: Princeton University Press, 1985); Bellour, "Psychosis, Neurosis, Perversion," in *A Hitchcock Reader,* ed. Marshall Deutelbaum and Leland Poague (Ames: Iowa State University Press, 1986); and Zizek, "In His Bold Gaze My Ruin Is Writ Large," in *Everything You Always Wanted to Know about Lacan (But Were Afraid to Ask Hitchcock),* ed. Zizek (London: Verso, 1992), 211–72.

51. Film "purists" prefer the recently released director's cut mainly because it eliminates the indeed overdone *noir* voice-over but especially because it eliminates the supposedly "cop-out" happy ending—meaningless, even idiotic preferences for any number of reasons; as if any MassCult production were not, in some sense, overdone or a cop-out!

52. See Althusser, "Ideology and Ideological State Apparatuses (Notes towards an Investigation)" [1969/70], in his *Lenin and Philosophy and Other Essays,* trans. Ben Brewster (New York: Monthly Review Press, 1971), 127–86; here esp. 174. In the meantime, a number of critics have (rightly) pointed out that in general the mechanism of interpellation is more contradictory and less necessarily debilitating or supportive of a functionalist status quo than Althusser implies; see perhaps most notably Göran Therborn, *The Ideology of Power and the Power of Ideology* (London: Verso, 1980).

53. See Mike Davis, *City of Quartz: Excavating the Future in Los Angeles* (London:

Verso, 1990), 83–88 ("Epilogue: Gramsci vs. *Blade Runner*"), and *Beyond Blade Runner: Urban Control, The Ecology of Fear* (Westfield, N.J.: Open Magazine Pamphlet Series, 1992). See further Norman M. Klein, "Building Blade Runner," *Social Text* 28 (1991), 147–52.

54. For example, it would certainly not be impossible—but would take a particularly rarefied and idealist frame of mind—to fold Worringer into the issues raised by the anthology *If You Lived Here: The City in Art, Theory, and Social Activism, A Project by Martha Rosler,* ed. Brian Williams (Seattle: Bay Press, 1991).

55. Deleuze, *Cinema 2: The Time-Image* [1985], trans. Hugh Tomlinson and Robert Galeta (Minneapolis: University of Minnesota Press, 1989).

56. See Deleuze, *Cinema 1: The Movement-Image* [1983], trans. Hugh Tomlinson and Barbara Habberjam (Minneapolis: University of Minnesota Press, 1986). For Deleuze, Alfred Hitchcock ("the last of the classics, first of the moderns") is the precise cinematic threshold between movement-image and time-image. See Deleuze, *Pourparlers* (Paris: Editions de minuit, 1990), 79.

57. Virilio, *Speed and Politics,* 147. See further his *Pure War,* with Sylvère Lotringer, trans. Mark Polizzotti (New York: Semiotext[e], 1983). For an important update, see Manuel De Landa, *War in the Age of Intelligent Machines* (New York: Zone Books, 1991).

58. As reported on CNN, after the war was over. "This Bud's For You (And All You Do!)" was of course part of a highly successful series of ads by the Budweiser Brewing Company. In it various kinds of traditional worker solidarity are effectively reconfigured (across class, race, and to a lesser extent gender lines) as modes of beer consumption— most notably of Bud, "The King of Beers."

59. *Selections from the Prison Notebooks of Antonio Gramsci,* 238. Compare and contrast Dante Germino, *Antonio Gramsci: Architect of a New Politics* (Baton Rouge: Louisiana State University Press, 1990). Jameson once suggested the possibility of a "Gramscian architecture," though he has left unclear what it might look like; see "Architecture and the Critique of Ideology" [1985], in his *The Ideologies of Theory: Essays 1971–1986,* Vol. 2, *The Syntax of History* (Minneapolis: Minnesota University Press, 1988), 35–60.

60. Ernesto Che Guevara, *Guerrilla Warfare* [1960], authorized trans. J. P. Morray, with an introduction and case studies by Brian Loveman and Thomas M. Davies, Jr. (Lincoln: University of Nebraska Press, 1985), 69.

61. See Deleuze and Guattari, *A Thousand Plateaus: Capitalism and Schizophrenia* [1980], trans. Brian Massumi (Minneapolis: University of Minnesota Press, 1987). Hereafter, *Plateaus,* with page numbers in text.

62. See Virilio, *Speed and Politics,* 38–41 and 134–35.

63. Heinrich von Kleist, *Penthesilea: Ein Trauerspiel* [1808], in Heinrich von Kleist, *Werke und Briefe,* 4 vols., vol. 2: *Dramen II,* ed. Peter Goldammer, with Anita Golz (Berlin [GDR]: Aufbau-Verlag, 1978), 120. *Penthesilea: A Tragedy* [trans. Humphry Trevelyan], in Kleist, *Plays,* ed. Walter Hinderer, foreword by E. L. Doctorow (New York: Continuum, 1982), 156–268; here 267.

64. See Geoff Waite, "On the Politics of Boredom (A communist Pastiche)," *Documents* 1 (Fall/Winter 1992), 93–109.

65. See Lenin, *The Development of Capitalism in Russia* [1886–99, first published 1899; 2d ed. 1908], in his *Collected Works,* 3:494. The properly Leninist point to be made today, however, is that the *structure* of this argument can still be applied both to the effects of the *dismantling* of the mining industry around the world (from the United Kingdom to South America to South Africa to the Urals, Lenin's own main focus), and to the concomitant shift to *post-Fordist* modes of production and consumption, and so on. Lenin himself stressed the ways that the fate of the mining industry reveals *uneven* development and

nonsynchronous overlap not only between older and new *technologies* but also between older and newer *social formations.* The young Lenin also savored the fable "The Metaphysician" by the writer I. I. Khemnitser, which he applied to intellectuals who ignore the importance of the national and global mining and metallurgy industries. According to Lenin, such idealists are lost in their *abstractions,* just like "the metaphysical philosopher who delayed climbing out of a pit while he pondered over the nature of the rope that had been thrown him. At last he decided: 'It is nothing but a rope!'" Lenin, "The Handicraft Census of 1894–95 in Perm Gubernia and General Problems of 'Handicraft' Industry" [1897/98, 2d ed. 1908], in his *Collected Works,* 2:355–458; here 453.

66. For a great attempt to obviate the difference between metaphysical or virtual and physical or real ascent and descent, see the unfinished novel by René Daumal (1908–1944), *Mount Analogue: A Novel of Symbolically Authentic Non-Euclidean Adventures in Mountain Climbing* [first published 1951], trans. Roger Shattuck (Boston: Shambhala Publications: 1992).

67. See Worringer, *Problematik der Gegenwartskunst,* esp. 13, 19–20, and 25–26.

68. Worringer, *Problematik der Gegenwartskunst,* 18.

69. *Videodrome* (Cronenberg, Canada, 1982). For a preliminary discussion of *Videodrome,* see Carol J. Clover, "Her Body, Himself: Gender in the Slasher Film" [1987], in *Fantasy and the Cinema,* ed. James Donald (London: British Film Institute, 1989), 91–133; Scott Bukatman, "Who Programs You? The Science Fiction of the Spectacle," in *Alien Zone,* 196–213; and especially Jameson in *The Geopolitical Aesthetic.* Also on Cronenberg, by way of his most recent film *Naked Lunch,* see the remark of film critic Stuart Klawans: "For a really good time with paranoia, see *Naked Lunch.* Based on the life and work of William S. Burroughs, *Naked Lunch* is the latest expression of writer-director David Cronenberg's one big idea. He believes the mind and the body to be a continuum, and that scares him silly. From *The Brood* through *Dead Ringers* he's been a film poet of somatic anxiety, simultaneously obsessed and repelled by the flesh but even more so by the emotions that shape and misshape the body. Now Cronenberg collides head-on with Burroughs, pseudoscientific rhapsodist of the mind-body split. Fog rises; shadows fall; and out of the unspeakable coupling slithers a great film." See Klawans's review of *Naked Lunch* (along with Oliver Stone's *JFK*) in *The Nation,* 20 January 1992, 62–64; here 63.

70. See Lenin, *The Proletarian Revolution and the Renegade Kautsky* [1918], in his *Collected Works,* 28:227–326; here 235.

71. Worringer, *Abstraktion und Einfühlung,* 57; *Abstraction and Empathy,* 22.

72. For an important reflection on one way that a "special culture of the eye" *might* be free from all spatial and existential coordinates, see Valery Podoroga, "The Eunuch of the Soul: Positions of Reading and the World of Platonov," *South Atlantic Quarterly* (Spring 1991), 357–408. Podoroga, a leading Russian literary theorist and philosopher, is developing certain theses about the relation of the visible to the invisible contained in the philosophical system of Merleau-Ponty but especially in the later works of the major Soviet science fiction writer, critic, and novelist Andrei Platanonovich Platonov (1899–1951). On this basis, Podoroga is working out the possibility of a new way of seeing that is radically opposed not merely to all—*Worringerian*—binary oppositions between "the inner" (whether "invisible," as in subjectivism and idealism, or "visible," as in objectivism and realism) and "the outer" ("the visible" from similar angles) but also to "a psychological representation of the inner." He then constructs what he variously terms an "objective nonrelative perception," a "disembodied eye," or (following Platonov) "the eunuch of the soul" *(evnukh dushi).* Such a gaze "makes a topological measurement of the external available to us—a more complex kind of measurement, whose analysis is not possible on the basis of the old inner/outer opposition" (358). While it is certainly possible to *read* Wor-

ringer in terms of this gaze, it seems unfair to Platonov to claim that such a perspective is actually present in Worringer's work, in light of Platonov's enormous, remarkably conscious achievement.

73. Gottlob Frege, *Die Grundlagen der Arithmetik: Eine logisch mathematische Untersuchung über den Begriff der Zahl/The Foundations of Arithmetic: A Logico-Mathematical Enquiry into the Concept of Number* [1884], trans. J. L. Austin, 2d revised dual-language edition (Oxford: Basil Blackwell, 1974), 19/19e. Also see a remark made by the American philosopher and semiotician Charles S. Peirce in 1891: "The straight line appears to us simple, because, as Euclid says, it lies evenly between extremities; that is, because viewed endwise it appears as a point." Peirce, "The Architecture of Theories" [1891], in *Philosophical Writings of Peirce* [1940], ed. and with an introduction by Justus Buchler (New York: Dover, 1955), 315–23; here 317. Finally, all this begins to sound rather like fractals and strange attractors, points and phase space—abstraction and empathy in chaos theory. See James Gleick, *Chaos: Making a New Science* (New York: Penguin Books, 1987), 134.

74. See Kandinsky, *Punkt und Linie zu Fläche: Beitrag zur Analyse der malerischen Elemente* [1926], 6th ed., with an introduction by Max Bill (Bern-Bümpliz: Benteli-Verlag, 1969). Not by chance, I think, Worringer later quite explicitly rejected Kandinsky's apparent development (read: misunderstanding) of his work in this regard. See, for example, Worringer, *Problematik der Gegenwartskunst,* 10. For Worringer at this time (1948), the specificity of *visual* art (as opposed especially to music) was its tragically irreducible, agonistic relationship to nature and to representation.

75. The etymological recollection that *ciphers* are simultaneously *nullities* as well as *signs* is also fundamental to one of the most productive impulses of Lacanian psychoanalysis. For example, Lacan's great early essay on the mirror stage concludes: "In the recourse of subject to subject that we preserve, psychoanalysis may accompany the patient to the ecstatic limit of the '*Thou art that,*' in which is revealed to him the *cipher* of his mortal destiny, but it is not in our mere power as practitioners to bring him to the *point* where the real journey begins." Jacques Lacan, "The Mirror Stage as Formative of the Function of the I as Revealed in Psychoanalytic Experience" [1949], in his *Ecrits: A Selection,* trans. Alan Sheridan (New York: Norton, 1977), 1–7; here 7 (my emphasis). In this case, the English translation works better for my purposes (but also in properly Lacanian fashion) than the French original, which has "moment" for "point." See "Le stade du miroir comme formateur de la fonction du Je, telle qu'elle est révélée dans l'expérience pyschanalytique," in his *Ecrits I* (Paris: Editions du Seuil, 1966), 89–97; here 97. For Lacan's later position on the cipher, explicitly in connection with the relation of political discourse to the Real, see his *Télévision* (Paris: Editions du Seuil, 1974), 59.

76. Kandinsky's line, along with the surface, creates a world, one described by him (*pace* Worringer) as a plane into which a human might walk. A walk-*through.* But, as such, presumably, a site of at least some sort of empathy-effect. Kandinsky wrote, for example: "The work of art is mirrored on the surface of consciousness. It lies beyond and after the termination of the stimulus, it vanishes without a trace from the surface. Here, too, like at a window, there is a certain transparent, but hard and stable glass that makes direct inner articulation impossible. Here, too, like with a door, the possibility exists to step *into* the work, to become active in it and to experience its pulsation with all senses" (*Point and Line,* 14).

77. Bataille, "Sacrificial Mutilation and the Severed Ear of Vincent Van Gogh" [1930], in his *Visions of Excess: Selected Writings, 1927–1939,* ed. and with an introduction by Allan Stoekl, trans. Allan Stoekl, with Carl R. Lovitt and Donald M. Leslie, Jr. (Minneapolis: University of Minnesota Press, 1985), 61–72; here 67. See further, also in *Visions of Excess,* "The Eye" [1929], and "The Pineal Eye" [c. 1930], 17–19, and 79–90, respectively;

and *Oeuvres complètes,* ed. Denis Hollier et al. (Paris: Gallimard, 1970–88), 1:258–70, 1:187–89, and 2:21–35.

78. For a brief introduction to Fichte's theory of the "implanted 'eye/I,'" see Manfred Frank, *What Is Neostructuralism?* [1984], trans. Sabine Wilke and Richard Gray, foreword by Martin Schwab (Minneapolis: University of Minnesota Press, 1989), 89–90.

79. Walter Benjamin, *Das Passagen-Werk* [1927–40], ed. Rolf Tiedemann, 2 vols. (Frankfurt am Main: Suhrkamp, 1983), 1:593.

80. See Richard Hamann's important review of *Abstraction and Empathy* in *Zeitschrift für Ästhetik und allgemeine Kunstwissenschaft* 5 (1910), 276–81. Michael Müller has discussed Hamann's analysis in the course of his comparison of Worringer's text to Adolf Loos's *Ornament als Verbrechen* (Ornament as crime), which, like *Abstraction and Empathy,* was first published in 1908. See Müller, *Die Verdrängung des Ornaments: Zum Verhältnis von Architektur und Lebenspraxis* (Frankfurt am Main: Suhrkamp, 1977), esp. 114–17. Müller relocates the debate about the ornament, which took on such urgency around the turn of the century in Europe, in its sociological and ideological context. I should add that Hamann was by no means entirely hostile to Worringer; he contributed an essay to the somewhat mysterious *Festschrift* for Worringer that was published in the Third Reich in 1943. See Hamann, "Die Kategorie der Stofflichkeit in der bildenden Kunst," in *Neue Beiträge deutscher Forschung: Wilhelm Worringer zum 60. Geburtstag,* ed. Erich Fidder (Königsberg: Kanter-Verlag, 1943), 143–50. Other prominent contributors to this volume included Ernst Robert Curtius, Guido Kachnitz-Weinberg, and Walter F. Otto.

81. See Karl Marx, *Capital: A Critique of Political Economy,* Vol. 1, *The Process of Capitalist Production* [1867], trans. Samuel Moore and Edward Aveling, edited by Frederick Engels (New York: International Publishers, 1967), 1:72, and Marx and Engels, *The German Ideology* [1845–46], in their *Collected Works,* various translators (New York: International Publishers, 1976), 5:19–539; here 44–49. But Marx's most relevant argument for today was neither his early work nor in *Capital* but rather in the *Grundrisse.* See Antonio Negri, *Marx Beyond Marx: Lessons on the "Grundrisse"* [1978], trans. Harry Cleaver, Michael Ryan, and Maurizio Viano, ed. Jim Fleming (New York: Autonomedia/Pluto, 1991). Also, for a rigorous demolition of the claim that Marx himself was a technological determinist, see (in addition to the oeuvre of Althusser) Richard W. Miller, *Analyzing Marx: Morality, Power and History* (Princeton: Princeton University Press, 1984).

82. See Debord, *La société du spectacle,* esp. 9–32 (my emphasis).

83. Pierre Bourdieu, *Outline of a Theory of Practice* [1972], trans. Richard Nice (Cambridge: Cambridge University Press, 1982), 191.

84. For example, Worringer attacks anyone who thinks that only one kind of art exists or that authentic, tragic, art for art's sake is ever reconcilable with social needs and with the public, by remarking that this false consciousness is the cultural equivalent of acting as if religion or gold were still being used in a secular, paper-money economy. See his *Problematik der Gegenwartskunst* (15) and his short (quasi-Simmelian) "parable" entitled "Papiergeld und Golddeckung: Ein Gleichnis," *Neue Zürcher Zeitung,* 11 October 1922. More tellingly, perhaps, Worringer in 1948 defends his own quintessentially *modern* and *conservative* political sensibility by quipping of *real* artists: "Whoever is convinced to work for the future, will for this reason not still demand unlimited power of attorney [*Blankovollmacht*] from the present." Worringer, *Problematik der Gegenwartskunst,* 18.

In short, for the later Worringer, artists and the general public, art and society, production and consumption, and so on, ultimately have *nothing* to seek from one another. But while this rhetorical "argument" pays lip service to the language of political economy, and is not ineffective in Worringer's (to some extent legitimate) claim that socialist culture politics had hardly freed itself from many bourgeois fixations. (Lenin himself would not necessarily have disagreed.) But none of this polemic constitutes an attempt to take issues of political economy *seriously* in the analysis either of the history of art, or of its current production and consumption. As even he admitted, "class analysis" was merely epiphenomenal to the more profound, incontrovertible, and insoluble *fact* that the "public" will never understand the greatest art, and ought not even try. See Worringer, *Problematik der Gegenwartskunst,* esp. 15–16 and 20–22. Cost, appropriation, expenditure, expropriation, labor, surplus—all are sacrificed to what Worringer called "the god" in whom "I believe most deeply, the *deo ignoto* of chance." Worringer, *Abstraktion und Einfühlung,* 13–14; *Abstraction and Empathy,* xii. And how on earth does one combat gods—"unknown," "ignoble," or other?

85. Jameson, "Postmodernism and Consumer Society," in *Postmodernism and Its Discontents: Theories, Practices,* ed. E. Ann Kaplan (London: Verso, 1988), 13–29; here 20.

86. See Jameson, *Postmodernism, or, The Cultural Logic of Late Capitalism* (Durham: Duke University Press, 1991), 19–21 (my emphasis). But then there is Mike Davis's powerful (though ultimately not unsympathetic) dismantling of the economic basis of Jameson's notion of postmodernism; see Davis, "Urban Renaissance and the Spirit of Postmodernism," in *Postmodernism and Its Discontents,* 79–87.

87. Worringer, *Form in Gothic* [*Formprobleme der Gotik* (Munich: Piper, 1911)], authorized trans., ed., and with an introduction by Herbert Read (London: Alec Tiranti, 1957), 159–60.

88. Kleist to Wilhelmine von Zenge, 16 and 18 November 1800, with an addition on December 30; in his *Werke und Briefe,* vol. 4, *Briefe,* ed. Wolfgang Barthel and Rudolf Loch, with Anita Golz, 151–59; here 153–54.

Bibliography

Publications by Wilhelm Worringer

This bibliography is based on the bibliography prepared by Wulf Schadendorf for the publication of *Fragen und Gegenfragen.* Works appear in chronological, rather than alphabetical order. Corrections and additions have been made where necessary. I wish to thank Magdalena Bushart for her invaluable assistance in preparing this bibliography.

English translations are listed separately. In the cases where no translation exists, an English title is given after the German citation. If a translation exists, that title is given.

Books

Abstraktion und Einfühlung: Ein Beitrag zur Stilpsychologie. (Dissertation 1907). Munich: Piper, 1908.

Lukas Cranach. Munich: Piper, 1908.

Formprobleme der Gotik. Munich: Piper, 1911.

Die altdeutsche Buchillustration. Munich: Piper, 1912. [Old German Book Illustration]

Künstlerische Zeitfragen. Munich: Bruckmann, 1921. Lecture (19 October 1920) for the Ortsgruppe München der deutschen Goethe-Gesellschaft, 1920. Reprinted in *Fragen und Gegenfragen,* 106–29. [Questions about Contemporary Art]

Die Kölner Bibel: 27 Holzschnitte von 1479. Introduction by Worringer. Munich: Piper, 1923. [The Cologne Bible: 27 Woodcuts from 1479]

Urs Graf: Die Holzschnitte zur Passion. Munich: Piper, 1923. [Urs Graf: The Woodcuts of the Passion]

Deutsche Jugend und östlicher Geist. Bonn: Friedrich Cohen, 1924. [German Youth and Eastern Spirit]

Die Anfänge der Tafelmalerei. Leipzig: Insel, 1924. [The Origins of German Panel Painting]

Buch und Leben des hochberühmten Fabeldichters Aesopi, Ulm 1475. Munich: Piper, 1925. [The Book and Life of the Famous Author of the Fables, Aesop, Ulm 1475]

Ägyptische Kunst: Probleme ihrer Wertung. Munich: Piper, 1927.

Otto Pankok. 24 charcoal drawings. Introduction by Worringer. Munich: Piper, 1927.

Griechentum und Gotik: Vom Weltreich des Hellenismus. Munich: Piper, 1928. [Greek Culture and the Gothic: On the Empire of Hellenism]

Über den Einfluß der angelsächsischen Buchmalerei auf die frühmittelalterliche Monumentalplastik des Kontinents. (Schriften der Königsberger Gelehrten Gesellschaft, Geisteswissenschaftliche Reihe, 8, 1). Halle: Niemeyer, 1931. [On the Influence of Anglo-Saxon Book Painting on the Monumental Sculpture on the Continent in the Early Middle Ages]

Problematik der Gegenwartskunst. (Lecture to the Leipziger Art Society [*Kunstverein*]). Munich: Piper, 1948. Included in *Fragen und Gegenfragen,* 139–54. [The Problematics of Contemporary Art]

Fragen und Gegenfragen: Schriften zum Kunstproblem. Munich: Piper, 1956. A selection of essays from 1919 to 1954. [Questions and Counter-questions]

Articles and Reviews

"Frank Wedekind. Ein Essay." In *Münchener Almanach. Ein Sammelbuch neuer deutscher Dichtung.* Edited by Karl Schloss. Munich: Piper, 1905, 55–64.

"Moderne Idealisten." In *Berner Rundschau* 2 (1907–8): 737–42.

"Die Ausstellung München 1908." *Masken* 4 (1908): 19–24.

"Gedanken zum Theater." *Neue deutsche Rundschau* (1908).

Review of *Impressionismus im Leben und Kunst* by Richard Hamann. *Monatshefte für Kunstwissenschaft* 1 (1908): 338–40.

"Transzendenz und Immanenz in der Kunst." *Zeitschrift für Ästhetik und allgemeine Kunstwissenschaft* 3 (1908): 592–98. Since 1910 this essay has appeared as appendix to *Abstraction and Empathy.*

Review of *Die Grundlagen bewusster Stilempfindung* by Albert von Hofmann. *Kunst und Künstler* 7 (1909): 468.

Review of exhibition, "Willy Geiger, Karl Arnold, Karl Felber-Dachau in München, Moderne Kunsthandlung." *Kunst und Künstler* 7 (1909): 328.

"Die Marées-Ausstellung in der Münchener Sezession." In *Der Cicerone* 1 (1909): 664–66.

"Die Marées-Ausstellung der Münchner Sezession." *Kunst und Künstler* 7 (1909): 231–32. Not identical to the essay with the same title in *Cicerone.*

"Die Münchner Frühjahrssezession." *Kunst und Künstler* 7 (1909): 369–71.

"Die Pietà Rondanini." *Kunst und Künstler* 7 (1909): 355–59.

Review of *Philosophie der Kunst* by Broder Christianssen. *Monatshefte für Kunstwissenschaft* 3 (1910): 293–95.

Review of *Gesammelte Aufsätze* by Adolf Hildebrand. *Monatshefte für Kunstwissenschaft* 3 (1910): 210.

Review of *Hans von Marées* by Julius Meier-Graefe. *Zeitschrift für Ästhetik und allgemeine Kunstwissenschaft* 6 (1911): 317–21.

"Der Baugedanke der Gothik." *Neudeutsche Bauzeitung* 7 (1911): 476–79. Excerpt from *Formprobleme der Gotik.* [The Architectural Principle of the Gothic]

"Zum Problem der modernen Architektur." In *Neudeutsche Bauzeitung* 7 (1911): 486–500. [On the Problem of Modern Architecture]

"Entwicklunggeschichtliches zur modernsten Kunst." In *Im Kampf um die Kunst: Die Antwort auf den "Protest deutscher Künstler."* Munich: Piper, 1911, 92–99. Reprinted as "Zur Entwicklungsgeschichte der modernsten Malerei," *Sturm* 75 (1911): 597–98. [On the Historical Development of the Most Modern Art]

"Entstehung und Gestaltungsprinzipien in der Ornamentik." Kongreß für Ästhetik und allgemeine Kunstwissenschaft. (Berlin, 1913). Stuttgart: Enke, 1914, 222–31. [Origins and Principles of Form in Ornamentation]

"Die Kathedrale in Reims." *Kunst und Künstler* 12 (1914).

"Geschlechterkampf." In *Zeit-Echo: Ein Kriegs-Tagebuch der Künstler* 2 (1914): 20–22. Title in table of contents only. [The Battle of the Sexes]

"Künstlerische Zukunftsfragen." (*Frankfurter Zeitung,* 25 December 1915). In *Kunst und Künstler* 14 (1916): 259–64. [Questions about the Future of Art]

"Geleitwort." *Katalog Freie Secession.* Berlin: Freie Secession, 1918, 9–12.

"Bemerkungen zum Kubismus." In *Jahrbuch der Kestner-Gesellschaft.* Hannover: H. Böhme, 1919, 145–52. [Observations on Cubism]

"Qualität und Gesinnung." In *Genius: Zeitschrift für alte und werdende Kunst* 1 (1919): 3. [Quality and Character]

"Kritische Gedanken zur neuen Kunst." *Genius* 1 (1919): 221–36. [Critical Thoughts on the New Art]. In *Fragen und Gegenfragen,* 86–105.

"Natur und Expressionismus." *Deutsche Kunst und Dekoration* 45 (1919–20): 265. Excerpt from "Kritische Gedanken zur neuen Kunst." [Nature and Expressionism]

"Papiergeld und Golddeckung: Ein Gleichnis." *Neue Zürcher Zeitung* (11 October 1922). Reprinted in *Der Neue Merkur,* 6 (1922): 528–31. [Paper Currency and the Gold Standard: A Parable]

"Dürers Apokalypse." In *Almanach 1904–24 des Verlags R. Piper & Co.* Munich: Piper, 1923, 19–32. [Dürer's Apocalypse]

"Zur Frage der gotischen Monumentalität." In *Vom Geiste neuer Literaturforschung: Festschrift für Oskar Walzel.* Edited by Julius Wahle and Victor Klemperer. Wildpark-Potsdam: Akademische Verlagsgesellschaft Athenaion, 1924, 211–23. Reprinted in *Fragen und Gegenfragen,* 39–64. [On the Question of Gothic Monumentality]

"Griechisch-Römisches." *Der Piperbote* 1 (1924): 2–4.

"Heinrich Wölfflin: Bemerkungen zu seinem 60. Geburtstag." *Neue Schweizer Rundschau* 17, no. 16 (1924). [Heinrich Wöllflin: Observations on the Occasion of his 60th Birthday]

"Nazarener" (1924?). In *Fragen und Gegenfragen,* 130–37. [The Nazarenes]

"Carlo Carrà's *Pinie am Meer.*" *Wissen und Leben* 18 (1925): 1165–69.

"Spätgotisches und expressionistisches Formsystem." *Wallraf-Richartz Jahrbuch* 2 (1925): 1–8. [Late Gothic and Expressionist Systems of Form]. In *Fragen und Gegenfragen,* 65–77.

"Byzantinismus und Gotik: Stilgeschichtliche Anregungen." In *Festschrift zum 60. Geburtstag von Paul Clemen.* Edited by Wilhelm Worringer, Heribert Reiners, and Leopold Seligmann. Bonn: F. Cohen, 1926, 329–34. Reprinted in *Zeitschrift des rhein. Vereins für Denkmalpflege* 19, no. 2 (1926): 80–85. [The Byzantine and the Gothic: Thoughts on the History of Style]

"Julius Meier-Graefe." *Widmungen zu seinem 60. Geburtstage.* Munich: Piper, 1927, 110–11.

"Michael Pacher." *Velhagen und Clasings Monatshefte* 42, no. 1 (1927): 409–25.

"Griechentum und Gotik." *Der Piperbote* 6 (1929): 2–6. [Greek Culture and the Gothic]

"L'Esprit grec et l'Art gothique." *Formes. Revue internationale* (April, 1931). [The Greek Spirit and Gothic Art]

206 Bibliography

"Lächelt die Mona Lisa wirklich?" *Thema. Zeitschrift für die Einheit der Kultur*
    2 (1949): 25–29. [Is Mona Lisa really smiling?]
"Jean Fouquet und Piero della Francesca." *Das Kunstwerk* 3, no. 1 (1949): 24–30.
"Zum Umgang mit Kitsch." *Die neue Zeitung* 35 (1951). In *Fragen und Gegen-
    fragen*, 177–179. [Coming to Terms with Kitsch]
"Paul Hankamer." In *Jahrbuch der Albertus-Universität zu Königsberg Preußen*,
    vol. 2. Freiburg im Breisgau/ Frankfurt am Main: Dirkreiter, 1952, 26–29.
"Kunstgeschichtliche Erkenntniskritik." *Die Kunst und das schöne Heim* 50, no.
    5 (1952): 168–72. [Critique of Art Historical Epistemology]
"Ars Una?" In *Fragen und Gegenfragen*, 155–63.
"Ein Mensch ohne Schablone." In *Stationen: Piper Almanach, 1904–1964*. Edited
    by Klaus Piper with Ernst Herhaus. Munich: Piper, 1964, 40–46.

Translations

Abstraction and Empathy: A Contribution to the Psychology of Style. Translated
    by Michael Bullock. New York: International Universities Press, 1953.
    Fourth edition, 1980.
Form in Gothic. Edited and with an Introduction by Sir Herbert Read. London:
    Putnam's, 1927. Reissue. London: A. Tiranti, 1957. Reissue. New York:
    Schocken Books, 1964. Schocken Paperbacks.
Form Problems of the Gothic. Translation unattributed, dedicated in 1918. Au-
    thorized American ed. for which translator has selected illustrative mate-
    rial, chiefly from American collections. New York: Stechert, 1920.
Egyptian Art. Authorized translation. Edited and with preface by Bernard Rack-
    ham. London: Putnam's, 1928.

Criticism

The works cited here deal directly with Worringer, an aspect of his influence, or
a closely related and therefore pertinent topic.

Arnheim, Rudolf. "Wilhelm Worringer on Abstraction and Empathy." In his
    New Essays on the Psychology of Art. Berkeley and Los Angeles: Univer-
    sity of California Press, 1986, 50–62.
Bakhtin, M. M., and P. N. Medvedev. *The Formal Method in Literary Scholar-
    ship: A Critical Introduction to Sociological Poetics*. Translated by Albert
    T. Wehrle. Baltimore: Johns Hopkins University Press, 1978.
Baum, Julius. "Der Geist der Gotik." *Die Kunstchronik*, n.s. 29 (1918): 145–50.
Behne, Adolf. "Moderne Kunstbücher." *Die Tat* 5 (1913–14): 936–42.
Brisch, Klaus. *Wassily Kandinsky (1886–1944): Untersuchungen zur Entstehung
    der gegenstandlosen Malerei an seinem Werk von 1900–1921*. Dissertation,
    Bonn, 1955.
Bushart, Magdalena. *Der Geist der Gotik und die expressionistische Kunst: Kunst-
    geschichte und Kunsttheorie, 1911–1925*. Munich: Silke Schreiber, 1990.
Buttigieg, Joseph A. "Worringer among the Modernists." *Boundary* 2 (1979):
    359–66.

Carrier, David. *Artwriting.* Amherst, Mass.: University of Massachusetts Press, 1987.

Dasenbrock, Reed Way. *The Literary Vorticism of Ezra Pound and Wyndham Lewis: Towards the Condition of Painting.* Baltimore: Johns Hopkins University Press, 1985.

Deleuze, Gilles, and Félix Guattari. *A Thousand Plateaus, Capitalism and Schizophrenia.* Translated by Brian Massumi. Minneapolis: University of Minnesota Press, 1987.

Dilly, Heinrich. *Deutsche Kunsthistoriker, 1933–1945.* Munich: Deutscher Kunstverlag, 1988.

Donahue, Neil H. "Analysis and Construction: The Aesthetics of Carl Einstein." *German Quarterly* 61, no. 3 (1988): 419–36. Included in his *Forms of Disruption.*

———. "Fear and Fascination in the Big City: Rilke's Use of Georg Simmel in *The Notebooks of Malte Laurids Brigge.*" *Studies in Twentieth Century Literature* 16, no. 2 (1992): 197–219. Included in his *Forms of Disruption.*

———. *Forms of Disruption: Abstraction in Modern German Prose.* Ann Arbor: University of Michigan Press, 1993.

Evans, Tamara S. "'A Paul Klee in Prose': Design, Space and Time in the Work of Robert Walser." *German Quarterly* 57, no. 1 (1984): 27–41.

Frank, Hilmar. "Nachwort." In Wilhelm Worringer, *Abstraktion und Einfühlung: Ein Beitrag zur Stilpsychologie.* Leipzig: Kiepenheuer, 1981, 118–34.

Frank, Joseph. *The Idea of Spatial Form.* New Brunswick: Rutgers University Press, 1990.

Frankl, Paul. *The Gothic: Literary Sources and Interpretations through Eight Centuries.* Princeton: Princeton University Press, 1960.

———. "Meinungen über Herkunft und Wesen der Gotik." In *Kunstgeschichte und Kunstwissenschaft,* edited by Walter Timmling. Leipzig: Teubner, 1923, 9–35.

Gluck, Mary. *Georg Lukács and his Generation, 1900–1918.* Cambridge: Harvard University Press, 1985.

Grace, Sherrill E. *Regression and Apocalypse: Studies in North American Literary Expressionism.* Toronto: University of Toronto Press, 1989.

Hamann, Richard. Review of *Abstraktion und Einfühlung. Zeitschrift für Ästhetik und allgemeine Kunstwissenschaft* 5 (1910): 276–81.

———. Review of *Formprobleme der Gotik. Zeitschrift für Ästhetik und allgemeine Kunstwissenschaft* 10 (1915): 357–61.

Haxthausen, Charles W. "A Critical Illusion: 'Expressionism' in the Writings of Wilhelm Hausenstein." In *The Ideological Crisis of Expressionism: The Literary and Artistic German War Colony in Belgium 1914–1918,* edited by Rainer Rumold and O. K. Werckmeister. Columbia, S.C.: Camden House, 1990, 169–91.

Hermand, Jost. *Literaturwissenschaft und Kunstwissenschaft: Methodische Wechselbeziehungen seit 1900.* Stuttgart: Metzler, 1965.

Hesse, Hermann. Review of Worringer's *Formprobleme der Gotik. Das Schweizerland* 1 (1914–15): 295.

Holdheim, W. Wolfgang. "Wilhelm Worringer and the Polarity of Understanding." *Boundary* 2 (Fall 1978): 339–58.

Howoldt, Jenns. "Krise des Expressionismus. Anmerkungen zu vier Briefen

Wilhelm Worringers an Carl Georg Heise." *Idea, Jahrbuch der Hamburger Kunsthalle* 8 (1989): 159–73.

Jennings, Michael W. *Dialectical Images: Walter Benjamin's Theory of Literary Criticism.* Ithaca: Cornell University Press, 1987.

Jones, Alun R. *The Life and Opinions of T. E. Hulme.* London: Gollancz, 1960.

———. "T. E. Hulme, Wilhelm Worringer and the Urge to Abstraction." *British Journal of Aesthetics* 1 (1960): 1–7.

Jung, C. G. "Zur Frage der psychologischen Typen" (1913). In *Typologie.* Freiburg im Breisgau: Walter Verlag, 1972, 7–17.

Korg, Jacob. *Language in Modern Literature: Innovation and Experiment.* New York: Harvester Press/Barnes and Noble, 1979.

Krannhals, W. A. "'Sehen' und 'Schauen': Worringers Querschnitt durch das Kunstschaffen." *Das Kunstblatt* 6 (1922): 234–40.

Kultermann, Udo. *Geschichte der Kunstgeschichte: Der Weg einer Wissenschaft.* Vienna: Econ-Verlag, 1966.

Kunisch, Hermann, ed. *Handbuch der deutschen Gegenwartsliteratur.* Munich: Nymphenburger Verlagsbuchhandlung, 1965.

Kunst, Hans Joachim. "Die Vollendung der romantischen Gotik im Expressionismus—Die Vollendung des Klassizismus im Funktionalismus." *Kritische Berichte* 7 (1979): 20–36.

Küntzel, Heinrich. "Alfred Lichtenstein." In *Expressionismus als Literatur: Gesammelte Studien,* edited by Wolfgang Rothe. Bern: Francke, 1969, 398–409.

Küppers, Paul Erich. "Kunstauffassung und Weltgefühl." *Das Kunstblatt* 1 (1917): 210–12.

Kurtz, Rudolf. *Expressionismus und Film.* Berlin: Verlag der Lichtbildbühne, 1926.

Lempertz, Heinrich G. *Wesen der Gotik.* Leipzig: Karl W. Hiersemann, 1926.

Lukács, Georg. "Größe und Verfall des Expressionismus" (1934). In *Werke: Essays über Realismus.* Luchterhand, 1971.

Manheim, Ron. "Expressionismus—Zur Entstehung eines kunsthistorischen Stil- und Periodenbegriffes." *Zeitschrift für Kunstgeschichte* 49, no. 1 (1986): 73–91.

———. *"Im Kampf um die Kunst": Die Diskussion von 1911 über zeitgenössische Kunst in Deutschland.* Hamburg: Verlag der Buchhandlung Sautter-Lackmann, 1987.

Masheck, Joseph. *Building-Art: Modern Architecture Under Cultural Construction.* New York: Cambridge University Press, 1993.

———. *Modernities: Art-Matters in the Present.* University Park: The Pennsylvania State University Press, 1993.

———. "Raw Art: 'Primitive' Authenticity and German Expressionism." *res* 4 (1982): 92–117. Reprinted in his *Modernities,* 155–92.

Müller, Michael. *Die Verdrängung des Ornaments: Zum Verhältnis von Architektur und Lebenspraxis.* Frankfurt am Main: Suhrkamp, 1977.

Müller-Wulckow, Walter. "Wilhelm Worringers *Formprobleme der Gotik.*" *Das Kunstblatt* 1 (1917): 216–18.

Nigro Covre, Jolanda. "Wilhelm Worringer prima e dopo: da un equivoco a un 'tramonto.'" *Ricerche di storia dell'arte* 12 (1980): 65–76.

Nachtsheim, Stephan. *Kunstphilosophie und empirische Kunstforschung, 1870–1920.* Berlin: Gebr. Mann, 1984.

Olin, Margaret. *Forms of Representation in Alois Riegl's Theory of Art.* University Park: The Pennsylvania State University Press, 1992.
Palmier, Jean-Michel. "Rudolf Kurtz et l'esthétique du cinéma expressioniste." In Rudolf Kurtz, *Expressionisme et cinéma,* translated by Pascale Godenir. Grenoble: Presses universitaires de Grenoble, 1986, 7–36.
Panofsky, Erwin. "Der Begriff des Kunstwollens." *Zeitschrift für Ästhetik und allgemeine Kunstwissenschaft* 14 (1920): 321–39.
———. "The Concept of Artistic Volition." Translated by Kenneth J. Northcott and Joel Snyder. *Critical Inquiry* 8 (1981): 17–33.
Pascal, Roy. *From Naturalism to Expressionism: German Literature and Society, 1880–1918.* New York: Basic Books, 1973.
Passarge, Walter. *Die Philosophie der Kunstgeschichte in der Gegenwart.* Berlin: Junker und Dunnhaupt, 1930.
Pehnt, Wolfgang. *Die Architektur des Expressionismus.* Stuttgart: Gerd Hatje, 1973.
Perkins, Geoffrey. *Contemporary Theory of Expressionism.* Frankfurt am Main: Herbert Lang, 1974.
Piper, Reinhard. *Briefwechsel mit Autoren und Künstlern, 1903–1953.* Edited by Ulrike Buergel-Goodwin and Wolfram Göbel. Munich: Piper, 1979.
———. *Mein Leben als Verleger: Vormittag–Nachmittag.* Munich: Piper, 1964.
Prange, Regine. *Das Kristalline als Kunstsymbol: Bruno Taut und Paul Klee.* Hildesheim: Olms, 1991.
Rank, Otto. *Art and Artist: Creative Urge and Personality Development.* Translated by Charles Francis Atkinson. New York: Norton, 1989. [Originally published New York: Knopf, 1932]
Read, Herbert. "Wilhelm Worringer." Obituary. *Encounter* 25, no. 5 (1965): 58–60.
Ringer, Fritz K. *The Decline of the German Mandarins: The German Academic Community, 1890–1933.* Cambridge, Mass.: Harvard University Press, 1969.
Roberts, Michael. *T. E. Hulme.* London: Faber and Faber, 1938.
Roskill, Mark. *Klee, Kandinsky, and the Thought of Their Time: A Critical Perspective.* Urbana: University of Illinois Press, 1992.
Schulze, Ingrid. "Wilhelm Worringer und die bürgerliche Opposition gegen den großdeutschen Nationalismus auf dem Gebiet der Kunstgeschichtsschreibung." *Wissenschaftliche Zeitschrift der Martin-Luther-Universität Halle-Wittenberg.* Gesellschafts und sprachwissenschaftliche Reihe 18 (1969): 65–85.
Selz, Peter. *German Expressionist Painting.* Berkeley and Los Angeles: University of California Press, 1957.
Sitt, Martina, ed. *Kunsthistoriker in eigener Sache. Zehn autobiographische Skizzen.* Berlin: Dietrich Reimer, 1990.
Soergel, Albert. *Dichtung und Dichter der Zeit.* N.s., *Im Banne des Expressionismus.* Leipzig: R. Voigtlanders, 1925.
Spanos, William V. "Modern Literary Criticism and the Spatialization of Time: An Existential Critique." *Journal of Aesthetics and Art Criticism* 29 (1970–71): 87–104.
Spector, Jack. *The Aesthetics of Freud: A Study in Psychoanalysis and Art.* New York: McGraw-Hill, 1972, 1974.
Stieglitz, Ann. "The Reproduction of Agony: Toward a Reception History of

Grünewald's Isenheim Altar after the First World War." *Oxford Art Journal* 12, no. 2 (1989): 87–103.

Tavel, Christoph von. "Der Lehrstuhl für Kunstgeschichte an der Universität Bern von den Anfängen bis zum Zweiten Weltkrieg." In *Jahrbuch des Schweizerischen Instituts für Kunstwissenschaft* (1972–73): 33–58.

Temborius, H. "Zur neuen Kunst." In *Westdeutsche Wochenschrift für Politik* 1 (1919): 83–85.

Thistlewood, David. *Herbert Read: Formlessness and Form: An Introduction to his Aesthetics*. Routledge and Kegan Paul, 1984.

Ulmer, Gregory L. "D. H. Lawrence, Wilhelm Worringer and the Aesthetics of Modernism." *D. H. Lawrence Review* (1977): 165–81.

Vallier, Dora. Introduction to *Abstraction et Einfühlung: Contribution à la psychologie du style*. Paris: Klincksieck, 1978, 5–32.

Walden, Herwarth. "Bemerkungen zu Worringer." *Der Sturm* 8 (1917–18): 178–79.

Washton-Long, Rose Carol. *Kandinsky: The Development of an Abstract Style*. New York: Oxford University Press, 1980.

Weise, Georg. "Das 'gotische' oder 'barocke' Stilprinzip der deutschen und der nordischen Kunst." *Deutsche Vierteljahrsschrift* 10 (1932): 206–24.

Weiss, Peg. *Kandinsky in Munich: The Formative Jugendstil Years*. Princeton: Princeton University Press, 1979.

Whyte, Iain Boyd, ed. and trans. *The Crystal Chain Letters*. Cambridge: MIT Press, 1985.

Wind, Edgar. *Art and Anarchy: The Reith Lectures, 1960*. London: Faber and Faber, 1963.

Zijlmans, Kitty, and Jos. Hoogeveen. *Kommunikation über Kunst. Eine Fallstudie zur Entstehungs- und Rezeptionsgeschichte des "Blauen Reiters" und von Wilhelm Worringers "Abstraktion und Einfühlung."* Leiden, 1988.

List of Contributors

Magdalena Bushart studied art history in Berlin, Vienna, and London before earning her Ph.D. degree in 1989 from the Free University in Berlin. From 1990 to 1993 she was assistant curator at the Staatliche Museen in Berlin. Since 1992 she has been assistant professor of Art History at the Technische Universität in Munich. She has written widely on German sculpture in the nineteenth and twentieth centuries, on the cultural politics of the Third Reich, and on Expressionist theories of art. Her book *Der Geist der Gotik und die expressionistische Kunst* was published in 1990 (Munich: Silke Schreiber).

Neil H. Donahue is associate professor of German and Comparative Literature at Hofstra University. He is the author of *Forms of Disruption: Abstraction in Modern German Prose* (University of Michigan Press, 1993) and has written articles on Carl Einstein; German-Japanese postwar fiction (including comparative studies of Alfred Andersch and Ōoka Shōhei, and Max Frisch and Yasunari Kawabata); Robert Musil; Rainer Maria Rilke; *Das Cabinet des Dr. Caligari;* Peter Handke, Patrick Süskind, and the New Historicism; and two articles on the poetry of Gerhard Falkner. In 1992–93 he received a National Endowment for the Humanities Fellowship for his study of Falkner and German poetry in the 1980s. He regularly reviews contemporary German literature for *World Literature Today.*

Charles W. Haxthausen is professor of art and director of the Graduate Program in the History of Art at Williams College, whose faculty he joined in 1993. He received his Ph.D. degree from Columbia University in 1976; from 1975 to 1983 he was curator of the Busch-Reisinger Museum at Harvard University. From 1975 to 1983 he taught at the University of Minnesota. His publications include *Paul Klee: The Formative Years* (Garland, 1981) and *Berlin: Culture and Metropolis* (coedited with Heidrun Suhr; University of Minnesota Press, 1990), as well as articles on Max Beckmann, Ludwig Kirchner, Kandinsky, Anselm Kiefer, Schlemmer, and Jasper Johns. He is currently completing a book on early twentieth-century art and art criticism, to be published by the University of California Press.

Michael W. Jennings is associate professor of German at Princeton University and author of *Dialectical Images: Walter Benjamin's Theory of Literary Criticism* (Cornell University Press, 1987), as well as articles on Kafka, Hölderlin, Musil, and the New Historicism. He is also the General Editor of Walter Benjamin's *Collected Works* (Harvard University Press, 1995), and coeditor (with Dorothea Dietrich) of an anthology of essays on politics and culture in Weimar Germany. He is currently at work on a book about figurations of space and political time in Weimar, with chapters on DADA photomontage, Thomas Mann, Erwin Piscator, Max Beckmann, Robert Musil, and Alfred Döblin.

Joseph Masheck teaches in the Department of Fine Arts at Hofstra University, where he also heads the graduate Humanities Program. He studied architectural history at Columbia University, where he received his Ph.D. degree in 1973, but he is better known as a historian and critic of modern and contemporary abstract art. From 1977 to 1980, he was editor of Artforum. His study of art in the 1970s, *Historical Present,* was published in 1984. He is also the author of two collections of essays: *Modernities: Art-Matters in the Present* (Pennsylvania State University Press, 1993) and *Building-Art: Modern Architecture under Cultural Construction* (Cambridge University Press, 1993).

Geoffrey C. W. Waite is associate professor of German Studies at Cornell University, where he offers courses in German literature (classicism and Romanticism), Marxist political theory, and visual studies. He is the author of *A Politics of Appropriation: The Nietzsche/Hölderlin Nexus from Heidegger to Nietzsche* (forthcoming) and "Nietzsche's Corps/e: Aesthetics, Politics, Prophecy; or, the Spectacular Technoculture of Everyday Life" (forthcoming). He has also published essays on Feininger, Velázquez, Leo Strauss, Alfred Hitchcock, Gramsci, Nietzsche, and Heidegger. He is currently at work on a book entitled "Visual Ideologies."

Joanna E. Ziegler is associate professor of the History of Art at Holy Cross College. She has lectured and published widely on religious art and architecture of the southern Low Countries during the late medieval and early modern periods. Her studies focusing on laywomen's art and religious experiences culminated in her *Sculpture of Compassion: The Pietà and the Beguines in the Southern Low Countries, c. 1300–c. 1600* (Brussels and Rome: Belgian Historical Institute of Rome, 1992). Her current research explores the historiography and phenomenology of dance as a paradigm for a feminist inquiry of the visual image.